Out of th

Tales from the T

Gerard Bourdillon

The events in this book are true, and I have made every effort to record them as accurately as possible (within the realms of reasonable memory). However, in some places I have changed the names of the officers, offenders or victims, or changed the location of the incidents in order to protect the identity of individuals. For my friends and colleagues who feature in this book... you know who you are!

Out of the Blue

Tales from the Thin Blue Line

ISBN: 978-0-473-72403-0 (Paperback)
978-0-473-72404-7 (E-pub)
978-0-473-72405-4 (Kindle)

Self Published by Gerard Bourdillon via The Publishing Launchpad.
www.thepublishinglaunchpad.com

First printed in October 2024, in Auckland, New Zealand.

www.outoftheblue-books.com
outofthebluebook@outlook.com

Dedication

This book is dedicated to Dom and James, and to all my other former colleagues who are sadly no longer with us.

To Toby and Carol,
With love,
Gerard.

Contents

Prologue

Why Would You?

For some time now I have been considering how best to write an honest and accurate account of policing in the UK. An account that would be useful for anyone considering a career in the police, or for anyone who has already joined up but may be struggling in some areas.

But this book isn't just for past, present, or future officers. It's also for their partners, friends, and family. It's for anyone who just wants to know what this often glamorised, regularly vilified, and totally unique job is actually like. And it's for anyone struggling to live with the effects of trauma.

There is no way of sugar-coating the fact that police officers (and paramedics) will be exposed to extreme trauma around 500 times during their career. Compare that figure to the general population who, on average, will only experience extreme trauma 3 or 4 times in their *entire lives.* As a result, at least one in five officers either suffer, or have suffered, from the debilitating effects of PTSD (Post-Traumatic Stress Disorder).

Trauma itself is hard to define. It goes way beyond something that simply upsets you, or you find difficult to process. In researching this book I have read multiple definitions of trauma from many different sources. Elements of them all resonated with me so I've cobbled them together as best I can: Trauma is a response to a severe and sudden adverse event (usually life-threatening or life-changing) that permanently affects your brain and negatively affects your ability to cope and function.

The symptoms of trauma (in particular of PTSD) include flashbacks and nightmares; feelings of hopelessness and isolation; anxiety and depression; insomnia and fatigue; cloudy thoughts and inability to concentrate; intolerance to stress; and irritability and sudden outbursts of anger. It can be life altering, leaving the sufferer stuck and unable to move forward with their life, and sometimes unable to work.

But this isn't a book about trauma (although trauma and my battle with its effects are a constant theme), it's about policing. I want to tell you, to show you, what it's *really* like to do this incredible job.

Amazingly, policing is a career that has no real job description, so I've done my best to break it down and define it in the following few paragraphs:

It's a thankless job of perpetually doing all the crap jobs that nobody else can (or will) do.

It's constantly dealing with the results of a failed society, or the failings of someone else to do their job properly in the first place.

It's a career where the first time you meet someone, you are invariably greeted with "Who the fuck called you?" or "What the fuck are you doing here?", "We don't fucking need you", or more often than not, just a simple "Fuck off!"

It's a career where you will be attacked (often verbally, occasionally physically) simply because of what you represent. You will witness horrors you will never forget. You will miss friends' weddings, family birthdays, Christmas dinners, New Year's Eve parties and FA Cup Finals. You will be at work when everyone else is asleep in their beds. You will be cold, wet, tired (more tired than you ever thought possible), bored, scared, saddened, frustrated, angry and hurt more often than you'll care to remember.

No one will thank you and you will constantly question what you are doing and why you are doing it.

But...you will also have one of the most exciting, challenging, and diverse careers out there. Every day will be different and at times you will have the most fun you could ever have whilst being paid for it. You will form the most amazing friendships with colleagues who you will literally trust with your life. It will open doors to worlds you otherwise wouldn't have access to. You will develop a humour which will see you through some of the darkest points in your life.

And, when it's finally all over you can look back and think "I stepped up, I did what I could, and I made a difference. It may only have been tiny, but I made a positive change in the lives of so many people" and ultimately that's what policing is all about.

For me joining up felt like an inevitability, an almost pre-determined fate. I came from a family of public servants. My father was an MI5 officer; my grandfather had been a colonial governor. Two of my uncles had been civil servants and one had been murdered by terrorists in the bombing of the King David Hotel in Jerusalem. I had three first cousins in the Royal Ulster Constabulary (now the PSNI), and other close relatives had served in the British Army, the National Health Service, in education, and as clergy.

As a small boy I obsessively read the Ladybird Easy Reading Book in the 'People at Work' series, titled *The Policeman*. The last two pages were my favourite, they were all about the mounted police and had a wonderful illustration of an officer astride his horse. I still have my well-read and battered copy and it sits proudly on my ten-year-old son's bookshelf.

More significantly, two of my earliest memories are of actual police officers.

My mum and dad sold their old bed to our local bobby. I was only about three or four at the time and was at home when the officer came around, in full uniform, to have a look at it. I was so excited, and so in awe of having a policeman in our home that I just stared at him, mouth slightly open. He must have picked up on my excitement as he let me try on his Custodian helmet and then gave me a Thames Valley Constabulary pocket notebook and a pencil. If I close my eyes I can still see my tiny self, reflected in the full-length mirror of my parents' bedroom, swamped by the enormous and heavy emerald-green lined headpiece, clutching the notebook. The same mirror now hangs in my own bedroom, a constant reminder of that life-forming moment.

A hazier but still extremely vivid memory is from a day out in London with my mum. It must have been about a year after my previous brush with the law, but I can't remember the specifics. I guess Mum had taken me to one of the London museums, probably the Natural History one, or maybe we had gone to see the Lord Mayor's Show. Wherever we were and whatever we were doing we had to get on the underground to get home. As we approached the tube station there was a mounted police officer sitting perfectly still outside the entrance. I can almost still smell the horse and the saddlery when I recall the moment of looking up in wonder at the enormous animal. His dark bay flanks were sleek and shiny and his hooves, below the pristine white fetlocks, were like glass. His perfectly combed tail swished occasionally to ward off the few flies that were attracted to his smell. The officer on top was also immaculately presented in his pressed tunic, riding gloves and mirror-like bulled riding boots. To top it off, a long, narrow brown-leather cylindrical scabbard hung down from the left side of his saddle, housing his baton. As a five-year old animal lover and police-nut I had never seen anything that wondrous so close-up before. And it was all so neat and shiny. My jaw almost hit the grubby London pavement.

As a teenage mod, and later as a scooter boy, my relationship with the boys in blue shifted somewhat. I got into many scraps which led to scrapes with the police. I got arrested at fourteen for fighting football casuals in London and spent six hours in a one-man cell with eight other teenage mods and skinheads. My dad was not amused and didn't talk to me for about a week.

I got pulled over and given a producer (form HO/RT1 requiring me to take my driving documents to the local police station) almost every time I rode my underpowered Vespa 50 Special, or later my tuned and customised Lambretta, and I was often stop-searched too. When a cop said "Pockets!" I immediately knew what he meant and what I had to do. "Haven't you got anything better to do?" I scowled at them "This is the third time you've stopped me this week."

As an art student I attended large protests in '80s London. I marched against Thatcher's Poll Tax, against student loans, and against the National Front. We were policed very robustly but none of my experiences made me hate the old bill. In a strange way they got me thinking about the police as a future career option. It seemed exciting, and a way of staying out on the streets, somewhere I loved to be. All my run-ins with the police and my street fights were like a teenage training camp for life as a cop.

When I left Art College I worked for a while as a graphic designer, but it didn't excite me. I wasn't a businessman and the private sector wasn't for me. I wanted to do more. I wanted to be more. I wanted to help more. And I wanted excitement. So I joined my local constabulary, Thames Valley Police.

My favourite early-childhood book

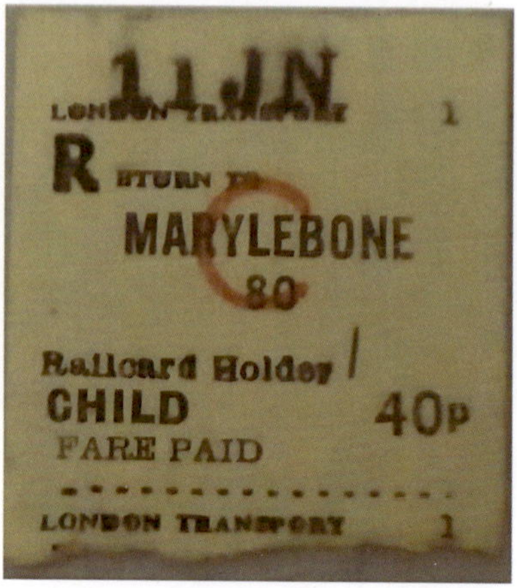

I've still got the train ticket from the day I got arrested

(l) At 16 on my Vespa PK50, and (r) at 18 on my Vespa PX200

Not Quite Chapter One

I tried to calm my breathing and keep myself as still as possible. I knew Frankie was holed up about five metres to my left. I couldn't see him; he was tucked in low, lying prone on the floor behind some shelving.

We were experienced firearms officers and knew how to conceal ourselves well. The seven principles of camouflage (the Seven S's) were ingrained into our consciousness. Shape, shine, silhouette, shadow, skin, sound, and sudden movement were all elements that could betray our positions.

I was crouched on one knee to the side of, and slightly behind, a chilled food counter and I was further concealed by a drinks display in front of me. The lighting was such that I was in the shadows... as long as I didn't move or make any noise then my only potential give-away was the light tone of my skin contrasting its dark surroundings. I was pretty sure I wouldn't be seen.

The threat was approaching slowly from my right, about ten metres away. His weapons were clearly visible in his hands, and judging by his cautious movements he knew we were close. I knew he was going to reach me before Frankie and every muscle in my body tensed as I tried to remain absolutely still. As I silently watched the man approach I suddenly felt the air move just past my right ear, and I heard an unmistakable loud crack.

Shit, there's someone else. They've seen me and I'm under fire! I had no choice. I had to break cover, I had to get out of there, and quickly. *Have they seen Frankie? Is he compromised, or is he still safe?* I thought to myself as I sprang to my feet and made a run for the hard cover of the supermarket wall behind me. My heart was racing with the adrenalin and the physical effort, giving me some much needed extra speed to reach safety.

I felt the impact of the blow to my left shoulder just as I dived for cover. I rolled onto my right side and glanced down to see the thick red liquid oozing and glistening as it started to run down my arm. Before I could do anything else I heard two more cracks as projectiles started to hit the wall in front of me, then another three in quick succession. *Where the fuck's Frankie?* I frantically thought to myself just seconds before he crawled up behind me.

"You've been hit!" he needlessly informed me. "I think Sly's down too." He grinned.

"Thanks for the sympathy." I sarcastically replied. "We need to move, we're sitting ducks here."

"I know, but don't worry, you're not going to die. It's only a bit of ketchup."

"I know it's only ketchup, but those hard boiled eggs fucking hurt when they hit you at close range!" I countered.

"Yeah, but half of them are soft, it's only the ones that were too close to the fire that have gone hard."

"I don't know what's worse, the bruising from the hard ones, or getting covered in rotten raw yolk!" I laughed.

Before moving we scanned our surroundings for further threats. I could see the remains of the five eggs dripping off the wall we had been hiding behind, but the boys from the Underwater Search Team were long gone. We were safe to move.

"Oh shit, Clarkey's got a fire extinguisher and he's heading our way!" Frankie giggled. "This is starting to get out of hand..."

I picked up my already heavily-shaken two-litre bottle of Coke and loosened its lid before throwing it at Clarkey's feet. As it hit the floor it started to spin violently, spraying my target (and anything else within about three metres of it) in a sweet, sticky liquid spray.

Clarkey swiftly jumped out the way of my soda-bomb and ran towards us. He raised the hose of the extinguisher, aiming it right at us as he pulled the trigger. White foam streamed in our direction as we fled, heading to stairs that led to a mezzanine level above the shop floor. Our pockets and hands were full of eggs, tomatoes, squeezy bottles of various sauces and mustard, and bottles of fizzy drink. The mezzanine would give us the perfect high ground to give us a real tactical advantage in this mother-of-all, inter-departmental food fight. As firearms officers, we were NOT going to be beaten by a bunch of boaties and scuba-divers.

It had all started the day before. A disgruntled (and presumably psychopathic) shopper had set and hidden a number of timed incendiary devices amongst the shelves of his local supermarket in Milton Keynes. The resulting fire had gutted half of the enormous shop, and the subsequent water damage caused by the fire service had rendered the remains of the building and its stock unusable. The entire contents were going to be destroyed, and the structure itself was going to be torn down and rebuilt.

At the time I was an AFO (Authorised Firearms Officer) posted to a small team that specialised in counter-terrorist and major crime searches. We had been tasked with ensuring there were no further unexploded or secondary devices hidden amongst the debris and wreckage of the store. As the site was so large we had been allocated three days for the job.

Six of us arrived early on the morning of the first day and suited up in our forensic suits, overshoes, work gloves and hard-top baseball caps (bump caps). We did a quick recce of the site and quickly realised what a monster of a job this was going to be.

We headed back to the van to have a brew and plan how we were going to attack the beast. Our van was well equipped with just about everything you could ever need to find something. At one end of the spectrum we had thermal cameras, endoscopes and sophisticated mapping software, and at the other end we had garden spades and bits of old metal poles for digging up gardens and poking around in bushes. Just as importantly we had a hot water boiler, a virtually endless supply of tea bags and a microwave oven.

We divided the supermarket into manageable search areas, prioritising the ones that seemed most likely to have secondary devices. We got into teams of two and each pair was allocated an area to search. We finished our mugs of tea and back we went into the literal bombsite. It was hot, sweaty, laborious, physical and generally unpleasant work. The section that Frankie and I got was all the worse because it had all sorts of household products, including bottles of bleach, in it. Many of the plastic bottles had melted and, despite our facemasks, the chemical fumes burnt the back of our throats and were overpowering.

After several tortuous hours of carefully removing soggy, or burnt, or melted detritus from the shelves we broke for lunch. I ripped off my face mask and drank in the fresh summer air as we left the building. I took off my gloves and we tore off each other's contaminated (and very sweaty) over-suits. I looked around at the others. Everyone seemed hot, tired and dejected. We were empty handed and had finished searching the areas where we were most likely to find something. We already knew our chances of discovering further devices was close to zero. Another two and a half days of this was an almost unbearable thought.

We discussed our options as we sat in the van eating our sandwiches and drinking our third or fourth cup of tea of the day.

"Let's bottom out the priority two areas, carrying on with a meticulous and methodical search. If we still don't find anything then I suggest we speed things up for the remaining areas... we'll just do visual searches and clear the shelves. Agreed?" Frankie said. "I want to get this done by tomorrow night. None of us want to be back here on Wednesday." We all agreed. To be fair I didn't even want to go back on Tuesday.

After a few more soul-destroying and fruitless hours we had completed our next search areas and decided to take a tea-break. As we headed for the exit Sly picked up a bottle of tomato ketchup and squeezed it all down Jon's back. Much to our amusement Jon was completely oblivious. Frankie grabbed a bottle of Coleman's mustard and emptied that onto Jon too. Still no reaction. We were now almost crying with supressed laughter. "What's so funny?" Jon asked. He was met with sniggers.

"Oh nothing, just something Sly said," I smirked. Jon seemed to accept this, shrugged and carried on towards the door, giving Sly the opportunity to write 'cock' in ketchup across his shoulders.

That was it. We howled with glee. Jon realised he must be the butt of some joke and stopped to check himself. He looked over his shoulder, saw the red and yellow gloopy mess and exploded.

"You wankers!" he shouted, struggling to contain his own laughter. He picked up a bottle of coke, shook it violently, and removed the lid as he pointed it at us. The sticky spray engulfed us as we scrambled to get away from Jon. We ran out of the store laughing our heads off.

The mini-food fight was over, but the germ of an idea had been planted.

"If we crack on I reckon we can get this done by tomorrow morning" Frankie said. "I think we might need to get the Underwater Search guys here to help us...shall we ask them to get here at seven?" he grinned.

We all knew what he meant. We didn't need their help. This was going to be a monumental ambush on a team we regularly worked closely with. Suddenly tomorrow wasn't looking bad at all. In fact it was going to be epic.

So Tuesday arrived, we got to Milton Keynes early, briefed the divers about what we wanted them to search and we completed the job and all the associated paperwork well before lunch. We had a quick cuppa and five of us disappeared inside to take up our positions, leaving Tom to suggest to the unsuspecting divers that they go back inside for one final check.

They took the bait and returned to the supermarket to be met with a hail of fruit, vegetables, sauces and eggs. The ensuing hour or so of carnage was probably the funniest and messiest sixty minutes of my career.

Unfortunately though, most days in the police aren't quite so much fun.

It's time to go back to the beginning of my story.

Day one of the supermarket search, looking for secondary devices

Day two, suited up and ready to meet the Underwater Search Team (above) and their truck at their base at Sulhamstead (below).

1

The Unwelcome Welcome

"What the..." I groaned as I rolled over and strained my half-open eyes to focus on the radioactive green glow of the hands of my little white Lorus travel clock. The almost non-existent amount of sleep I had that night had been shattered by the shrill beeping of the alarm. I felt sick and my head was groggy...I couldn't believe it was time to get up already. I had never been an early morning person, but surely this was the middle of the night? I squinted again at my clock. 4:30 am. Yep, as painful as it was, this was going to be my new reality and half-past four in the morning was time to rise and shine.

I practically fell out of bed and struggled in the dark to get into my freshly-ironed 'half-blues', the heavy woollen black trousers with black leather belt and light blue cotton shirt that made the basis of my uniform. This was the accepted way to dress for travelling to and from work...quick to kit-up on arrival but indistinct enough so as not to be easily recognised as a police officer during the commute. At the station I would add the epaulettes, clip-on tie, NATO pullover, handcuffs, truncheon and radio that would complete the TVP uniform.

Once dressed I crept downstairs in the dark, trying not to wake my mum and dad, and made my way to the kitchen where I could finally turn on the lights. I tried to eat some breakfast, but between the nerves, the excitement, and the awful time of day (night?) all I could manage was a glug of tea and a mouthful of Alpen. I grabbed my Batman lunchbox that I had prepared the night before from the fridge, pulled on my shiny, new, eight-hole Dr Martin boots and collected the bags of newly-issued kit that were waiting for me by the front door.

Once outside, my first job was to scrape the ice off the windscreen of my old white Ford Escort parked in the street directly outside my parents' house. I was getting anxious...this was an unwelcome delay and I was desperate not to be late on my first day. When I finally set off I was relieved to find the only traffic on the road consisted of a few newspaper delivery vans and couple of electric milk-floats, so my drive to Windsor took much less than the half-hour I had predicted.

I got to work far too early for the 6am shift start and as I didn't yet have the access code to raise the carpark barrier I had to wait for one of the night-shift panda cars to let me in. I parked up under the yellowish haze of the rear yard's lighting and realised I couldn't get into the nick either. So, there I waited, kit bag at my feet, standing by the back door on a dark and freezing December morning, hugging myself and stamping my feet trying to stay warm. After what seemed like an eternity, but was in reality only about ten very cold minutes, a car pulled into the yard and the driver got out and walked up to me.

"Are you the new boy?" he asked cheerily. "I'm Andy".

"Oh, are you Andy Grenfell?" I replied.

"No" he said rather unhelpfully as he punched the code into the door lock. I followed him inside into the warmth and asked where I should put my stuff. He pointed down the corridor and said "The lockers are down there on the left...there might be an empty one if you're lucky, but you'll need to get a key from admin once they're in". I hauled my stuff down to the locker room, a cramped and windowless area with a dozen or so tall, grey, single doored metal storage units lining each wall. Luckily there was an open, vacant locker on the right hand side, right next to one with a sticker on it with "PC Grenfell" scrawled on it. That's a bit of luck I thought.

As I was emptying all sorts of items I couldn't yet identify into my new locker, a mountain of a man with a shaved head and very bloodshot eyes opened the locker next to me. He looked like he hadn't slept for a week, and completely ignored me.

"Hi I'm Dillan" I said. "Are you Andy Grenfell?"

He looked at me with suspicion and appeared to be slightly confused. "You're my tutor constable" I explained.

"Like fuck I am" he muttered as he slammed his locker door shut and marched out of the room, shouting angrily "Where's the fucking sergeant?!"

That was my welcome to Thames Valley Police.

With my parents at my Passing Out Parade, Police Training Centre, Ashford

(l to r) PK, me, Ady and Nick. TVP graduates from Ashford looking forward to getting out on the streets

Out of the Blue

2

Trains and Brains

Andy, as it turns out, was quite wrong. He *was* my tutor constable. He was also not only my tutor constable, but he was a bloody good one at that. First impressions aside (I later found out he had been having a tough time at home and no-one had pre-warned him he was getting a probationary constable to look after) he was a great bloke with a wealth of knowledge and experience. He had previously served on Support Group and was one of the specialist firearms officers deployed to the mass shootings at Hungerford to apprehend Michael Ryan. He had a very hands-on, honest, no nonsense approach to policing which I largely adopted during my career. I had huge respect for him and continued to seek out his advice long after he was no longer my tutor. I was gutted when, several years later, he transferred up to the Lake District.

Shortly after I first met Andy, I found myself sitting next to him on my first night shift in our H-reg Vauxhall Astra panda. It was around 10.30pm on another freezing cold winter's night when the call came over the car radio.

"Lima Alpha One Two Five"

"Go ahead" I replied, still feeling rather self-conscious using the radio.

"LA125, we've had a call about a man on the railway line at Sunnymeads Railway Station. BTP have been informed and are en route, but you're the closest unit."

BTP (British Transport Police) are a uniquely trained force who are solely responsible for policing our railways and ports, and take primacy in those areas.

"Roger, en route" I excitedly replied.

Andy looked across at me from behind the steering wheel. "This could be messy. Have you ever seen a dead body before?"

"No" I replied, my feelings of excitement rapidly being replaced with feelings of anxiety, inexperience and naivety.

"Okay, put some gloves on and just do what I tell you. Oh, and don't go near the track until we've had the all clear and we know the power's off and all the trains have stopped".

As we pulled up outside the station I saw a few shocked-looking passengers walking out into the darkness of the carpark to catch taxis to finish their journey home from Windsor. We walked onto the strangely silent, dark and cold platform to be met by the station master and a visibly shaken train driver. We were told the track was still live and we would have to wait. The now-empty train was stationary on the far track, its first few carriages overshooting the end of the platform. We slowly walked along the platform, heading towards the front of the train and saw what looked like a man with an unusually small head lying sandwiched between the rails almost out of sight under a carriage. Although clearly lifeless there didn't appear to be any damage to the body, and there was none of the blood and gore I had been expecting. I was oddly both relieved and disappointed.

The delay gave us time to talk to the driver. He told us the train wasn't due to stop there, but as he was approaching the station he saw a man stagger and sway on the platform's edge before falling onto the track. The driver had no time to brake, and watched in horror as the guy tried to roll out of the way. He told us he could read the man's lips saying "Oh shit!" as he tried to tuck his head down and out of harm's way. Tragically he wasn't quite quick enough.

I heard a phone ring and the station master walked off to answer it. He returned a couple of minutes later to inform us it was now safe to approach the body. I jumped down off the platform and walked over to the man, who I could now see was probably in his early forties. His jacket and trousers were slightly torn and his head was wedged against the rail, with the top part of his skull missing. There was a faint trail of dark red blood and black hair along the top edge of the track, leading to where the train had finally stopped. We walked along the track and I found a palm-sized piece of his cranium about 15 metres from the body. We marked its position with my coat and went back to the platform to wait for everyone to arrive: the duty CID officer; the duty SOCO (Scenes of Crime Officer) who would photograph the scene; the BTP officers; a doctor who would certify the death; and the undertakers who would take the body to the morgue.

Once the full team was assembled the scene investigation was carried out and the train was moved allowing the doctor (and us) easy and safe access to the body. The doctor confirmed death and it was time for the body to be moved. Andy, two BTP officers and I had that unsavoury job. One of the BTP guys had already picked up the bit of skull and was carrying it in a transparent evidence bag. The four of us went to lift the corpse. I had his left shoulder, Andy his right and the others took hold of his legs. "One, two, three, lift!" came the command from somewhere near his feet.

As we stood up I heard a sickening "schloop" as his head was freed from the rail. Almost simultaneously his head dropped back and slightly to the left, allowing his brains to exit his open skull and land on my boots. I just stood there and stared at my feet in total disbelief.

"Oh for fuck's sake" said the BTP officer holding the evidence bag. He let go of his end of the body, leant over, scraped the brains off my boots and dropped them into the bag containing the bit of skull as casually as if he were throwing an empty can into a rubbish bin.

"Well come on, let's get on with it" he said as he retook hold of the guy's leg. With considerable effort we hauled him up onto the platform. I was immediately surprised by just how heavy and hard a dead body was to move, and it occurred to me that we don't use the term 'a dead weight' for no reason. Once on the platform we dropped him onto the undertakers' trolley and left him there for them to bag up and take away to Wexham Park Hospital in Slough.

The SOCO looked at me and decided he needed to lighten my mood. "That's why I don't drink much. You always end up with a splitting head in the morning!"

"Yeah, and I often lose my head after a few drinks' chuckled the detective constable in reply.

Andy looked at me with a straight face and said "But seriously, there's a valuable lesson to be learnt here."

"Yeah? What's that" I asked, hoping for some words of wisdom from my tutor.

"It's vital you keep a good head on your shoulders in a crisis."

That was my introduction to the dark humour that is so intrinsically linked to policing. Although to bystanders it may at times seem heartless, unkind or inappropriate, it actually performs a vital role in relieving pressure, stress and grief for the officers involved. The jokes that night didn't erase my shock and horror, but they did help enormously in normalising death and getting my head ready to deal with the next job that was already waiting for us to attend.

Back then, all the larger police stations had a police bar...a non-profit licensed premise, usually somewhere on one of the top floors of the nick. It would be run by a mix of staff paid for through our Sports and Social Club membership fees and officers volunteering to help out. These bars became contentious when the "canteen culture" of the police came under scrutiny following the Stephen Lawrence Enquiry and the subsequent Macpherson Report.

Although I fully understand why the idea of police bars became so unpopular, I still think it's a shame they disappeared. They provided an invaluable place where officers could go after a shift to relax, let off steam, talk out the stresses and horrors of the day, and to bond as a team...all in a totally safe and judgement-free environment. I think it was vital to have somewhere to go where we could talk openly without the worry of being overheard and misunderstood by the public, and to be able to lighten the mood with our typical dark humour. I don't think the positive impact these bars had on our mental health can be questioned and I wonder if the numbers of officers failing to cope have increased since they closed.

Perhaps the police *service* is better off without the bars, but I'm certain that the police *officers* are not.

SOCO photos from the scene

SOCO photos showing placement of body

3

The Bloody Burglar

It was an unusually mild and still Wednesday night in Windsor, one of those nights where even in the early pre-dawn hours you didn't need your jumper. I was a little bored, single-crewed, patrolling the empty residential streets of Dedworth when a call came over the radio to break the monotony. A concerned woman had seen a light flashing around inside her neighbour's house. She knew the house was unoccupied as the family were away on their summer holidays and so she assumed they were being burgled.

A colleague, Mick, was already en route, making his way to the front of the house to check it out so I drove to an access road at the rear.

"I can see torchlight inside the premises" Mick informed me over the air as I was turning into the narrow street. "There's a white guy with a shaved head wearing a red football shirt in the front downstairs room. Oh shit, he's seen me" A pause, then "He's running, he's heading out the back towards you. Dillan, are you there?"

"Yes" I said as I jumped out of my panda and ran towards the row of terraced houses, trying to guess which one it exactly was. A bare-chested male in his early twenties with blond closely-cropped hair came running out of an alley to my left. He looked startled when he saw me and immediately jumped up onto the roof of a bank of lock-up garages behind the houses. "He's on the garage roofs" I called up. "Can we get a dog unit?" On hearing me ask for a dog, the lad must have decided he'd rather take his chances with me than trying to outrun what is in effect a trained wolf. He jumped down and started running.

Game on. I was a keen competitive triathlete and I considered it a matter of personal pride to never lose a foot chase. I caught him quickly but he started to struggle violently, pushing me away and wildly punching and kicking. I swept his legs away, taking him to the ground. He continued to fight and I worked hard to restrain him, finally subduing him enough to handcuff him with my brand new pair of 'Quickcuffs'...rigid cuffs that our force had recently acquired, replacing the now outdated traditional chain linked ones.

I called up to let control room know I'd got the suspect and we could cancel the dog handler. I searched his pockets, got him up onto his feet and walked him over to my panda. Mick informed me over the radio that he had found a red football shirt near the back door of the house, and he could see the door had been forced open. On hearing this the prisoner became very agitated and started to struggle again. As he was still handcuffed it was fairly easy to restrain him, holding him down on the bonnet of the Astra with one hand as I used my free hand to call up on the radio for Mick to come and give me a hand transporting the burglar to custody.

The next thing I knew, the guy lifted his head, looked me straight in the eye and half-smiled, half-snarled at me. That's strange, I thought. And then, completely out of the blue, "BANG!" He violently slammed his face into the car, smashing his nose sideways across his face, and leaving a dent and blood on the otherwise clean, white bonnet. I was stunned and before I could react he spat a mouthful of blood at me and laughed. "I'm going to have your fucking job for that!" It took me a second or two to process what had just happened. *Shit, who's going to believe me?* I thought, starting to panic. *I wouldn't believe me! Shit, I'm going to lose my job. Or worse. Shit.* I looked up and around to see if there were any CCTV cameras that could save me. There weren't any. *Fuck, fuck, fuck!*

No CCTV, no colleagues, no independent witnesses. Just a handcuffed prisoner with a broken nose and split lip, a dent on the bonnet of my car, and his blood all over me and my car. And he was going to say I attacked him.

I went cold. My panic turned to anger. "You bastard" I said as I grabbed hold of the cuffs by the rigid plastic centre grip, and twisted them violently as I pulled him away from the car. He winced in pain, crying out "Fuck!" as I marched him to the side of the panda, opened the passenger door and almost threw him into the back seat. I had an overwhelming urge to hit him. I wanted to hurt him. Luckily for me my self-control won out over my anger, as I turned around to see my Sergeant, Lucy had just turned up to help.

"So you got him?" she asked, although I wasn't sure if it was a question or an observation. "Well done". Then hers eyes caught the mess on the bonnet and she raised an eyebrow before looking into the back of my car at my prisoner. "What happened Dillan?" she asked.

"You're never going to believe this" I said as my heart sank. I told what had just happened. She looked at me unemotionally, slightly tilted her head to the side and shrugged her shoulders. "Of course I believe you. Something similar happened to me a few years ago. As strange as it seems, it actually happens quite a lot. Some criminals will do all sorts of crazy stuff if they think it'll somehow get them off." She continued "Just make sure you write it up exactly as it happened in your statement. He'll probably think better of it in the morning...Don't worry too much about it, I bet he doesn't even make a complaint."

Relief swept over me "Okay, I'm not going to lose my job", and then I quickly remembered how I had intentionally hurt him, twisting and pulling on the cuffs. I was lucky I hadn't broken his wrists... there would have been no way I could have justified that. I was still in my probation and that would definitely have been the end of my career.

Just as Lucy had predicted, he never made a complaint. He admitted to the burglary, and half a dozen or so others on top and was sent to prison for a few months. Despite the praise I received for the arrest I never really felt great about it. I had been provoked and I had bitten. Not as hard as I could have done, but I had still reacted unprofessionally and I had let myself down.

I learnt a few lessons that night.

I learnt to always expect the unexpected.

I learnt that controlling my emotions was an essential policing skill. To stop and breathe before the red mist of anger clouded my decisions was a skill to develop and value.

I learnt to have faith in the process. To act in good faith and strive to do the right thing. If I did so I should be fine.

I learnt not to cross the line, and if I ever did cross it then I should expect to be judged and for there to be consequences.

And I learnt not to let myself down. It's just not worth it.

As a young officer in Windsor (l)

4

A Sledgehammer and the Nut

"Humpff" I tried to suppress my laugh.

"Hey love, try not to hurt yourself until we've had a chat, okay?"

We had two bail hostels in Windsor then, one on Vansittart Road and one in Old Windsor. Only one survives, as Vansittart was demolished about 20 years ago to make way for some expensive new apartments. Bail hostels were a sort of half-way-house between prison and life on the outside. Some of the residents had jobs, many didn't but all had strict bail conditions and a curfew. We would often go there to deal with people who had breached their bail conditions in some way, usually staying out late and getting drunk.

We got a call late one afternoon from the Vansittart Hostel to say one of their inmates was threatening to kill himself. I was crewed that evening with Cookie, a large (and larger than life) ex-Welsh Guardsman and ex-Regional Crime Squad detective. He spoke softly with a Welsh accent and had a tendency to call everyone "love".

On arrival we saw a guy leaning out of a first floor window, holding what looked like a large shard of broken glass. He started screaming at us "If you come anywhere near me I'll fucking kill you!"

"Okay love" came the quiet, calm reply.

"I'm fucking serious. I'll fucking kill you and then I'll kill myself. Fuck off and leave me alone!"

"Alright love, just you calm yourself down now, okay?" said Cookie, barely looking at the man as we walked under his window to the hostel entrance. There we were met by the warden who ushered us inside and explained that the man had totally barricaded himself into his room and the only other way in was through the window he was currently hanging out of.

The warden showed us up to the room and I knocked on the door. I received an immediate reply: "Fuck off!" I turned the handle and tried to open the door but I could feel the resistance of a pretty heavy bit of furniture behind it.

"That's not budging mate" I said to Cookie "What are we going to do now?"

"You can fuck right off" came a voice from behind the door "that's what you can do now". He continued "You can't get in, and if you try I'll fucking kill you, so leave me alone".

We moved away down the corridor out of earshot from the room. "I think we should get kitted up" I almost whispered. In those days our pandas didn't routinely carry the extra items of PPE we were needing, things like stab-proof vests, shields and visored helmets, so I called up for another unit to bring them to us. In the meantime Cookie started to knock on the corridor walls. "There's no point fucking knocking, I'm not going to let you in!" I looked at the others rolling my eyes and smiling. Despite his anger this guy was actually quite amusing. Cookie quietly mouthed "It's just plasterboard" and motioned for us to move further away from the room so we could speak freely. The warden led us back down the stairs to the foyer where Cookie spoke to him

"Right love, we can sort this out for you but we're going to make quite a mess and damage your walls, is that okay?" The warden sighed. "Yeah, okay, I suppose so. I mean we can't just leave him in there, can we? I guess you boys have to do what you need to do."

It was starting to get dark when Bob arrived in the Transit van with the bags of PPE. "Seeing as you're here now love, you may as well stay and help." Bob agreed and so the three of us suited-up in the hostel carpark while Cookie briefed us with his plan. I collected a sledge hammer and crow bar from the boot of the panda and we went back into the hostel. Cookie asked the warden if he had access to the building's fuse box and if he would be able to pull the main lighting fuse for us. "Sure" he replied.

He had a look about him I would see in members of the public many times during my career, a mix of excitement and bewilderment with just a touch of fear or panic.

I looked at my watch, it was a couple of minutes to six, so we asked him to kill the lights at exactly 6pm...that gave us plenty of time to get ourselves into position outside the room. We crept upstairs as quietly as possible, and waited silently in the corridor.

Right on cue the lights went out and Cookie (being the largest of the three of us) started to demolish the room's wall with the sledgehammer. I was crouched next to him, ready to strike. As the smallest and most agile of the trio I was to be the entry man, and as soon as the hole was big enough I scrambled through it into the pitch-black room and tackled the guy to the ground. I was pumped with adrenalin and was expecting a fight, but instead I was greeted with "That was fucking brilliant! You guys are ace! That was the best thing I've ever fucking seen!"

With some difficulty Bob crawled in behind me just as I was handcuffing the man. The lights came back on and I was able to properly see the mess the room was in. The bed and a chest of drawers had been pushed up against the door, there were bits of plasterboard and dust everywhere from Cookie's handiwork, and a mirror on the opposite wall had been smashed, with jagged pieces of broken glass all over the floor, including one large dagger-shaped one. I looked back at my prisoner and saw he had cuts to his hands, I assumed from holding the improvised glass weapon.

Bob and I moved the furniture so we could leave the room through the door and were met outside by a sweaty looking Cookie and shocked looking warden. "These guys are fucking class!" the prisoner grinned to the warden, who I imagine was wondering how long it was going to take him to write up the damage report.

We left the hostel to be met by a small crowd of nosey neighbours who had come out to see what all the commotion was about. Our man seemed delighted to have an audience and shouted out to them "These guys are fucking awesome. I didn't think they could get me, but they came through the fucking wall! It was fucking awesome man!" It was hard not to laugh. "Okay love, mind you head as you get in" Cookie softly said as we stepped him up into the cage at the rear of the police van. He was still singing our praises as I slammed the van doors shut. "That was the best fucking thing I've ever seen!"

Yet again, I learnt to expect the unexpected (it's a regular theme in police work).

Fighters don't always fight...sometimes a calm manner can defuse even the most violent situations. We clearly don't call everyone "love", but sometimes it helps!

Generally speaking though, I learnt that keeping calm, taking the time to properly plan and prepare, and working in a team with clear communication would see me through most incidents. And I never forgot the humour, to look for it in every situation...it made the job so much less stressful, and so much more fun.

5

Kicking Off at the Castle

To many TVP officers, Windsor was seen as a cushy posting...a nice, posh town where the Queen lived. It had a castle, a beautiful Royal Park, boats on the River Thames, historical old lanes, and soldiers marching through the streets in red tunics and bearskins. It had the Long Walk, botanical gardens, a race course, and a safari park (now Legoland) and, just across the bridge, one of the oldest and most exclusive schools in the world...Eton College.

But it also had its darker side. Like almost anywhere in the UK it had plenty of crime, and this was exacerbated by the town's close proximity to Slough, one of TVP's most crime-ridden centres.

Historically Windsor had some interesting skeletons in its closet too. In 1963 Buster Edwards, one of the Great Train Robbers, went into hiding in the adjacent village of Wraysbury before he fled to Mexico. In the 1980s the infamous 'Windsor Chapter' of the Hells Angels had had their club house on the Dedworth Road, before finally moving out in the early '90s, much to the relief of their neighbours. And there is the still-unsolved rape and murder of a 7 year-old girl from 1951. She popped out from her town-centre home to see if she could catch a glimpse of her hero, the boxer Sugar Ray Robinson who was staying in a nearby hotel. She mingled with the excited crowd outside the hotel but was tragically never seen alive again.

Windsor also had a serious problem with drunken disorder on Friday and Saturday nights, particularly during the summer. The combination of the historic centre, the castle, the easy rail links, and its lively pub and club scene made it a highly attractive destination for a night out. And adding to the town's swelling evening crowds, of course, was the number of soldiers. Windsor had two barracks. Victoria Barracks was home to various Guards Regiments (the Scots Guards were there in the early '90s when I was a young PC) and was situated right in the centre of town. Combermere Barracks was home to the Household Cavalry and was just out of town on St Leonards Road.

To be perfectly fair the squaddies didn't cause us that much trouble. Although many of them had little (or no) respect for the civilian police, and some enjoyed a Friday night pub fight, they had a real and understandable fear of the military police. If we needed to calm things down all we often had to do was offer them a 'blue light taxi' ride back to barracks. They knew that being kicked out of the back of a panda at the gates would likely lead to a swift dose of summary justice from the duty Red Caps. Nine times out of ten the mere suggestion of a lift home would stop any further problems. But, like many others who visited the town centre on a Friday night they still enjoyed a few drinks and having the opportunity to blow off a bit of steam. Fights were commonplace and kept us busy.

My first taste of serious public disorder happened very early in my career. It was a warm summer evening and I was in the passenger seat of LA115 (the town centre panda) which was being driven by the only female constable on my shift, Helen.

We were keeping an eye out for a group of some of our most prolific burglars and thieves who, we had been briefed, were out in force. One of their number had recently died in prison and his funeral had been that afternoon. His brother and about half a dozen of his closest mates had headed straight into town to drown their sorrows in the local pubs. They weren't the nicest of lads at the best of times, but drunk and grieving they were a real problem, and we knew it was only a matter of time before someone was going to get hurt.

We were driving slowly down Thames Street in the shadow of the castle walls, enjoying the buzz of the crowds, when we spotted Bob on foot patrol just ahead of us. We decided to pull over to have a chat with him, but as we were slowing his attention was drawn away from us and onto something happening outside McDonalds. I followed his gaze and saw the group we were looking for spill out of the restaurant doors and onto the street. Almost immediately one of their number, Kerry, threw a punch at some poor lad who promptly dropped to the floor.

Bob was off, sprinting the ten metres or so to the group, and promptly tackled Kerry to the ground just as he was about to put the boot into his prone victim. I was out of the panda door and running before Helen even knew what was happening. I reached Bob just as it all started to kick off. Kerry's brother and a couple of their mates pushed and punched Bob in an attempt to free their friend. I pushed them away and drew my baton, shouting at them to back off, but they were drunk and angry and clearly weren't about to go anywhere without Kerry. I heard a familiar voice on the radio call up for urgent assistance and looked up to see Helen rushing towards us to help, the panda car abandoned by the side of the road.

Helen and I managed to create a bit of space between Bob and the rest of the group, but Kerry was struggling violently and Bob couldn't get him under control. Neither Helen nor I could do anything to help him as we were now under attack from the lads who were screaming abuse, throwing punches and kicking out wildly at us. We were swinging our batons in front of us, trying to give ourselves some safe space and to stop the gang from getting to our colleague.

We had hoped Bob could get his prisoner to our panda, but our assailants were between us and it, ruling that out as an option. I looked around frantically for a safe area. I could see Bob was on the ground, rolling around in a desperate fight. He was going to struggle to keep hold of Kerry much longer and I feared he was going to get seriously hurt. We had slowly been pushed back down the hill towards the Windsor Castle Pub (now the King and Castle). There is a small alleyway to the far side of the pub that leads to a carpark and to Alexandra Gardens. If we could get there, I thought, then that would buy us some time until help arrived... one of us could hold the entrance to the alley whilst the other helped Bob restrain his prisoner.

Just as we got to the passageway help arrived. Unfortunately the only local help available was one single officer, the duty sergeant, also called Bob. This Bob was a small, wiry man who was known to be fairly hot headed. Although not physically imposing he was definitely the sort of person you wanted on your side in a fight, and it didn't take long for him to get stuck in.

We were now in the narrow alley. Helen and I were at the front, relentlessly pushing back the group which by now had considerably grown in size, and was continuing to grow by the minute. It's amazing how many ordinary people, when fuelled by alcohol, will join a violent attack on the police when the opportunity arises. We were jabbing our batons into the mob, trying to keep them out of our space as the two Bobs were now struggling on the floor with the prisoner. Finally the handcuffs went on, and an exhausted Bob, complete with missing tie and ripped and bloodied shirt, got to his feet to help us. The sergeant was left on the ground to control the prisoner, who continued to struggle.

Any brief thoughts I may have had that we were winning were quickly dashed as curious drinkers started to pour out of the pub's rear door, which happened to lead directly to the back of the alley. They also appeared to find the opportunity to attack a small number of cornered police officers too good to miss, and we were now trapped. I quickly dropped down to the bottom of the alley, leaving Helen and Bob at the top.

"Where's our backup?" I screamed over the radio. The situation was rapidly deteriorating and we had no chance of gaining control. There was a real danger we were going to get seriously hurt if our fragile lines were crossed.

"We've got units making from Maidenhead, Slough and Reading, including dogs. No ETA yet. I'll get back to you" came the reply in my earpiece.

Strangely, the crowd at the rear of the alley, despite having no apparent involvement in the initial situation, were just as violent as those at the front. The repeated jabs from my baton were only just holding them back. Despite still being on the ground, wrapped around the prisoner, the sergeant helped me as best he could by kicking out at anyone who got too close.

Things were getting desperate when I finally heard the distant sound of sirens. First to arrive was Matt, a dog handler. His dog, Hogan, was ferociously barking and snarling and the crowd at the top of the alley quickly moved out of his way. With them now at the entrance Bob was able to join me at the back, fighting to keep the drunks at bay. I could hear more sirens and I became aware that at least four officers from Slough and another pair from Maidenhead had joined us. I could also hear the barking of a second dog. I wasn't alone in realising that the situation had suddenly and dramatically changed. The group of twenty or so at the bottom of the alley quickly disappeared back into the pub, no longer liking the odds.

My relief was short lived. I knew the fight was far from over. If anything, it had intensified at the top end of the alley and the group's number had now swelled to about fifty. The relief officers had managed to form an arc at the entrance and had slowly been pushing the crowd back across Thames Street towards the castle walls. The deafening noise of the sirens, the dogs barking and the mob screaming was pierced by the sudden sound of shattering glass as a bottle exploded as it landed by my feet. It was the first of a dozen or so bottles, glasses and other bits of assorted rubbish that were thrown at us from the far side of the road.

"Missiles!" someone shouted from our ranks, but without shields or helmets there wasn't much we could do to protect ourselves. Clearing the crowd was now a matter of real urgency before someone got seriously hurt. It would have been nice to arrest some of the offenders, but restoring the peace was our prime concern. The dogs advanced across the road, straining on their leads, snarling and snapping, drawing back their gums to show their teeth, with their handlers struggling to hold them back. We advanced behind them, batons drawn, shouting at our attackers to drop their bottles, to back off, to go home. Some of the cops from Slough grabbed a prisoner or two, wrestling them to the ground. The message was clear and as quickly as it had started it was over. The crowd melted away, either back into the pubs or to start their drunken walks home.

It had been exhausting but exhilarating, and I was instantly hooked. Public order policing brought back the feelings of excitement and danger that I had often felt as a young scooter boy and as a student demonstrator. I wanted more of it, and it turned out that Windsor was one of the best towns in the TVP area for that sort of policing. I had well and truly landed on my feet.

Over the following weeks and months Kerry, along with his brother and their mates, continued to be a thorn in our sides, and it wasn't long before I came across him again.

A few weeks later I arrested a lad who had been kicked out of Windsor's biggest nightclub, Mirage. He was fighting with the door staff and clearly had some sort of an issue with them. Once he had calmed down he explained his behaviour to me. He said the bouncers had searched him on entering the club and had found some drugs (I think a small quantity of ecstasy pills), which they had seized. So far, so good. But...he alleged that they were then selling his drugs (and more they seized off other patrons) inside the venue. He had confronted them about it and had been very physically ejected. He said it happened all the time and was common knowledge amongst the clubbers.

It immediately occurred to me that although our Town Centre Patrol Team did occasionally get called to the club to pick up confiscated drugs, the calls were infrequent and the quantities were small. Mirage was a busy, popular and large nightclub, and everyone was searched on the way in. I would guess that they were seizing considerable amounts of drugs every night. Where were they ending up? His story made some sense.

I went to see Lucy, my sergeant, to get her advice on what to do next. She suggested I come to work the following night in my best dancing clothes and go and have a look at what was going on inside the club. Sweet. I was a single male in my mid-twenties and I was going to get paid to go clubbing! This was my first plain-clothes operation and, filled with my own self-importance I headed into town with just a covert radio for company. A couple of uniformed town centre officers were briefed on what I was doing and were to be on foot patrol in the vicinity to respond if I needed help.

My first hour in the club was uneventful and I saw no evidence of the bouncers selling drugs. In fact I didn't see any drug dealing going on at all, but the night was still young and the club was still steadily filling up. The vibe was upbeat and energetic but (perhaps because I was slightly removed from it all) it had a slightly sinister feel to it. I couldn't relax and had the constant urge to check my back. Would I be recognised? Would the bouncers work out what I was up to?

The music picked up tempo and the stage area was filling with the most extroverted dancers. The place erupted when the slow introduction to 'Sandstorm' kicked into its frantic, trancelike beat. A huge cheer went up and everyone's arms were in the air, hands open-palmed and moving in time with the music. And then, there he was. Despite being on bail, with strict curfew conditions of being at home from 6pm to 6am, Kerry was on stage, front and centre, showing the world his best moves. I didn't want to blow my cover, but this was too good an opportunity to miss. I went to find the quietest spot I could and called up the PCs outside the club to come and get him.

They walked in, escorted by a couple of door staff, and were met with jeering, boos, and looks of surprise and confusion. The greatest look of surprise, however, came from Kerry when they arrested him for breaching his bail. As he was being led out he looked furiously around the club, presumably trying to work out who had grassed him up, and then he spotted me. He froze and stared at me with a mixture of hatred and disgust. He was going to take this particular arrest personally and wasn't going to forget about it any time soon.

I couldn't risk staying in the club any longer so headed back to the nick to change into my uniform. I went to see Lucy to update her and work out what to do next.

"Well, you haven't got any evidence. All you've got is the word of someone who has a grievance with the nightclub. You've submitted a report to LIO haven't you?" The LIO was our Local Intelligence Officer who collected and distributed information from officers, informants, other agencies, and members of the public.

"Yes, I did that yesterday."

"Okay. If you want to do anything else I suggest you go and see the manager one afternoon when the club is closed. He won't want his bouncers dealing drugs, he knows that could get him shut down. Leave it up to him to deal with for now. If we get any further reports or some actual evidence then we may be able to do something more positive."

So a week or so later I found myself knocking on the large double doors at the front of the club. A young woman dressed in black let me into the cavernous entrance hall with a wide staircase which led straight up to the bars and dancefloor. We didn't go upstairs, but instead she led me through a door on our left into a dark, narrow corridor, lit only by the light of the hallway behind us. She knocked on the first door on the left.

"What is it?" came the gruff, slightly irritated reply.

"There's a policeman here to see you" she said.

A couple of seconds later the door was opened by a large man in a cheap-looking and slightly crumpled suit. He looked like a retired heavyweight boxer and, despite being close to 60, he still looked like someone you wouldn't want to get on the wrong side of. And he knew it.

"Come in" he ordered as he turned back towards his desk at the far side of the cramped, dingy and windowless room. The lack of natural light combined with the low ceiling and the smell of stale cigarette smoke made the room claustrophobic. Hesitantly I entered. Even at this early stage in my career I had learned that you wanted to avoid places with no easy means of escape.

"Sit down" he said, nodding to an old and dirty armchair by the desk. It wasn't a request, it was an instruction. I shook my head. "It's okay, I'll stand."

As I turned to face him I realised we weren't alone. Standing in the shadow of the corner of the room behind the door was one of the door staff.

"So what do you want?" the manager demanded, no pleasantries offered.

"Could we talk privately?" I asked, glancing at the bouncer to make it clear I wanted him to leave.

"No, he stays." This guy wasn't going to negotiate anything. His club, his rules. I was nothing, an irritation to get rid of as quickly as possible. I wasn't feeling comfortable and was starting to wish I hadn't come alone. Maybe he sensed my unease, I don't know, but the next thing the manager did was to walk back over to the door and lock it. He folded his arms and repeated his question.

"So what do you want?"

Unnerved by his behaviour I said as confidently as I could "I need you to unlock that door, ask your man here to leave, and then we can talk."

He just shrugged, making no attempt to acknowledge my request or to unlock the door. He exchanged a glance and a subtle nod with the bouncer, an unspoken but understood command of some sort. He was clearly trying to intimidate me, and to be honest he was succeeding. I briefly considered calling on my radio for assistance, but thought better of it. If I wanted to escalate things then that was the best way to go about it.

I tried another tack.

"I'm not sure what the drama is, this is just a routine courtesy call. I just wanted to check if you're having any issues here at the club that we need to be aware of?" I said, being deliberately economical with the truth.

He snorted by way of reply. I clearly wasn't fooling him.

"I know you've been sniffing around the club lately. What do you really want?"

"I'd rather we spoke privately" I pressed, slightly panicked.

He just shrugged and the bouncer made no attempt to move. Oh well, I'd have to face this head on.

"What sort of quantity of drugs do you find on an average club night?"

"You know how much. One of your colleagues collects it from the office every week."

"Is that all of it?"

"Yes. Why?"

"It's not very much and sometimes there isn't any at all."

"So?" he snarled. I was clearly pissing him off. I looked across to the bouncer. He looked like he wanted to kill me. I was painfully aware that I was stuck in a locked and windowless room with two men twice my size who very clearly didn't like me or my questions. It occurred to me that these men were more than just nightclub staff and maybe I had inadvertently stumbled through a doorway into a world of gangsters and organised crime.

"You do search all your customers as a condition of entry?" I pushed on, despite my desire to leave.

"You know we do. It's part of our licencing conditions."

"So where are all the drugs going?" I was pushing my luck but figured, despite the obvious intimidation, they weren't actually going to hurt me. They just wanted me to know that here, in the club, they were in charge and I wasn't. They want to scare me into not coming back again, and they were doing a good job of it.

"What are you saying?" He looked like he was going to explode.

"We've had an allegation made against your door staff" I said, glancing across the room to the bouncer. He returned my look, staring distastefully at me whilst failing to suppress a sneer.

"What allegation?" the manager snapped back at me.

"That drugs are being taken off customers at the door and then sold by your bouncers inside the club." There was a pause whilst the manager thought about his answer.

"Have you got any evidence?" he asked slowly and deliberately.

I answered with a slight shrug and raised eyebrows.

"Then you can fuck off" he spat as he turned and unlocked the door. I was escorted out of the club and onto the street by the bouncer.

I drove back to the nick relieved but dejected. I clearly hadn't resolved anything. In fact all I had managed to do was alert the club that we knew what they were up to, possibly blowing the chance of a future drugs operation there. But at least I knew the management were either complicit or didn't care. I submitted a report to the LIO, with a copy going to our licencing officer. Someone else could deal with this now, it wasn't a job for a lone probationary constable.

So, was Windsor a cushy posting in a pretty town with a castle? Yes, to some extent. But if you scratch the surface anywhere you'd be surprised at what you may uncover. And that's what policing is about...discovering what goes on behind closed doors, in worlds most of us don't even know exist.

Top companies advertise vacant posts in the 'Observer': 01753 523355 W May 24, 1996 THE OBSERVER 31

SALLY HENSON joins the Friday police patrols in Windsor town centre

KEEPING UP A HIGH PROFILE

HANDLING minor disputes and major fights are all in a night's work for Windsor police who were out in force on Friday.

As officers strive to stamp out crime and the fear of crime, the 'Observer' joined Windsor police patrols last Friday.

More than 20 officers were policing the town, both uniform and Specials, two police horses, a dog handler, and two traffic cars from Taplow were in the vicinity.

There is a high-profile policing campaign on and wherever you looked, there was an officer watching over proceedings.

Reporting for 'duty' at 7pm, things started quietly with foot patrol around the town to see what was going on.

In River Street car park, PC Alan Boyce was called over to referee a battle between two irate motorists who both insisted they had spotted the last remaining parking space first.

The man and woman had each driven their respective vehicles half in to the space and stalemate had been reached.

PC Boyce heard from both drivers before pointing out it was time to 'be adult' about the situation. A toss of a coin fell in the man's favour. He parked and the woman drove off in her BMW in a huff.

At 8.40pm it was back to the police station to collect a car.

Once mobile, PC Gerard Bourdillon is collected from the High Street as the two are paired up for the night.

On route there was a quick stop off to find out where the driver of a Land Rover parked on double yellow lines in Victoria Street was. The vehicle had been spotted earlier and with security threats in the town at a high, inquiries were made at the nearby pub. The driver was 'just popping in to deliver some eggs'!

Driving around, the two PCs are on the look-out for known criminals, for signs of tampering, broken locks, windows on stolen vehicles.

Several drivers are pulled over: "It gives us a chance to have a chat and check out the cars. If nothing is wrong people are usually quite comfortable about it," explained PC Boyce.

He explained: "It is a quiet evening but it is noticeable more and more people are gathering in the town.

"Our focus is to be seen in the town, high-profile policing. We also have to bear in mind the security situation at the moment."

Demonstrations

At 9pm, Sgt Pete Downing and PC Neil Jones from the mounted section based at Milton Keynes arrive.

Their horses, Windsor and Chesham (all police horses are named after towns in the force area) known as Clyde and Arnie respectively, will be patrolling the town for about three hours, assisting officers on the ground.

PC Jones explained their duties involve maintaining public order at events, including demonstrations, concerts, football matches, Newbury by-pass, Royal Ascot and Windsor Horse Show.

As they tack up their horses, Sgt Downing added: "Not only do we police events we also travel around the force area to patrol in the evenings.

"It takes up to a year to train a police horse, you can't expect them to go straight into the job, it is not just a matter of the horse having the right temperament."

At 10pm the next shift report for duty. Sgt Chris Parker briefs his team on who is working with who and where.

Friendly rivalry is good for morale and amicable bets on who gets the first arrest are bantered about.

Reports of a missing teenager come through and we head off to Dedworth.

The 15-year-old girl has not been seen since that morning and checks need to be made with her boyfriend and grandmother.

The car pulls in at the Clarence Road petrol station to check out a gang of lads. Recognising some, the PCs radio through to control to see if the names given come up as wanted people. All clear and off again.

The boyfriend's family have not seen the missing girl and as the car heads for the next address a suspect disqualified driver is spotted.

A quick U-turn and the car pulls over. The occupants are quizzed. They are on their way to see a nameless friend in a road they don't know the name of.

The officers find a stolen tax disc and two of the three are arrested on suspicion of theft and driving with no insurance.

After booking the two into custody at Maidenhead, it is back to Windsor as it is nearing pub closing time.

The call comes through a fight has broken out in Thames Street as we enter the town.

Hundreds of people are about as officers, two on horseback and dog handler PC Matt Sharp with a fierce-looking, but muzzled Hogan, are breaking up the fight and dispersing the on-lookers.

An hour later when all is quiet and 11 people have been arrested, PC Bourdillon explained: "Having the horses there was invaluable. If a horse goes up to someone they are far more likely to move on, if they don't you can pick them up by the scruff of the neck and move them on.

"The problem was people were hanging around to see what was happening. You can only ask them to move on and warn them they could be arrested so many times.

"It's now a matter of sorting out who arrested who, who said what to whom and everyone getting back to the jobs they were doing before the call."

It is 12.15am and the radio controllers are trying to establish which officers are where, who has who's handcuffs, truncheon and so on.

A check of an address regarding the missing girl is carried out.

At the Mobil garage in Maidenhead Road, the PCs speak to some young men hanging around when a report of a noisy party or domestic fight comes over the radio.

Heading to Hanover Way, PC Boyce said: "You never know what's going to be going on on the other side of the door if it's a domestic. There could be fighting and someone hurt or they may not want us to be involved."

It turned out to be nothing, just a group of people, slightly the worse for drink.

It is nearing 1am and time to go to Maidenhead to deal with their prisoners and ready for nightclub closing times. At 5am, the two PCs sign off duty.

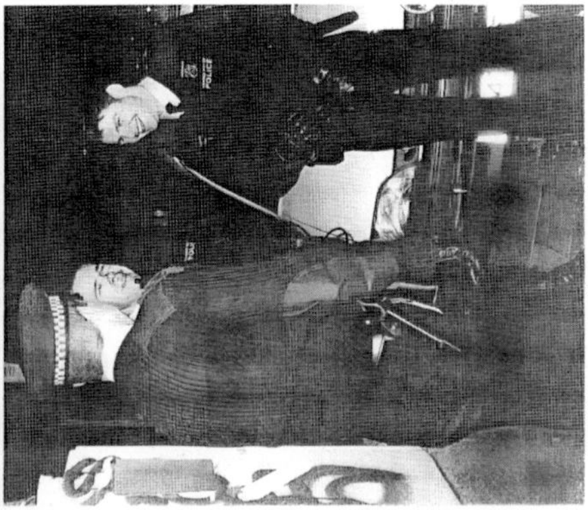

A LIGHTER moment for officers on patrol in Windsor on Friday.

Local newspaper article about another typical Friday night shift in Windsor

6

Confessions of a Killer

Often the most routine and mundane jobs turn into something else altogether. MisPers (Missing Persons) and domestic disputes are some of our most regular calls and although many are 'groundhog day' jobs, often things are not quite what they seem.

Whilst still a keen and highly motivated probationer, I was sent at the start of a night-shift to a local mental health clinic. I was crewed with Steve (my newly promoted sergeant) and we were there to take a MisPer report for an in-patient who had taken himself off for the day and hadn't returned. He was both bi-polar and suicidal and the staff were extremely concerned for his wellbeing.

As I opened my briefcase and started to sift through the astounding number of different forms I had to carry around with me everywhere I went, optimistically looking for a 'MisPer 1', the clinic's front door opened and a big guy in his forties walked in. "Oh, it's George" said the nurse. "Okay" Steve replied "we'll just have a quick chat to check he's alright and then we can leave you to it." I could, however, already see he wasn't alright. He looked confused and agitated and was sweating despite it being a cool night. We tried talking to him, but it was immediately obvious he didn't like the police and wasn't going to cooperate with us. The decision was made to call an ambulance as we suspected he may have taken something in an attempt to take his own life.

Despite our requests he refused to wait and told us he was going to leave. The staff were not happy as he was under their care and we couldn't just let him walk out...the risk to his life was too great.

"You can't go anywhere mate until the ambulance is here. We just need to check you're alright, ok?" I said to him. He didn't like that and started to become aggressive and abusive.

"Fuck you. You can't fucking stop me. If I want to kill myself I will."

"No" I replied, "I can't let you do that. You're not going anywhere just yet mate."

I felt the air move in front of my nose as he threw his first punch. My reflexes were sharp enough that I pulled my head back just in time, avoiding contact from his fist. Steve lunged forward and was promptly knocked to the ground.

Shit I thought, *here we go.* I shoulder barged him with all my might, pushing him back up against the wall. He was angry and considerably bigger than me and I knew I wouldn't be able to hold him for long. Luckily Steve didn't appear to be hurt and quickly got back up onto his feet, just in time to grab one of George's arms before he could break free from my grip. We now had hold of one arm each, but due the guy's size, strength and mental demeanour we knew it wasn't over yet and we had a real battle on our hands.

Then, inexplicably, "Shit, I'm sorry. Oh god, I'm sorry, I'm sorry, I'm sorry.' He stopped resisting and almost went limp as the aggression left him. "I'm so sorry. I don't know what came over me, I'm sorry." I slowly released my hold on him as he started to sob. I looked at Steve who had also released his grip. He shrugged. I could tell he was thinking the same as me...this guy hasn't really hurt us, he's clearly unwell, let's just get him medically checked and we can leave it at that.

We didn't have to wait long for the ambulance to arrive, and when the two paramedics entered the clinic's large entrance hall and approached George, he immediately became agitated again. He stepped back from them, almost recoiling, and said "Fuck off, you're not touching me."

"It's okay George" I said softly "they just need to have a quick look at you and then we can all leave you in peace."

"Fuck off, all of you!" he shouted as he moved side to side, transferring his weight from one foot to the other and alternately clenching and relaxing his fists.

"Come on George, calm yourself down mate, we're all here to help you, okay? The last thing you want is to get yourself arrested."

Once again there was a sudden and dramatic change in his behaviour. "Shit, sorry. Sorry, sorry, sorry..." he muttered as he calmly walked towards the paramedics. One of them smiled at him and said "Okay George, I just need you to come outside with me to the ambulance so I can check you over." His reaction was immediate and violent. He threw himself at the paramedic whilst wildly kicking and punching him to the ground. Steve and I reacted in unison, springing forward and quickly taking him to the floor where we were able to properly restrain him.

And again, the total transformation in his behaviour from extreme violence to a calm and sobbing apology. This time he remained calm, and looking like a harmless, sad and broken man he allowed the paramedics to examine him. They were happy that he hadn't actually taken anything and that he was in no immediate physical danger. Their only concern was for his state of mind, and seeing as he was currently an in-patient at a mental health clinic they saw no point in taking him to hospital.

The clinic were happy for him to remain there under their care and supervision, and the paramedic didn't want to press charges for the assault. That was that. Job done, so we left.

That *was* that, until I got to work the following afternoon to find a hand-written message in my docket (back in the days before we had e-mail) asking me to pop down to the ambulance station to talk to the guys about the incident. So off I went in one of our unmarked Vauxhall Corsa 'enquiry' cars, and was met at the door by one of the paramedics who had been at the clinic the night before. It was impossible not to notice that he was limping badly...clearly his lower right leg was injured and he appeared to be in some pain.

Very apologetically he explained that one of George's kicks had connected just below his knee and it had badly torn his calf muscle. It was a much more serious injury than he had first suspected. He would be off work for a number of weeks and his calf may require surgery. The NHS has a zero-tolerance attitude to violence against its staff and he had no option but to file a complaint. Fair enough, I thought, but I knew no action would actually be taken due to George's considerable mental health issues.

Out came my trusty briefcase and after filling out the crime report (form CID1, of which I had plenty) I took a statement and filled out a medical disclosure consent form, allowing me to access full details of his injury from the hospital. I then headed straight back to the clinic to see if I could speak to George. I received a very frosty reception, the staff were extremely unhelpful and appeared not to want police in their building (unless, that is, they called for them). They explained that he was too mentally unstable for me to see him, so instead I obtained all George's details so I could at least file my report. I was now completely convinced that this case was going to be marked 'NFA', or 'No Further Action' on the grounds of mental diminishment.

Back at the nick I carried out all the necessary checks on him, but I could find no police record of someone with that name and date of birth. I was surprised as I assumed someone that violent must have come to police attention at some point in his life. "Have you got anything similar?" I asked the PNC (Police National Computer) operator on the other end of the phone. There was a pause, then "We've got an Alex George Rees, spelt REES, not REECE, with a slightly different date of birth. Same day and year but born in August, not September." That sounded hopeful "Okay, what's he known for?" I pushed. "He's wanted by Nottinghamshire Constabulary for robbery. Oh, and he's absconded from prison." Now I was getting excited "What's his description?" The description I was given could have been him, but equally it was vague enough that it could have been any 40 year-old, six-foot-something white guy I had come across in my career. "Have you got a photo of him I can see?" Another pause while she furiously typed into her keyboard "Apparently there's one in an old edition of the Police Gazette"

"Great! Can you fax it through to me?"

"No, we don't have those here. You'll need to get that from the Archives Department at Headquarters, but they'll be closed now...they work normal office hours" I looked at my watch, it was already around 7pm, my shift ended at 11pm and then I was into a couple of rest days. This was going to have to wait until Thursday when I was back on earlies.

Three days later I was back at work and after a quick call to Archives I was holding a faxed photograph of the wanted man. Unfortunately the photo resolution was poor and that, combined with the steaks of black ink from the old fax machine, made the picture almost as useless as the description. I still had no idea if it was him or not. I knocked on the Sergeant's office door, and waited to be called in. I showed the fax to Steve who just shrugged his shoulders. I was getting really frustrated now...this guy may be an escaped prisoner but we've got no way of identifying him. I decided to head back to the clinic to show the photo to staff there. If anyone was going to recognise him it would be them.

"Yes, that's George" said the lady at reception cheerfully.

"Okay, well this is a lot more serious now. He's coming with me now, no matter what you say. It'll be up to the court to decide if he comes back here or goes back to prison, not you."

"No, he can't go with you" she replied.

I sighed. "Yes he can, and he will."

"No, you don't understand, he discharged himself this morning and we don't know where he's gone."

I was furious and my irritation with the clinic was showing "You knew I needed to speak with him. If he was well enough to discharge himself he was well enough to talk to me. Why didn't anyone contact me?" She just shrugged and apologised, saying they go by the doctors' orders. I left her a list of contact numbers and the job's URN (Unique Reference Number) to quote should he return, and I left feeling totally deflated.

I guessed Rees could still be in Windsor so before going off duty I left a short screed in the briefing file so the late and night shifts would know the basis of the job should he turn up and the clinic call.

At 6.30 the following morning I was greeted at work with the news that "there's one in the traps for you mate". I phoned custody to be told that Sgt. Allen had arrested Rees at the Vansittart

Arms pub the previous evening, and my prisoner was ready to be interviewed. I collected the case file from my docket, grabbed a set of car keys and drove over to Maidenhead Police Station, which held the designated custody suite for our area.

After a brief chat with the Custody Sergeant I went down to the cell block to check we actually had the right person and to see if he wanted a lawyer for his interview. With a loud metallic thud I dropped the heavy door hatch to his cell and peered through the opening. I instantly recognised him. "Hi George. I'm going to be interviewing you in a bit and I just wanted to check you're okay and see if you want a duty solicitor?" He shook his head. "A cup of tea then?" I asked.

"Never mind that," he replied "there's something I need to tell you."

"Not now mate, you can tell me whatever you want during the interview, but we can't talk here."

"No, bollocks. I need to talk to you right now" he insisted.

"No George, not now, in the interview, okay?"

"Look, I've killed someone. I need to talk to you now."

Shit. He's just confessed to a murder but he's not under caution and there's no tape recording of this. What am I going to do now my thoughts were running away from me. This was suddenly becoming a lot more difficult than I had been expecting. I was still in my probation and, not surprisingly, hadn't dealt with a murderer before. I didn't want this to go horribly wrong and get kicked out of court because I messed up the procedure.

"Look George, don't say anything more until we get you a solicitor" I said firmly.

"I don't want a fucking solicitor, I want to tell you I killed someone in London. Surely someone's looking for me?"

I tried again "Okay George, I hear you but you really do need a solicitor present if you're going to talk about this."

"I don't want a fucking solicitor" he repeated. I could see he was getting irritated, and I didn't want him to change his mind and clam up.

"Okay, I'll call the Met and see if they know anything about it. Whereabouts in London was it?"

"I was near the Barbican. I stabbed a guy."

Slightly stunned, but with a rush of adrenalin in my blood, I returned to the custody office and spoke to the sergeant. As it wasn't a Thames Valley crime he was happy for me to follow things up myself and not hand it immediately over to CID. I got out the navy blue national police phone directory to look up the number for the Barbican under the Metropolitan Police's list of stations. I couldn't find it and realised that the Barbican is actually right in the City, and the Met don't police the square mile of the financial centre. That job was down to the tiny 'City of London' force, distinctive in their almost entirely black uniforms with red and white check cap bands. I found the relevant number in the phone book and called the nick.

I introduced myself and asked the front-desk officer if he was aware of any unsolved murders on his patch. He sounded bored and totally uninterested but said he'd put me through to CID anyway. His complete lack of interest made me wonder whether George had made the whole thing up and was sending me on a wild goose chase...something that's not as unusual as you might expect.

The phone seemed to ring forever before an only marginally more interested Detective Sergeant picked it up. I repeated what Rees had told me, along with his previous history. "Okay, has he told you anything else" he almost sighed in reply. "Well they're not interested. What a waste of my time" I thought to myself morosely, but instead cheerily said "Hang on a minute, I'll go and ask him".

I went back to his cell "George, I'm on the phone to a DS now...he wants to know if you can tell me anything else?'

"I stripped the guy naked, tied him to a chair and stabbed him to death" came a shocking reply that I hadn't expected...I had assumed this had just been a street fight gone horribly wrong. I rushed back and picked up the phone in the office, relaying the horror of what I had just been told. The DS now sounded slightly more interested "Has your guy got any tattoos?" I hadn't noticed any, so back I went to the cells.

"George, have you got any tatts mate?" He rolled up his sleeves and showed me some small do-it-yourself type of black inking on his wrists and forearms, mainly dots and a few centimetre-long crosses. I went back to the phone. Now the DS was sounding interested, almost excited. "I need a bit more before I come all the way out to see him".

"Like what?"

"Ask him if he took anything from the victim."

Back again to the cells, and now Rees was getting really pissed off "What the fuck do they want now?" He growled "How fucking hard is it to confess to a murder?!!"

"Sorry mate, just one last thing. Did you take anything?"

"Yeah, I took his watch. A nice one. An Omega."

Back to the phone for the last time "This should help, he says he took the guy's Omega watch."

The voice on the other end of the line almost exploded with excitement "Right! I'll get my team together and we'll be down as soon as we can!"

"Okay, I'll go and nick him now for the murder" I said, my head spinning that I was going to make such an important arrest.

"No, don't do that, we don't want the clock to start ticking until we get there. I'll do that later" replied the DS. I was instantly deflated...that was an arrest I wanted recorded on my PDP (Probationer Development Portfolio). Oh well, at least I had been the one to find this guy and I still felt pretty chuffed with that.

It turned out that Rees hadn't actually killed the guy, but not through want of trying. By some miracle the victim had survived the horrific attack, despite being stabbed multiple times. He had managed to get himself free from the chair once George had left, and crawled to a neighbour for help.

The City of London Police had had a full Incident Room running for months with little evidence and no suspect, and now, totally out of the blue they had a full confession. It really was quite unusual and an amazing result all round.

I didn't think much more about it until around a year later I was reading an article in the paper about an ex-soldier who had been sentenced to 15 years in prison for a brutal attack. As I read on I realised it was Rees. The story said that he had joined the Army at 16, and there he had been bullied and sexually abused. He had spent most of his short career either in military custody or absent without leave. On leaving the Army he had developed a pathological hatred of homosexuals, which started to manifest itself violently. He started to exact his revenge for the abuse he had suffered by going to gay bars, picking up men and robbing them once outside.

Over the years the attacks had become ever more violent, culminating with the City of London case (although Rees also maintained he killed a man in Amsterdam, a claim never substantiated).

During the trial his psychological assessments revealed that his offending was getting worse and that his intent was to carry on killing until he got caught. By his own admission he was a danger to society and the judge stated in his summing up that Rees had all the hallmarks of becoming a serial killer.

So, although this turned out to be a highly unusual job, it started off as something very routine and I learnt some really useful lessons from it. As a police officer you never really know what (or who) you're dealing with, so it's really important to do all the checks possible, not simply the necessary ones. Dotting all the 'i's, crossing all the 't's and doing a proper 'belt and braces' job is vital.

With overflowing trays of crime reports and case files it's easier said than done, but as officers we shouldn't be in too much of a rush to get rid of jobs, to file them away or write them off...sometimes they may just be the biggest jobs of our careers or the one investigation we're most proud of.

In my case this job was a great piece of evidence to show how diligent an officer I was when, several years later, I applied to join the Mounted Section. But more important than any of this, I almost certainly saved the life or lives of Rees's next victim or future victims.

Policing doesn't get much more rewarding than that.

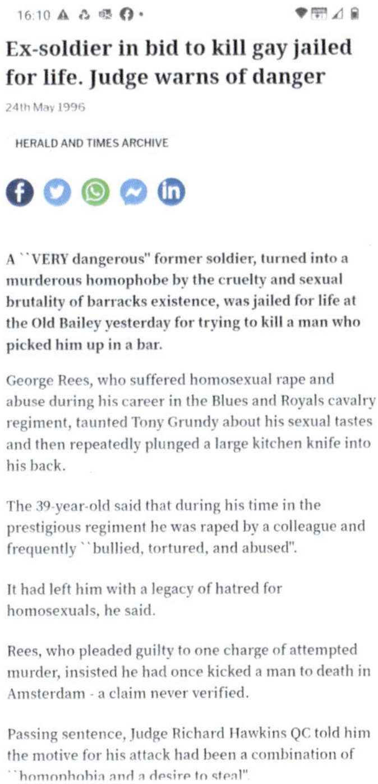

16:10

Ex-soldier in bid to kill gay jailed for life. Judge warns of danger

24th May 1996

HERALD AND TIMES ARCHIVE

A ``VERY dangerous'' former soldier, turned into a murderous homophobe by the cruelty and sexual brutality of barracks existence, was jailed for life at the Old Bailey yesterday for trying to kill a man who picked him up in a bar.

George Rees, who suffered homosexual rape and abuse during his career in the Blues and Royals cavalry regiment, taunted Tony Grundy about his sexual tastes and then repeatedly plunged a large kitchen knife into his back.

The 39-year-old said that during his time in the prestigious regiment he was raped by a colleague and frequently ``bullied, tortured, and abused''.

It had left him with a legacy of hatred for homosexuals, he said.

Rees, who pleaded guilty to one charge of attempted murder, insisted he had once kicked a man to death in Amsterdam - a claim never verified.

Passing sentence, Judge Richard Hawkins QC told him the motive for his attack had been a combination of ``homophobia and a desire to steal''.

16:08

INDEPENDENT

Subscribe

Menu

NEWS SPORT VOICES CULTURE LIFESTYLE

News

Ex-soldier gets life for 'gay hatred' attack

Jojo Moyes • Thursday 23 May 1996 23:02 BST

• Comments

Sign up to our free breaking news emails

Email

SIGN UP

I would like to be emailed about offers, events and updates from The Independent
Read our privacy notice

A former soldier who warned that gay men would never be safe from him was jailed for life at the Old Bailey yesterday for the attempted murder of a man who picked him up in a bar.

George Rees was left with a "festering hatred" of homosexuals after he suffered homosexual rape and was "bullied, tortured and abused" during his career in the Blues and Royals Cavalry Regiment, the court was told.

Various news reports from the trial in 1996

Out of the Blue

7

Fires and Fools

My shift were on duty the night Windsor Castle caught fire.

The fire burned for fifteen hours, destroying one hundred and fifteen rooms, including St George's Hall. Incredibly the Royal Library survived and only two works of art from the Royal Collection were lost.

Two hundred and twenty-five firefighters used thirty-six pumps to discharge one and a half million gallons of water to fight the flames. Six people were injured but luckily no one was killed.

I can't tell you anything else as I wasn't there.

It happened a year before I first drove into the backyard of Windsor Police Station as a brand new probationary recruit.

A few years later however I did find myself at the scene of another large fire in Windsor, but this one received little or no media coverage.

I was on my way to some mundane job driving along the Windsor Relief Road towards Slough. It was a blisteringly hot summer's day so I wound down the windows of my panda in attempt to get some relief from the heat. I was enjoying the coolness of the fresh breeze that was rushing past my right arm and rumpling my hair. I breathed in deeply and realised the air wasn't quite as fresh as it should be. It was only the faintest hint, but could I smell something burning?

I glanced to my right and, in the distance, I could see plumes of brownish-grey smoke coming from the fields on the Eton side of the river. I stuck on my blue lights and slowly pulled over to the side of the road so I could safely get a proper look. When I looked again the smoke had doubled in size and was getting closer. The hot, dry, afternoon wind had picked up and it was fanning the flames and rapidly pushing the fire towards the road.

"Sierra Alpha from Lima Alpha One One Five" I called over the radio.

"Go ahead One One Five" came the familiar reply from the Slough Control Room. I reported the fire and explained my concern that it was rapidly baring down on the busy dual carriageway that connected the main centres of Slough and Windsor. It wouldn't be long before flames would be whipping across the road, and the thick smoke would reduce visibility to dangerously low levels.

"You're the second call we've had about this" the radio operator replied. "The fire service are already en route. Can you make your way to roundabout below the M4 motorway? We need you to close the road from that end and divert traffic either back onto the M4 or through Slough. We'll get another unit to close the road at the Windsor end."

"Roger that." Blue lights still flashing, I made my way as quickly as I could to my traffic point. The front of the fire was now almost at the road and was about one hundred meters wide. As a result 'quickly' actually meant 'painstakingly slowly' as it was getting difficult to see through the thick grey smoke.

I stopped my panda right across the exit of the roundabout that leads onto to the Relief Road, blocking it off. I put on my cap and high-vis jacket, grabbed some cones from the boot and spaced them out behind my car, giving me a relatively safe space to stand in.

The first few cars came racing down off the motorway, not expecting to find their exit closed. The drivers looked shocked and irritated to see a police car blocking their path. Despite the obvious inferno raging only a few hundred meters down the road, every single one of the first dozen or so cars to exit the motorway stopped to complain, and then every third or fourth car thereafter.

"Why have you closed the road?"

"Can't you just let *me* through? Then you could stop all the traffic after me."

"But I live/work/have to collect my kids/ have a meeting/need to see my granny in Windsor"

"Is that *really* necessary? It doesn't look *that* bad to me"

"Well, if I can't go that way *you'll* have to tell me how I get home."

"No one will know if you just let *me* through. I only live down the road."

And of course, plenty of "For fuck's sake, just let me through. I'm late for (a, b or c)"

The incessant questions, demands and complaints were all equally idiotic, unreasonable and entitled. Could these motorists not see the inferno that was raging in front of their eyes?

"I can't let you through because, as you can clearly see, the road's on fire." I informed every single one of them, in an increasingly bored and irritated tone. I was standing in the full sun, on the hottest day of the year, close to a massive fire, wearing thick black woollen trousers and a bright yellow jacket. Sweat was slowly trickling down my spine, and I didn't have any water. I was very definitely not enjoying myself and knew it was going to be a long, hot afternoon dealing with idiots.

About an hour and fifty or so stupid drivers later a shiny black Range Rover stopped beside me and the passenger window opened. I sighed. Here we go again. Another self-important prick is about to tell me why they should be exempt from a lawful direction.

"Officer!" came a strong and very familiar Scottish voice. "I see the road's on fire." The voice wasn't just familiar now, it was unmistakable. I leant forward to look across to the driver. The long dark hair and big smile confirmed my identification. "I think I'll go the long way home today" said Billy Connolly.

"That would be great. Thanks. You know which way to go?"

"Aye, I do. Thank you officer."

So...the only person to say anything sensible to me (and the only one who didn't think he should get any special treatment) was one of the world's greatest comedians.

Funny that.

Out of the Blue

8

Hoping to Help

Most of us join the job because we genuinely want to help others and actually make some sort of a difference. How we think we should help varies greatly from officer to officer. Some believe the best way to improve society is simply to lock up as many criminals as possible. Some think the best way is via community involvement – visiting schools, setting up youth clubs and Neighbourhood Watch schemes, attending community meetings, and by being generally visible and accessible. Some strive to reduce the number of accidents and deaths on our roads. Some choose to focus only on the most dangerous members of society whilst others protect us from terrorism. I believe all are equally valid, and on the whole I feel most UK police forces balance these different approaches well.

Where I think we get the balance wrong is by not focussing enough on proactive policing (preventing crime) and spending too much of our time and resources on reactive policing (detecting crime). Unfortunately it's hard, if not impossible to measure crime that we've stopped from happening, whereas detection rates are easy to measure so that is what the government wants from us.

One pitfall of this desire to help is that it can lead you into trying to help one particular person over an extended period of time, in effect becoming a sort of untrained social worker. We just don't have the time or the skills to do this. Worse, we will inevitably let the person down as we are unlikely to be able to be there for them when they need us most. Like many young officers, I fell into this trap early in my career.

Datchet was experiencing more than its fair share of crime on our area and as a result my shift (Team 5 at Windsor) was spending quite a lot of time there getting to know the local "problem" families. I was often crewed with another young officer and good friend, Dom, and we quickly formed a bond with an unlikely trio who were regularly finding themselves on the wrong side of the law. As I got to know them I realised that they weren't particularly *bad* kids, they just had pretty bad problems at home.

Jamie's parents were divorcing and as a result he had moved home and school several times in the previous year. His mother was unable to cope with him and so he was currently living with his older half-sister, despite the fact she was only in her early twenties herself and didn't appear to care about what he got up to or whether or not he went to school. Jolene was from a local gypsy family but appeared to want to escape that lifestyle and chose to hang around with the local kids rather than others from the travelling community. Leon was a mixed-race kid from a broken home and seemed to struggle to fit into an almost entirely white village with an unusually high proportion of travellers.

They were twelve or thirteen and were at an age where their future paths were already being set. Jolene would almost certainly turn out okay, she had a heart of gold and wanted to mother the others but was easily led. Jamie was much more of a worry, he appeared to be totally disenfranchised and I guess he felt rejected by everyone who should have cared for him. He almost certainly had ADHD or similar behavioural issues and his frustrations often boiled over into anger and violence. He was usually (but not always) happy to chat with me and Dom but had a deep mistrust of all other police officers.

That left Leon. He was a quiet and intelligent lad who wanted to be an illustrator or designer. He seemed to really enjoy spending time with us, and as my previous career had been in graphic design he was always picking my brains about art school and the creative industries. Unfortunately he lacked any self-belief and just couldn't accept that he could succeed in life and realise his potential. I don't think he thought he was good at anything, or that he deserved success. Crime was an easy option for him and tragically at only thirteen he had already given up. I could see so much promise in him and I wanted him to see it in himself. It was clear that Leon neither needed nor wanted a life of crime but just couldn't accept that an alternative life was possible.

Over the course of the next couple of years I spent many, many hours in Datchet giving these kids (amongst others) as much of my time as possible. I watched as Jamie's behaviour deteriorated and his face appeared on our daily briefing sheets ever more frequently...wanted for car crime, burglaries and the occasional assault. His attitude towards me and Dom also changed and he would openly hurl abuse at us if he wasn't in the mood for pleasantries. I had to arrest him on a number of occasions and it quickly got to the point where he considered me to be just like any other cop, the enemy. He was more than happy to punch and kick me in an attempt to avoid arrest and the good relationship we had had become unsalvageable. I came across him a handful of times over the following twenty years and sadly he never changed, in and out of prison and never able to sort his life out.

Leon struggled with Jamie's choices. His offending didn't escalate during those couple of years and he still dreamt of a better life. I think he found it awkward or even embarrassing when his mate was being abusive to us, he genuinely liked us and was still seeking our guidance. He desperately needed a strong male mentor, but all he had was Jamie – possibly the worst role model he could have chosen. Due to his association with Jamie his name would also occasionally pop up at our briefings and I would often find myself saying "Okay, I'll go and talk to him", still hopeful he could find his way off the path he had found himself on.

Some of my colleagues wondered why I was bothering. Leon wasn't an informant, either he didn't know or wouldn't tell us about the crime that was going on so they thought I was wasting my time. But that wasn't the point. I really believed I could actually make a difference, that I could change his life's direction – not just for his sake, but for the benefit of the whole community. Datchet didn't need another Jamie, the one it had was already causing more than enough misery.

Life moves on though, and my roles changed. Firstly I stayed local but then I joined the Area Team meaning I still spent some time in Datchet, but much less than I had been. This was followed a couple of years later by realising my own dream and getting selected to join the Mounted Section, meaning a permanent move away from the Windsor and Maidenhead area and making it extremely unlikely I would patrol Datchet again.

One damp, grey and miserable afternoon around the turn of the Millennium I found myself back in my old area, doing a patrol on horseback in Maidenhead town centre. A call came in about a lad in a hoodie acting suspiciously in an open-air carpark behind the shops. I was just around the corner so trotted off to see if I could find him. As soon as I turned into the carpark I saw Leon, who looked surprised to see a police officer on a horse. I was actually pleased to see him.

"Leon!" I called cheerfully over to him. He didn't reply, but just stared at me.

"Leon, come over here mate" I said. His stare wasn't warm, and he appeared to be thinking about what to say. Maybe he hadn't recognised me?

One more try "Leon, it's me, Dillan. Come over here and have a chat mate."

"Fuck you!" The words spat out of his mouth with real ferocity. I was momentarily stunned...I don't think he had ever sworn at me before. I manoeuvred my horse over to him, but he immediately turned his back on me and stated to walk away.

"Leon, I need to talk to you mate. Just wait there, okay."

"Fuck you, pig" he shouted as he turned, his face filled with hate and rage.

"Come on mate, calm down. I just want to chat to you. Why are you so angry? You know I'll be fair."

"Fuck you, you're all cunts" came the furious reply, and he turned to walk away again.

No more pleasantries. My tone changed "Right, stay where you are Leon, you're not going anywhere until I've checked you out." He ignored me and continued to walk away. I followed him closely as I began doing the necessary checks over the radio. As I did so a local panda turned up and the officers detained him for a search. I rode over and started to give them Leon's details, but was interrupted.

"Oh, we know Leon VERY well" the officer turned towards him "don't we mate?"

"Fuck you!" came his reply.

The results of my PNC and local intelligence checks came back through my ear-piece and made for depressing listening. In the few years since I had last seen him Leon had amassed a lengthy criminal record and had already spent some time inside. I was crestfallen. All his hopes were gone and ultimately his lack of self-belief and poor friend-choices had destroyed his life. I have no idea how things ended up for him. I never saw him again. I hope he found a way out and built a new life for himself, but I very much doubt it.

So, what's the point in me telling this story? There is no happy ending, and I failed to help anyone. Am I suggesting I shouldn't have bothered? No, not at all. But I needed to understand that a police officer's best way to help, to make a difference, was not to focus on the individual victims or criminals, but to focus on themselves. Being the best cop I could be, making the best decisions, looking after my own mental and physical health would enable me to do the best job I could. I was not a social worker, a probation officer or a counsellor. I was not a mentor or a stand-in parent. But that didn't mean I couldn't be a role model. I believe police officers should, and must, lead by example.

By focusing on myself and the service I provided, I learnt that I could (and in fact *did*) make a difference – probably more than I ever knew.

I just learnt not to expect anyone to thank me for it.

9

Sticks and Screwdrivers

"Is it necessary? Is it reasonable? Is it justified?"

Three questions we as police officers need to ask ourselves every time before we act. The longer I am out of the job, the more I believe these are questions we should *all* be asking ourselves before doing anything. Whether that may be making important decisions, commenting on social media, disciplining our kids, or reacting to conflict. I think if we did, then the positive impact on our communities would be considerable.

These questions become particularly critical when you're a police officer dealing with a confrontational situation. Just because someone has committed an offence doesn't mean it's necessary to arrest them. Because we arrest so many people we don't often stop to consider the impact of removing someone's most basic human right...their right to freedom. Even if it's only for a few hours, that complete loss of control of your own life can be a really impactful experience for some people, particularly if it's their first time.

Most importantly though is to use these three simple questions before using any force. All police use of force needs to be *reasonable*, a term that is often misunderstood, and difficult to define, as every situation is unique. Very clearly, reasonable force when arresting a scared and compliant twelve-year-old girl for shoplifting bears almost no resemblance to the reasonable force necessary to arrest a violent armed offender who has just shot his wife and has now pointed his gun directly at you.

Sometimes 'use of force' may simply be placing a gentle hand on someone's shoulder, or standing in someone's way to prevent them from leaving. On other occasions it may involve placing a suspect in handcuffs to enable officers to safely search them, or to transport them safely and securely to a police station. Often it is both reasonable and necessary to push, strike or even take to the ground a non-compliant or violent offender, in order to effect a controlled arrest. In some instances it will involve using pepper spray, a baton strike or firing a Taser. Dog handlers and mounted officers regularly use their animals to disperse crowds or arrest people, and that can actually involve quite a high level of force that needs to be carefully considered. And then there's the highest level of force there is, deadly force. This is an option that usually (but not always) falls into the hands of highly trained firearms officers.

Like many young officers, I wanted clear guidelines from my trainers about what 'reasonable force' actually meant in reality. I suppose I was after a sort of A+B=C flow chart where my actions would be pre-determined in any given situation. There is no such chart. There are no clear answers. I was however given one very good piece of advice by a training school sergeant who, when I pushed him for an answer, simply pointed to his chest and said "The answer's here. It's in your heart. You'll know, you'll feel it. Do I *need* to do this?"

"Actually" he continued "it'll be crystal clear afterwards. Did I need to do that? Was it necessary or was I just angry? Did I just do what had to be done, or did I try to punish them too? Trust me, in your heart of hearts you'll *know* if it's reasonable or not."

His words stuck with me and although at times I did act out of anger or fear (we're all human, and this is an emotional job), for the vast majority of my career I lived by those words and they served me well.

Three years or so into my service I was attached to the Area Team, a small pro-active policing unit which performed a mixture of uniform and plain-clothes operations. My years there with Millsy, Pikey, Jim and Dougie were without doubt the best (and happiest) in the job for me. We were a very close team and, as long as we were getting results, were left alone to pick and choose our operations and hours. We did a lot of uniformed public order work, whether that was policing the town's pubs and clubs or larger disorder at events like football matches and demonstrations. As well as being MAST trained (what the press like to call 'Riot Police') we were also MoE (Method of Entry) trained...which basically meant we were taught how to use the various bits of equipment available to properly kick a door in. A key role of the team was to execute most of the area's search or arrest warrants, often early morning raids looking for drugs, stolen property or 'wanted' suspects. When we weren't needed for these types of commitments we were free to choose how best to spend our time, and that's when we often utilised the skills we learnt on another course...surveillance.

Nowadays police in the UK have a strict legal framework that dictates when, how and which surveillance tactics can be used. The legislation introduced in 2000 was the Regulation of Investigatory Powers Act, commonly known as RIPA, but in the mid '90s (when I was on the Area Team) no such guidance existed. So, if we were at a loose end then more often than not we'd simply change out of our uniforms and go and follow known criminals and see what they got up to. It was fairly easy pickings for us as some of them were extremely prolific and, as long as they didn't spot us, we usually didn't have to wait long before they got up to no good.

Our other favourite tactic was to set up 'O.P.s' (observation posts) in crime hotspots such as carparks that were suffering a spate of thefts. Essentially we would hide up in a car, building, hedge or anywhere else we could find and sit and wait for something to happen. It could be incredibly boring...hour after hour of hot/cold/cramped/wet/hungry nothingness, just waiting and hoping. But sometimes we would get an arrest before we had even finished setting up the O.P. It was proper 'old school' policing where patience got results, and I loved it.

At the start of the summer, Datchet Railway Station had been experiencing an explosion in the number of thefts from vehicles left in its carpark. Regular patrols from panda cars and local beat officers didn't seem to be slowing the crime rate there, so Dougie, Jim and I decided to do a focussed job on it.

We started by visiting some of the local car dealerships with a view to borrowing an old and indistinctive run-around for a few days. We were lucky enough to find a dealer who was happy to lend us an old Toyota, and he didn't seem to care when we told him it may come back in considerably worse condition than when we took it. "No problem, just happy to help and do my bit!" he beamed in a very used-car-salesman sort of way. So, off we went to Datchet in our lovely 'new' old banger to try and find a suitable O.P. and started knocking on the doors of a row of red-bricked terraced houses that overlooked the carpark. This took a little bit more patience than getting the car, and after a number of refusals (and some no replies), the last house in the row was opened by a lovely lady in her seventies who couldn't have been more delighted to help. She invited us in and showed us upstairs to the rear bedroom which had a perfect and unobstructed view of the station and its parking. She said we could use it for as long as we needed and offered to bring us a tray of tea and biscuits each day. How could we refuse?

The carpark was getting hit mostly mid-week, in the middle of the day...when it was full of commuters' cars but there were very few people around and so little danger of anyone disturbing the thieves. As it was Tuesday afternoon we decided to start the operation the following day and run it until Friday, if necessary. Our plan was to park up the Toyota somewhere in the carpark where it was easily seen from the O.P. and leave a laptop case on the rear parcel shelf as bait. We would all be in plain clothes with one of us in the house with binoculars and a radio (and tea and biscuits) and the other two would be the strike team, sitting in an unmarked car just out of sight (and without tea and biscuits). Dougie (as acting sergeant) pulled rank and chose the option which included refreshments, leaving me and Jim in the car.

It was a hot, sticky, uncomfortable and boring wait on the first morning, with absolutely nothing going on. Our only distractions were updates coming over the radio from Dougie, informing us of his latest choice of biscuit from the selection box he'd been given. After about four hours of slowly cooking inside the Vauxhall, my back was stiff, I was fed up and I desperately needed the loo. Jim was equally miserable and we were just about to suggest to Dougie that we call it a day when my radio's earpiece crackled.

"Three lads have just got off the London train and have headed straight into the carpark."

"We're on!" I said to Jim as the adrenaline started to pump through my veins. I was eager to get out of the car, even just to stretch my back, but the potential strike was a much more exciting prospect.

"They're in the carpark now. They're looking into vehicles. Standby."

"Any second now Jim" I said as I checked my seatbelt was off and patted myself down to make sure my radio, handcuffs and baton were all securely attached to my belt.

"They're approaching our car now" Dougie calmly informed us. I silently inched my door open, in order to save me a fraction of a second when the call came.

"They've smashed the quarter light. One's in the vehicle, Strike, strike, strike!"

I was already out of the car and running by the time Dougie's third "strike" rang in my earpiece, and Jim was right behind me. We knew we had a problem before we got out of the car...there were three of them and only two of us, but Dougie was already onto it "I'm making from the O.P." he called into his radio.

"Police! Stay where you are!" I screamed at the top of my voice as we approached the scene. One of the lads was climbing out of the back of the car, laptop case in hand and Jim quickly grabbed hold of him. The other two were already running, star-bursting in different directions. I went after the one who headed to my right, away from the railway line. He was the biggest and oldest looking of the trio and I assumed he was the ringleader. The third lad was small, skinny and took off through the carpark running parallel to the tracks. I could see Dougie over my right shoulder, desperately sprinting across the tarmac trying to catch up with the little guy who, by now, had at least a fifty metre head start on him. My guy exited the carpark onto a quiet, tree lined, suburban, residential street. I was quickly gaining on him, and on seeing me he ducked into a gravel driveway beside a large detached house. I followed, expecting him to be fleeing over a fence at the back of the property, but to my surprise I almost ran straight into him. He had stopped and had turned to face me, standing in the driveway holding a screwdriver threateningly in his right hand. I could now see he was about 20, a lot bigger than me, around 6'2" tall and very large and solidly built. His face and body language told me everything I needed to know...he wasn't going anywhere with me quietly.

"Put the screwdriver down!" I commanded.

"Or what?" he snarled.

"Put the screwdriver down now!" I repeated as I pulled my baton from my belt. He looked at me and snorted as he half-smiled and raised the weapon.

"Put the fucking screwdriver down" I yelled as I extended my baton and raised it to my shoulder whilst he simultaneously lunged at my chest with the weapon. Instinctively I swung my baton, which connected with his left temple with a sickening crack. There was a fleeting look of bewilderment on his face as he sank to his knees and then fell heavily onto his side. I looked down to see him lying motionless on the ground with blood starting to trickle from his skull.

I hesitated, I guess in shock. *Shit, I've killed him* I thought, then quickly dropped to a kneel putting my baton away as I did so. I was just about to check him for signs of life, my left hand reaching for the transmit button on my radio to call for an ambulance when he groaned. I was totally caught by surprise as he shook his head and got back on his feet. I went to grab hold of him but he caught me off-balance and shoved we away, hard. I stumbled and as I fell backwards I watched him take off, running past a builder's van as my backside hit the pavement. A couple of workmen were unloading something from the back of the vehicle "Police! Stop him!" I shouted, but they just looked at me, slightly confused, and made no attempt to stop him as he turned into another driveway and disappeared out of my sight.

I called over the radio for a dog unit as I jumped to my feet, but my call was answered by Jim. I had forgotten we were "back-to-back" on our radios, in effect using them like walkie-talkies and bypassing the control room. "You'll need to change channel mate" he said "and we can't help you... I'm with my prisoner and I've got no idea where Dougie is. Still chasing the other guy I guess." I was wasting valuable time and it sounded like I was on my own. As I started to run back down the street I changed to the local radio channel only to be told there weren't any dogs available. I passed the builders and muttered a sarcastic "Thanks for your help" as I turned left into the driveway of another immaculately kept detached home. I could see straight down the side of the house to a beautifully manicured lawn, with an equally beautifully shaped privet hedge at the back. Beautifully shaped that is, except for a person-sized dent in it close to the back right hand corner of the garden. I ran across the lawn and scrambled my way through the damaged hedge, only to find myself standing on the lawn of the house behind. From there I could see that the drive led out onto the main road to Windsor, but by the time I got onto the street there was no sign of anyone on foot.

I walked down the road, checking driveways and hedges as I went, but without a dog I knew I had little chance of finding the thief, so I started heading back to the carpark.

"Dillan, I'm back at the car, do you need picking up?" Jim called up.

"Wait there mate, I'll be with you in a couple of minutes" I replied. As I approached the car Jim looked at me inquisitively. "He got away" I shrugged, disappointedly. "Did Dougie get the other guy?"

"No. He's going to bring the trap car back once he's collected everything from the O.P."

I sighed. One out of three offenders was not the result we would have hoped for, and I hated losing people in foot chases. All in all I was feeling pretty dejected.

We set off back to Windsor (in those days Windsor police station still had a small custody suite which has since been converted into locker rooms) and as we entered the town I spotted the back of a familiar figure walking along the footpath at the front of the Riverside Railway Station.

"It's him!" I couldn't believe my luck "Pull over Jim!" Before the car had even come to a stop I was out of the door and running. The guy turned right onto Thames Street, heading towards the Eton Bridge. Perfect, he had his back to me and had no idea I was behind him. Having no idea if he was still armed or not I ran straight at him, using a combination of my momentum and a leg sweep to take his legs out from under him. For the second time that day he fell heavily to the ground, but this time I was on his back before he could get up, and I quickly handcuffed him. I looked up to see a crowd of bewildered pedestrians staring at us and realised I wasn't in uniform. "It's okay, I'm a police officer" I reassured them. As they started to drift away back to their usual Wednesday afternoon business I noticed one person remained, grinning at me.

"Hello Robin!" I greeted my old friend from college. "That was ace mate" he beamed from ear to ear. "Thanks" I chuckled as I searched my prisoner. Unfortunately he no longer had the screwdriver on him, and I had lost a valuable piece of evidence. I got him up onto his feet and escorted him back to the car, where his behaviour rapidly started to deteriorate and by the time we got back to the nick he was getting pretty aggressive, kicking the back of my seat and making all sorts of violent threats to me.

Once in front of the custody sergeant he took no time to deny any wrongdoing, to claim he hadn't had a screwdriver and to demand his right to make a complaint against me for my baton strike.

"This fool" he said in a very Mr T kind of a way. I tried not to snigger, that wasn't an insult prisoners generally used and it sounded particularly funny coming from a white lad (albeit a white lad who clearly thought he was some kind of gangster). "This fool" he repeated "hit me with his baton. He hit me on the head. That's a Red Zone, fool. You never hit in a Red Zone. You're going to lose your job."

"Well, perhaps you shouldn't have tried to stab me then" I suggested. This really angered him and he lunged at me "I'll take your fucking head off, fool!" he yelled as Jim stepped between us and pushed him up against the wall. The custody sergeant was getting fed up with the whole performance and almost sighed "PC Bourdillon, did you strike the prisoner on the head?"

"Yes Sarge."

"Why did you do that?"

"Because he tried to stab me with a screwdriver."

"Did you attempt to stab this fine officer?" he asked Mr T.

"No, I didn't try to stab this fool, and if I did where's the screwdriver?"

"Have you found the screwdriver?"

"No Sarge."

"Can I inspect your baton?" I handed my baton to the custody sergeant who looked at it (I don't know exactly what he was looking for, but I guess it was an attempt to show Mr T he was listening to him). He examined it thoroughly, turning it to view it from every angle. He looked impassive, almost bored then shrugged and handed it back to me saying "I suggest you go and look for the missing screwdriver, constable."

I was taken aback that my prisoner was so well versed with 'red zones'. The term came from a brand new national training module for our new extendable side-handled batons that had recently replaced the traditional wooden truncheons. The course taught us multiple techniques for using our batons, and gave us a simple 'use of force' picture guide...an image of the human body split up into different traffic-light coloured zones of green, amber and red. The zones were graded according to the potential level of injury from a baton strike with red being reserved for the most dangerous areas to hit...the head, neck and groin. In those pre-internet days it was beyond me how he would be aware of any of this, but it made me acutely aware that if he did make a complaint then being able to prove he had a weapon was vital.

Jim and I headed back to Datchet to look for the screwdriver. We started our search at the last place I had actually seen it, the driveway where I had struck him. It wasn't there, so we started to retrace his steps down the road towards the builders van. One of the builders (who must have been watching us) approached me "Are you looking for this?" he asked, holding out a screwdriver.

"Yes, where did you find it?"

"The lad you were chasing threw it away when he ran past us and I picked it up. Sorry we didn't help but I didn't realise you were Old Bill until it was too late. Did you get him?"

"Yes, I found him in Windsor...he must have got on the train or hitched a lift. Anyway, thanks for keeping this for us" I was relieved, at least now I had the weapon and contact details for a couple of witnesses to corroborate my account. I knew my baton strike was reasonable and justified to defend myself from being stabbed, but was it necessary? We had been taught various blocking techniques with our batons, but they were complicated and I didn't have total faith in their effectiveness. My instincts had told me to strike, not block and I was still standing, so job done. I knew though that without the screwdriver and witnesses it would have just been my word against his, and that wasn't a situation I wanted to be in.

I returned to custody and told the sergeant about our progress. "Excellent" he said "His solicitor's waiting so you'd better go and interview him."

Before doing so I carried out some basic background checks on him. He came from Feltham, just over our border with the Met and had an extensive criminal record for theft and assault, including assaulting police. I decided to call the LIO (Local Intelligence Officer) at Feltham to find out a bit more about him. He warned me to be careful...my prisoner was often violent to police and was prolific in his complaint-making against officers. Apparently he had tried to stab a Met officer a couple of weeks earlier and had made an official complaint after being struck with a baton in what sounded like a carbon-copy case of mine. This was a dangerous man, someone happy to stick a knife in you and to complain if you dared to fight back.

I interviewed him, and as expected he replied "no comment" to all my questions. The custody sergeant charged him with theft from a motor vehicle and possession of an offensive weapon, and bailed him to court with conditions not to enter Datchet or Windsor. As I was about to escort him out of the nick he said to the sergeant "I still want to make a complaint about this fool hitting me in a red zone!"

"Oh well, you can't do that I'm afraid" replied the sergeant "because you need to see the Duty

Inspector and he's not here right now. You'll have to come back tomorrow to see him." He paused. "But of course you can't come back because I've just given you bail conditions not to enter Windsor. Never mind. Maybe in future you shouldn't try to stab one of my officers. Now I suggest you fuck off out of my custody suite."

I supressed a snort of laughter as I said "Okay mate, let's get you out of here."

"Fuck you, fool" he replied as I led him outside into a lovely summer's evening. I smiled as he walked off towards the town, not a bad result in the end.

The Area Team boys. With Millsy, Dougie and Jim (above) and with Pikey (below)

10

The Angels are Angry

My friend Gary was interested in joining the police so I arranged for him to come out with me and Jim one summers evening for a 'ride along' in the Area Team car. I chose a Friday (usually the busiest day of the week) and hoped he would get a proper feel of what the job is all about.

The evening started off busily enough with us searching an embankment for the missing and presumably dead driver of a car that was stuck upside-down more than two metres up a tree (yes, really). We didn't find him, but he was later located safe and well, but somewhat shocked, at home. This was swiftly followed at dusk by a foot chase and subsequent fairly physical arrest of my old mate Jamie who had been breaking into cars in a residential Maidenhead street. So far, so good and we were only a couple of hours into the 6pm to 2am late shift. Gary was having a great time.

At around 9pm we got a call to say a group of Hells Angels were at an out-of-town Chinese

Restaurant just off the A4 and were refusing to pay the bill.

"Hells Angels, yeah right." I scoffed. "The amount of times we get sent to deal with Hells Angels...it never is. It's usually just a few kids on motorbikes." I explained to Gary, who looked slightly alarmed at the prospect of dealing with a proper biker gang. "Anyway" I continued "we can't make them pay for a meal if they're complaining about it...it's a civil dispute, not a crime. Basically we'll just pop up there to keep the peace and to encourage them to pay some of the bill. It'll be a nothing job."

When we arrived at the restaurant I was surprised to see there were no bikes in the carpark, just a few cars and a couple of old transit vans. Rather than walking straight in we decided to walk round to the back and look in through the windows to get an idea of what we were actually dealing with. To my amazement we saw a large table around which was seated a group of a dozen or so fully grown men, some with beards, some with shaven heads, and all wearing full Hells Angels colours and patches. There were a lot of empty beer glasses and bottles strewn around the table, along with several untouched and half-eaten plates of food.

I told Gary, who was staring at me with eyes like saucers, to go back to the car and not get out under any circumstances. As he walked back to the panda the owner noticed us and came out to speak with us.

"They refuse to pay."

"Why?' Jim asked.

"They say they didn't like the food" he replied.

"How much have they actually eaten?"

"Most, but they did not eat three dishes".

"Okay" Jim said "we can't force them to pay but we'll see if we can get them to pay for their drinks and maybe half the food."

"No! They owe me. I want it all." He said defiantly.

"Well, we can ask but it doesn't sound like they will. I can't legally make them pay, and to be honest I don't think any of us want to end up with a brawl in the middle of your restaurant. People could get hurt and they could do a lot of damage."

The owner clearly hadn't considered this, but still insisted "But they need to pay!"

"No," I butted in "what they need to do is pay for their drinks, contribute to their meal costs... ideally paying for the food they've actually eaten... and then leave peacefully so you've still got a restaurant tomorrow." He looked unhappy, but Jim and I walked into the restaurant before he had time to argue.

On seeing us the table went quiet and one of the Angels stood up and approached us. He was about 6'2", in his mid-40s and was physically very imposing. He had a thick beard, and a shaved head with a large C shaped scar at the back. He was wearing a leather motorcycle vest over his t-shirt and I noticed it was patched with a large "Windsor Chapter" on the back, and a much smaller "President" on the front. He was clearly in charge and looked like a man who wasn't used to being told what to do.

"Hello mate." I opened cheerfully "There seems to be some debate over the bill."

"Yeah. The food was shit. We're not paying." he said flatly. He continued "You know Black John?" I nodded. Black John was a notorious local Hells Angel who had died about a year ago. "Well it's his anniversary and I've invited representatives from all over Europe to come here to pay their respects and we've been given this shit" he nodded towards food "It's insulting so we're not paying."

I glanced at some of the other jackets, there were patches of presidents from Germany, Holland and various UK Chapters. This was a big deal, and the issue was one of respect rather than the food itself.

"Fair enough, I understand why you're upset. But to be fair you have eaten most of the food so it can't have been that bad."

"It was shit. We're not paying" came the flat reply again.

"Okay, but the owner's not happy. The bill's nearly four hundred quid, and I can see a lot of that was the beer...you can't tell me that was no good too?" I replied, treading carefully to try to find a compromise.

"Yeah, fair enough" he conceded "the beer was okay. We'll pay for that."

It was a good start, but I pressed for more. "Great. How about you give the guy some money to cover his losses on the food? Maybe pay for the meals you actually ate?"

"Why should we? It was shit."

"Because nobody wants this to turn into something it doesn't need to. You're hosting an important evening and you don't need us spoiling that for you" I bluffed. "How about you give the guy three hundred quid and you can go and carry on your evening somewhere else."

He looked down at me, as if I was some minor irritant he wanted to get rid of, whilst he mulled over my suggestion. He stuck his hand into the pocket of his battered and faded black jeans and pulled out a large wad of bank notes. He quickly thumbed through them, removing four fifty pound notes and four or five twenties which he casually dropped onto the table amongst the half-eaten dishes and empty beer glasses. I nodded to him in acknowledgement, he shrugged and walked out of the restaurant without another word. The other Angels got up from the table and followed him out to the car park.

The owner came over to us. He wasn't happy. "But they still owe me!" he protested.

"I'd take that as a win" I suggested. "I'm sure you've more than covered your costs and your restaurant's still standing. I could see he wanted to argue but we didn't give him the opportunity and before he could say anything more Jim and I left. I was surprised to see another panda was parked next to ours in the carpark as we were very short-staffed that night. I went over to let the officers know that the job was sorted and they could go, only to find it was Dougie who was crewed with a young and inexperienced Special Constable (a part-time volunteer officer) called Sarah.

"Just as well it didn't kick off in there as we're your only backup tonight" Dougie shrugged. As the Area Team we were only supposed to be backing up the local shift officers, but for one reason or another there weren't any and we were now the only available response in Maidenhead. We re-joined Gary and Jim started the car and reversed out of our space. It felt like we were running the gauntlet as we slowly drove out of the carpark, with the Angels lined up on either side and coldly staring at us as we turned left onto the A4 and headed back towards town.

I turned to face Gary in the back of the car. "Well, that could have gone horribly wrong!" I chuckled, slightly out of relief. I was just about to call up Control Room to tell them to close the job and that we were now available for the next commitment when Dougie calmly came over the air.

"Can you ask PC Bourdillon and PC Adams to return to the restaurant please?"

I shook my head in disbelief. "What's Dougie done now?" I half-joked to Jim as he swung the panda around and put his foot down, accelerating hard back towards our colleagues. As we turned into the carpark for the second time that evening I could see the two officers were out of their vehicle, standing on the gravel and Dougie was holding onto one of the bikers. They were totally encircled by the remaining Angels who were clearly angry and becoming aggressive.

"For fuck's sake, what's he doing?" I asked in exasperation. "We really don't need this tonight!" I turned and spoke to Gary again "Whatever happens, stay in the car. Put your hands behind your back so it looks like you're handcuffed. They'll think you're a prisoner so should leave you alone, Okay?" He nodded, looking somewhat alarmed by the situation. Jim got on the radio to ask for any available units to head our way as we got out of the car and pushed our way into the circle to join Dougie and Sarah. Their prisoner was the smallest of the bikers and had long unkempt hair and a straggly beard. He looked more like a member of a Heavy Metal covers band than a Hells Angel.

"What's going on?" I quietly asked Dougie.

"He threw a handful of gravel at our panda as we were leaving" came the surprising reply.

"What?!! And you arrested him?!" I was in total disbelief. "Has he actually damaged the car?"

"No, I don't think so."

"Then let him go and we can all get on our way."

"No. I've arrested him. He's coming in."

"It's just not worth it mate. Drunk and Disorderly? Or Attempted Criminal Damage? Really? Swallow your pride and de-arrest him." I almost whispered into his ear. But he was having none of it.

"No, he's coming in" Dougie flatly ended the discussion.

I realised I needed to use the very limited rapport that I had built with the Angel inside the restaurant. "Look, your man here's been a bit stupid, throwing stones at a police car. He needs to come to the nick and sober up overnight. I'm pretty sure he'll get released without charge in the morning, so if you can get your guys to move out of our way we can get out of your hair."

"No!" he snarled, clearly no longer in the mood for bargaining. "He's not going anywhere with you."

We were stuck. Neither Dougie nor the biker were going to back down. Our odds weren't looking good...we were outnumbered three-to-one by men well known for their violence and our nearest back-up was coming from either Slough or Reading, a good fifteen minutes away. I knew we desperately needed to stall for time so started to negotiate further when, totally unexpectedly, another panda pulled into the carpark. Les Allen, the Duty Sergeant, had managed to get away from whatever he had been dealing with and I let out a sigh of relief to see this large and extremely experienced officer get out of the car. Despite not being liked by many officers for his abrupt and no-nonsense style of leadership, I had great respect for him as he was a highly capable officer.

He spoke briefly with Dougie and I thought he would tell him to let his prisoner go. I was amazed by his response though. He looked straight at the bald guy I had been dealing with and said "I guess you're in charge here."

It was the perfect opening line. The biker flushed with pride and was obviously pleased that his authority had been so publicly recognised.

"Yes, I'm in charge. These are my boys" he gestured to the others "and they'll do exactly what I tell them."

"Okay, I can see that" said Les "and these are my troops and they'll do exactly what I say" he countered.

The Angel looked as us and sneered. "Well, there's not much you can do here then, is there?"

Les reached for the transmit button on his radio and bluffed "Ah, but all I have to do is press this and I can get a dozen or more officers here in minutes."

"Well, I suggest you fucking do that then. But of course we both know you're fucking lying."

Les immediately dropped the pretence. "It was worth a try, but yes, you're right of course. I may be able to get one or two, but any more will take much longer."

"So let my boy go and no one needs to get hurt" came the menacing reply.

Good idea I thought *Go on Les, tell Dougie to let him go and we won't get killed!*

"Sorry, but I can't do that" Les replied, much to my dismay. "He's been lawfully arrested and he needs to come back to the station with us." There was no uncertainty in his voice, Les was not in the mood for negotiation either.

"Well, I can't let you take him. He's coming home with us." He looked at one of his underlings and flicked his head, indicating to one of their vehicles. The biker left the circle and quickly headed to one of the vans, opening its rear doors and jumping up inside. I could hear the metallic crashing sound of things being moved around inside the van and assumed he was getting weapons of some sort. The circle closed in on us and I believed we were in immediate danger of being attacked so instinctively I drew my baton. I immediately regretted my decision...the bald Angel looked down at me and almost laughed. The look of complete contempt on his face said "Put that away now son before I shove it up...." Without either of us saying a word I quietly returned it to its holder on my belt. I didn't want to antagonise things further.

Les spoke again "I fully understand our predicament" he stated calmly. "We're heavily outnumbered and your boy is getting who-knows-what weapons from your van. This isn't going to end well for us, but a law has been broken and it's our job to uphold the law and that is exactly what we are going to do."

The bald guy looked perplexed. He must have been thinking "Are you for real? There's no way you can win this. We could kill you all right now if we choose to." I couldn't tell if he was starting to respect Les or whether he thought he was crazy.

Les chose his words carefully. "So, you can let us leave, with our prisoner, or you can take him back by force. We will use all necessary force to protect ourselves, but you will win and we'll get hurt, badly. And you're right, no one is coming to save us. But you need to consider this carefully. For you to get your man back you are going to commit some serious assaults on my officers. If things go horribly wrong you may even kill one of us. We're outnumbered tonight, but do you have any idea how big our gang is? Do you understand the lengths we will go to hunt you down and lock you up if you go down this path? And for what? This man" he indicated to our prisoner "has let you down. Throwing stones at police like some sort of delinquent kid. He's let you down.

He's dishonoured the Hells Angels name with his drunken stupidity. Your organisation is better than that. You outgrew that type of childish behaviour many years ago, you're professional businessmen now, not thugs." He continued "This lad will be out in the morning once he's sober. If he even gets charged it will be with a minor offence. No one's going to prison. But if you hurt us, if you seriously hurt us, then we'll come for you. Do you want to give us the opportunity to investigate your businesses, to search your premises? You've got colleagues from all over the world here...do you want to drag them into this, to drag them down with you? Just for a stupid drunken mistake? Think about it."

It was a good speech. I looked at the head Angel, who was thinking it all through, trying to choose between pride and good judgement. We stood in silence for the best part of a minute before he gave our prisoner a disdainful look, shaking his head in disgust. Without saying a word he turned and walked away to his van. The others quickly turned and followed, leaving the five of us and our prisoner standing in the middle of an empty carpark trying to process what had just happened.

As we returned to our panda I realised I had totally forgotten about Gary, who was still sitting in the back, with his hands behind him. He looked stunned. Jim and I laughed, as much out of relief as anything.

"One of them opened the door and tried to help me escape!" he exclaimed.

"What did you do?" I giggled.

"I didn't know what to do, so I just sat there and shook my head." We all laughed, it was the perfect bit of light relief we all needed. I wish I'd seen it!

I'm not sure if it was because of that evening, but Gary never asked if he could come out on patrol with me again! He didn't talk much about becoming a police officer after that, so I guessed I had put him off the idea. It must have triggered something in him though as about five years later, much to my surprise, he asked me to help him fill out a police application form. He was accepted and after a number of years on the beat in and around Slough he was promoted and is currently serving as a Neighbourhood Policing Sergeant, a role he is perfectly suited to.

Neither Tony nor the cannabis are from this story, but the photos were taken around the same time

11

The Attitude Test

So, just to be clear, this isn't actually my story but comes from one of the funniest guys I have had the pleasure of working with.

Tony was a big character. He had a healthy disrespect for rank and authority, liked to joke, and loved to swear. He had a great fondness for the C word and used it as often as he could, but in such a way as it was almost impossible to tell if it was being used as an insult or a term of endearment. He particularly liked to aim it directly at (and I mean to the faces of) our sergeants and inspectors. He did it with such harmless humour that amazingly he always got away with it.

Tony had a nickname for everyone on our team, and our inspector was no exception. Inspector Price was a well-respected and experienced firearms officer who had a bit of an OCD clean-freak thing going on and always sterilised his desk and keyboard at the start of each day, so 'TCP' (the disinfectant brand) seemed an appropriate moniker for him. Or that's what he thought. The rest of us knew that Tony called him that because it also stood for 'That C#*t Price'.

To this day I have absolutely no idea if the inspector knew this or not, but if he did he never let on.

We all looked forward to the daily early-morning pantomime of Inspector Price arriving at work. He would go straight to his office, almost without a word, to wipe down the surfaces. He would re-appear a few minutes later, expecting to be handed a cup of tea by one of us, only to be greeted by Tony asking "Have you made the tea yet you cunt?" Without a flicker of emotion the inspector would instantly reply "Have you made the tea yet you cunt, *Sir*!" We never got tired of it!

Anyway, I digress. This chapter isn't necessarily about swearing, it's about a much-used tool in our toolbox...the 'Attitude Test'. Most non-traffic officers hate dealing with minor traffic offences and predominantly use them as an excuse to pull over and talk to known or suspected criminals. Our usual response to no seatbelts, or driving slightly above the limit is a simple "Put your seatbelt on mate" or "Slow down chap, it's not worth it" with no ticket given. *But*, there is a baseline of decent behaviour you need to pass to get away with just a warning. It's so easy to pass the attitude test, all you need to do is smile and say sorry. I am astounded by the number of folk who want to argue and say things like "Well that's a bit fucking petty. Why don't you go and catch some real criminals?" They may as well just ask for a ticket.

One day, many years ago, Tony was on duty driving down the Windsor Relief Road when he was undertaken by a Porsche 911 driving on the inside lane. Tony was driving to the speed limit, so the Porsche was clearly speeding.

"Bollocks" he sighed, "I can't have that" and changed lanes to get behind the car so he could properly gauge its speed. The Porsche's driver was in such a hurry that he didn't notice he was being followed by a marked police car and carried on speeding and undertaking other vehicles. By the time they reached the roundabout at the bottom of the dual carriageway Tony had seen enough and illuminated his blue lights to pull the Porsche over.

The guy was immediately remorseful, and politely apologised. He went on to explain that his wife was sick and had called him in the middle of a meeting to ask if he could leave work early to pick their young son up from primary school. He was late, and was stressed that his son would be alone and worried.

So far, so good, but not quite good enough for Tony who was still deciding whether to bother writing the man a ticket or not.

"I've been watching you for the best part of a mile, and that was some pretty crappy driving" he said. "There's a word I use for people who drive like that..."

Without missing a beat, the reply was instantaneous.

"Does it begin with a C?" the driver asked with a wry smile. Tony was absolutely delighted and chuckled as he replied "It does indeed! And you, my friend, have just talked yourself out of a ticket!"

The man himself (above, 2nd from r), many years later. With me, Sly and Frankie. Having a quick cuppa on the M40 during a murder search on the motorway and (below, 2nd from l) on a joint-services training exercise

12

Horses for Courses

What's the old showbiz saying? Never work with children or animals? Unfortunately, as with most things in the police, you don't get the luxury of choice. You get sent to the jobs you get sent to. Dealing with any cases of harm or neglect to children, cruelty to animals or dangerous dogs is never pleasant.

That doesn't mean, however, that you can't choose to work with *police* animals. In fact positions on our animal departments are highly sought after and the competition to become a dog handler or a mounted officer is fierce. Once selected though you don't get to choose the actual dog or horse you are allocated, and that can be a bit like a game of Russian roulette.

Before I could start working as a mounted officer I had to learn how to ride properly. I also had to learn how to drive Heavy Goods Vehicles and get my HGV licence so I could drive our large 4-berth horse boxes. I had to become a qualified search officer, learn mounted public order tactics and become a 'Football Spotter' (an officer who can identify all the main hooligans from their local clubs and not, as the title may suggest, someone who's good at Spot the Ball competitions).

The Basic Riding Course was a massive sixteen weeks long and took me from a novice to a competent rider. I spent three hours a day, every day, in the saddle with the remainder of my time learning the basics of horse husbandry, general equine care and tack cleaning. Paramount for the riding part was learning to have excellent control over your horse, but the course also taught reasonably difficult elements such as tiny lateral movements (extremely useful in controlling large crowds) and jumping.

Now, our horses were mainly failed hunters. They were often offered to us by hunts who had found them too slow and steady to be good hunting animals and thought they were more suited to police work. They were generally mixed breed and part heavy-horse, Irish Draught, Welsh Cobb or Clydesdale, and they were big. A minimum of 16 hands and often stocky. As such, their attitude and aptitude to jumping was mixed.

Some were fine, happy to jump and pretty much did it all for you. No drama and a dream to learn on. George, Arnie and Clyde were in this coveted group and we all loved them.

Some just plain refused. You had to be very much in charge if you wanted to get them over even the lowest rungs. They could be hard work, and on one occasion I was thrown over a jump by Rodney when he decided to abruptly stop just as he was about to take off. Before I knew it I was out of the saddle and over his neck. I landed on the other side of the obstacle, shocked and embarrassed but luckily unhurt.

"Get back on and we'll try that again" Donna, my riding instructor, said without any hint of concern or emotion.

A couple of them were a little too enthusiastic though. They *loved* to jump. It didn't matter how low the jump was, they were going to fly!

Monty was one of our favourite horses. He was a pure white, totally bomb-proof Irish Draught. He was a dream to ride at public order commitments as nothing phased him and he was as steady as a rock. But he had a strong personality, so strong that sometimes I wonder if he actually had a sense of humour.

He would always lie in his own poo the night before a Royal or military event, leaving a massive greenish-brown stain down his hindquarters. It would never brush out properly and we'd have to paint plimsoll-whitener over it to hide the mark. I think he enjoyed seeing the stress it caused us and he revelled in all the attention he would get.

He also knew if you were a novice rider and, if you were, stand-by, because he was going to make life difficult for you. The first time I got to jump him he knew how inexperienced I was. I could swear he actually laughed at my incompetence. Right from the moment we entered the riding school he wasn't going to do anything I wanted. He sensed my anxiety through my saddle (we used to call it having an electric arse), took one look at the jumps and thought "I'm going to have some fun here with this idiot".

I struggled to get him to even trot, and his transitions to a canter and back were on his terms, not mine. When we finally lined up for the first pair of jumps he started to pull on. I could feel his excitement, and he could feel my fear. He got faster, and faster, and faster as we made the approach. I tried to rein him back, but he was having too much fun. He leapt into the air, taking six feet to clear a two foot jump. "Whoa! Shit!" I exclaimed.

"Get a grip of that horse!" shouted Donna who rather unfortunately had decided to film the lesson.

Monty landed and almost immediately took off for the second jump.

"Fuck! Whoa! WHOA!" I shouted as he jumped even higher. He squealed with delight as he landed and, rather than slow for the sharp left hand turn, he accelerated towards the wall at the end.

"Shit, he's going to throw me over the wall" I thought.

"Whoa, whoa, WHOA! WHOA!" I screamed, totally out of control of my horse. I could hear Donna chuckling as she carried on filming. "Pull up Dillan!" she yelled. What the fuck did she think I was doing?

And then, a couple of metres from the wall, Monty turned. Hard. He went left. I went straight on. I was out of the saddle, my left foot exited its stirrup as I veered violently to my right. My heart was in my mouth. This was going to hurt. I was going to be slammed into the wall, six feet in the air.

I closed my eyes, waiting for the inevitable. But the pain never came. I felt myself drop back down into the saddle, and Monty slowed to a walk. He had timed his prank to perfection. He wasn't going to let me fall off, but he wasn't going to let me know that. For the rest of the lesson he was a dream to ride and did everything I asked, right on command. I could swear he was still silently laughing to himself though.

Monty wasn't the only one who was laughing. When I finally got to dismount I had to suffer the humiliation of walking back into the office to be met by a round of cheery applause. Donna had shown everyone the video of my miraculous escape. I almost wondered if the whole thing had been a set up...

Once I was fully qualified I didn't have to wait too long before I was deployed to my first public order event as a mounted officer.

TVP had been policing a long running animal rights protest at Hillgrove Farm in Witney since 1997. The Animal Liberation Front were targeting the farm as, alongside being a traditional working farm, it was the last cat breeding facility in the UK for animals destined for laboratory vivisection. The protests happened almost weekly, normally on a Saturday, and often turned nasty. Despite some of the participants being violent anarchists who seemed intent on causing damage and fighting the police, most were genuine and peaceful protestors and I had some sympathy for their cause.

I had felt slightly conflicted prior to first attending the site (several years earlier as a public order officer on foot) as I felt no desire to protect such a place. I was an environmentalist and I loved animals. I was a member of Greenpeace and the Woodland Trust and I donated regularly to the RSPCA.

My reservations about policing these people were quickly dispelled when I was subjected to the usual anti-police abuse, was threatened with violence, and was repeatedly told "You're no better than the guards at Auschwitz" and "The Nazis were just following orders too". That stung a bit. I hated the far-right and as a teenager I had literally fought with National Front skinheads. On top of that, I wasn't 'guarding' anything. The role of the police was to facilitate the protest whilst preventing any serious crime or disorder. My role was mainly to *allow* them to have their say.

Much as I disagreed with the breeding of cats at Hillgrove, I thought comparing animal breeding to the holocaust was something of a stretch. It was insulting to the memory of all those who suffered and died in the concentration camps, and just highlighted the ignorance of some of the protestors. I quickly became indifferent to policing these protests, and found it easy to reconcile myself to supporting the cause but opposing the actions of extremists.

My first outing to Hillgrove on horseback came towards the end of the campaign, in 1999 when the violence reached its peak. The day started peacefully enough, with the usual vigil and chants in the fields to the front of the farm. There was a ring of public order officers positioned outside the temporary fortress fencing that enclosed the farm. We had evidence-gathering teams filming, photographing and recording the protestors, and back-up officers and dogs on standby. We, as mounted officers, were either on standby too, or were out in pairs patrolling the perimeter.

I was approached by several protestors during the morning who told me they intended to free my horse from oppression. I laughed and told them Dexter was fine and he actually quite liked me.

One blocked my path by laying down in front of me and declared that my horse wouldn't harm him because he was a vegetarian. I told him that I was also a vegetarian but that hadn't stopped Dexter from treading on my foot several times and it bloody hurt. He refused to believe me. Luckily for him some bobbies picked him up and moved him out of my way before he found out that I wasn't lying and Dexter really didn't care what he had or hadn't had for lunch.

Things started to turn more sinister in the afternoon, with a small minority trying to find gaps in our defences so they could break into the farm. They were dealt with swiftly and robustly, but that aggravated some of the crowd who started to jeer and throw lumps of brick and flint from the fields at the farm house and at us. This was all pretty usual and expected, so we were all kitted out in full public order gear, complete with Perspex shields for the foot troops and even our horses had their own body armour.

What was less usual and expected was when the 'animal rights' protestors started to throw rocks at us. By us, I mean me, my colleagues and our horses. The last time I checked, our horses were animals, so this behaviour made no sense at all. It also made me angry that Dexter was being hurt. I rode over to a group of them. "What the fuck are you doing? You're throwing bricks at my horse. You claim to be here for the rights of animals, but you're hurting our horses."

"Your horses are acting as oppressors too" came the banal reply "but don't worry, we will free them from oppression too." The guy sounded like Neil from the Young Ones.

I shook my head in disbelief.

"You do realise that you're also stoning the farmer's geese that are just the other side of the fence, don't you? Two or three have already been killed by you fucking morons." They looked a bit shocked by this news, but quickly regathered their composure and started to scream "Fucking Nazi scum" at me as I rode back to my team.

The missile attack intensified and the farm house was starting to suffer some real damage. I was hit several times by lumps of stone, mud and flint, and Dexter was getting distressed and starting to dance around on his toes. I looked behind me to see extraction teams starting to form. We were going to disperse the crowd and grab some prisoners as we did so. I waited for the command for a mounted dispersal. It would be my first time cantering through a hostile crowd and my adrenaline was pumping. Six of us formed up, drew our long batons, put our visors down and waited to go. We were now under a sustained attack from a large and violent mob, and officers were getting hurt.

The order came and we were away. From standstill straight to a canter, our batons in the air above our heads. The crowd ran as we rode hard towards them. Even the most hardened vegans decided now wasn't the time to lie down in front of a horse. We only had to go once. The message was clear. We weren't going to tolerate that sort of behaviour. The energy and intensity of the crowd quickly vanished. They didn't have the stomach for a proper fight and it wasn't long before many of them slowly drifted away, back to their cars or off to the pub to tell their war stories.

Luckily Dexter was unharmed. As I now look back on that day I have to question who the animals were in this story. The irony of it all isn't lost on me either. I (and my mounted colleagues) clearly cared for the rights and welfare of animals far more than many of the so-called animal rights protestors. No animals were harmed that day by us, but they could not even begin to claim the same.

But horses and violent anarchists weren't the only animals I had to deal with whilst at work.

I got bitten by dogs twice in my career.

Once was by a small, aggressive Jack Russell terrier who had a go at my right ankle when, as a firearms officer, I was part of a team carrying out an early-morning raid on a gypsy site. We were looking for (and found) several stolen caravans, vehicles and firearms. Luckily there was no serious injury, but I did need to see my doctor to get a tetanus booster and some antibiotics when the puncture marks got infected.

The other time I was bitten was very early on in my career. I was still in my probationary period, and the dog was a large German Shepherd called Shadow. Yes, I got bitten by a police dog. I stupidly assumed that our service dogs would somehow either recognise police uniforms or know instinctively who the good guys were. Ripped trousers and a puncture wound to my left thigh were a quick way to learn not to ever get between a police dog and the burglar he's tracking in the middle of the night.

Whilst a fresh-faced constable at Windsor I also had cause to try to rescue, with varying degrees of success, a Muntjac deer, a badger and a swan.

The Muntjac had been hit by a car on the outskirts of Slough and was bleeding quite heavily. Unfortunately for the deer, it had been discovered in the access road to a block of lock-up garages by a group of unruly primary school children who were enjoying this distraction to their long summer holidays. They were shouting and screaming in excitement and some were waving sticks and throwing stones at the cornered and clearly distressed animal.

My first job was to get rid of the kids. This wasn't easy. They were either oblivious to the presence of a uniformed police officer or had absolutely no respect for anyone in authority. The latter was confirmed when a woman in her late twenties, who I assumed was one of their mums, approached me and said "Good luck mate, they never listen to a fucking word I say".

I wanted to keep my voice low and calm so as not to stress the deer any further, but I quickly realised that asking nicely and appealing to their better nature was a complete waste of both breath and time.

"Leave it alone!" I boomed. They went quiet and turned to look at me, assessing their options. After a brief pause one of them threw a stone at the cornered animal, and they all started shouting again.

"Stop it!" I shouted "Leave the poor animal alone. Can't you see it's hurt?" They went still again and looked at the deer. It didn't appear to have occurred to them that the Muntjac might not being enjoying their attention. They finally backed away, giving me an opportunity to catch the deer. I approached it slowly and quietly and when I was close enough I threw my coat over its head and pounced, wrapping my arms around its middle and holding on as tight as I could.

Although only small deer, Muntjac are the size of medium-to-large dogs and it was quite a struggle trying to hold onto the injured animal. I realised I couldn't deal with it on my own so called for another unit to come and collect me. We delivered it, shaken but alive, to Mrs Tiggywinkles, the local animal rescue shelter where it made a full recovery before being released back into the wild.

My coat, however, wasn't so lucky and required incinerating. I went home that afternoon covered in blood, to the inevitable "Shit, what happened to you?" question, and the generic "Don't worry it's not my blood" reply.

The badger got me called in for my first proper bollocking, administered by the Chief Inspector at Windsor. Wasting valuable police resources and money apparently.

I had been driving along a pitch-black country road near Bray in the early hours of the morning when my headlights picked out a badger by the side of the road. As something of an animal lover I naturally stopped to check it out. It was alive but badly injured, I assume having been run over. I called out an emergency vet. The vet arrived half an hour later, said the poor animal's back was broken and promptly put it to sleep.

On my next set of earlies I was called upstairs.

"What the bloody hell did you think you were doing?" the Chief Inspector screamed at me.

"I was just..." I tried to explain.

"You were just nothing" he shouted. "You weren't bloody thinking. You should have got your truncheon out and hit it over the head. Or you should have run it over and put the bloody thing out of its misery. Now I've got to authorise the vet's bill out of our budget. Do you know how much it costs to call a bloody vet out in the middle of the bloody night?"

Well, that told me. Another lesson learnt.

The swan was an altogether more difficult animal to deal with than its furry friends.

Windsor has the Thames running through it, and the Thames has a large swan population. The Windsor Relief Road is a large dual carriageway that crosses the Thames and, by all accounts, looks a lot like the river from the air…or it does from a flying swan's point of view at least. This leads to a fairly regular number of calls to police about swans causing traffic jams on the Relief Road. This is one of those type of jobs that I've talked about before, you know, the crap ones we go to because no one else can, or will.

It became apparent over the years that we weren't actually very good at catching swans, and swans are bloody big, angry animals who don't like being caught anyway. Think of the swan that gets in the police car at the end of Hot Fuzz (Simon Pegg's hilariously accurate film about policing in the nineties/noughties) and you'll get the general idea. To compound matters, we can't in any way hurt the swans…they belong to the King (or the Queen in those days) and are protected.

Luckily for us there's a Swan Sanctuary in Eton, and they ran a one-day course for us to attend so we could learn how to catch these enormous birds without breaking either their wings or our arms. I don't think any of us took it particularly seriously or paid too much attention, much to my later regret.

Catching a swan is much harder than it sounds, and surprisingly is much more terrifying than fighting a violent criminal.

I got the call one hot Thursday morning that the traffic was backing up on the Relief Road as a swan had landed heavily in lane two and was just walking around, stunned and unsure what to do with itself.

"Great" I replied, sarcastically. As, yet again, I was single-crewed I got another panda to come and help me. Dom turned up a minute or two later and judging by the look on his face he was even less happy about being there than I was. The two of us spent the best part of ten minutes performing a highly entertaining but pathetically embarrassing pantomime of chasing an uncooperative bird up and down the road in front of an audience of dozens of motorists.

Whenever we got close enough to grab it, the swan would hiss, flap its terrifyingly huge wings, lower its head and aggressively run towards us. We would, rather bravely, scream "Oh shit!" and quickly get out of its way. Feeling extremely pleased with itself the swan would turn and walk straight back into the traffic. I lost count of the number of times we repeated this charade.

We were hot, sweaty, tired and embarrassed. Thank goodness it was back in the days before smart phones and social media...if it had happened today we would have been a viral sensation.

We were running out of ideas, and we were running out of energy. "I wish this swan would just piss off" Dom muttered. And then, right on cue, the swan flapped its wings and slowly lifted off, gently rising into the sky above the cars before banking to its right and swooping down towards the waiting water of the river.

Yep, never work with animals if you can avoid it.

Oh, and they won't thank you either.

On my Equestrian Course at Milton Keynes (with Dexter and Arnie)

Mounting up before a day at Hillgrove Farm

On George at Hillgrove Farm

All kitted up for a long day in the saddle

13

Horses and Hooligans

You idiot

You stupid fucking idiot. How have you got yourself into this? You stupid fucking idiot! My thoughts were racing. *Fuck. Here we go. Fuck. Fuck. Fuck. But I'm not going down alone, I'm taking at least one of you fuckers with me.*

My baton was drawn, sitting high on my right shoulder and I was staring right into my target's eyes. The red mist was rapidly closing in. My head was starting to spin as a potent mix of stress, fear and adrenaline was forcing my attention onto the group's leader. My brain had no choice but to fade out the other dozen or so Reading hooligans who were baying for my blood. The sound of my breathing was almost deafening and the veins in my temples thumped with each beat of my heart. Either my feet had turned to lead or my boots were glued to the tarmac of the road beneath them. I didn't know which, but knew I was unable to move.

I wanted Costar to know it was him and me. I wanted him to know I was ready for him and I intended to hurt him. The rest of his firm could deal with the ten or so Cardiff boys behind me. I pushed away the thought, and the fear, of the possibility that the whole Reading group would attack me whilst the Welshmen just watched. Or worse...they would join the locals in their attack on a lone copper. I made the most practical choice I could with my brain in such a scrambled state and glanced over my shoulder.

"I'm with you. Let's have these fuckers!" I didn't wait for a reply, but said a silent prayer that they weren't going to jump me from behind. I figured they owed me one and would return the favour. Besides, I was pretty sure they hated Reading more than the police.

So, how did I end up here, alone, standing in the middle of a busy dual-carriageway with traffic backed up in both directions? All 5'8" and 12 stone of me, in my jodhpurs and riding boots, surrounded by about 25 football hooligans at least half of whom wanted me dead, and all I had for protection was my extendable baton and a radio.

It had all started months earlier when two of my Mounted Section colleagues had witnessed Reading's 'top boy', a nasty white supremacist, seriously assault someone. He was arrested and charged with Assault Occasioning Grievous Bodily Harm (GBH), a serious offence that carries a lengthy prison sentence. The subsequent court case was heated, Reading boys would turn up outside court each day to intimidate and threaten the officers and witnesses giving evidence. Despite their best efforts the case didn't go the crew's way and their leader was sent down for a few years, much to their disgust. They somehow thought that we, the Mounted Officers, had broken an unwritten rule. They felt we should only really police the away fans and should look after the Reading boys at home games. It was true that we had a good working relationship with most of them and knew them all by name, but our job was purely to keep the peace, not choose sides.

They took the conviction very badly, almost personally, and started to make open threats towards the officers on our small department. They would happily approach local bobbies in Reading and tell them that they intended to kill a mounted officer in revenge. These threats were taken seriously by intelligence officers and at pre-match briefings we were always warned to stay in pairs to keep ourselves safe, and the PSUs (teams of MAST trained public order officers) were told to keep an eye on us and make sure we never got isolated.

The week before I found myself alone and in trouble Reading had played away in Bournemouth. After the match a few of the Reading hooligans found a lone police dog handler and viscously attacked him and his dog. He was kicked to the ground and had his nose broken. As they walked away, one of the Reading boys spat on him and said "You're lucky you've only got a fucking dog, if it was a horse you'd be dead now."

On the day of the Cardiff match the pre-game lunchtime period was marred by the usual fights in and around the town centre, and it was a struggle to keep things under control, particularly around the favoured pubs. Things quietened down after lunch when all the fans made their way to the Madjeski Stadium in time for kick-off. Once all the supporters were safely inside it was time for us to grab a meal break, leaving the stewards to control the crowds within the ground. We made our way back to the horsebox to rest and feed the horses and to get ourselves some lunch and a brew.

We would normally head back out to our post-match positions about a quarter of an hour before the end of the game, but Andy and I were bored so decided to head out early and do a patrol of the carparks, hopeful we might catch someone breaking into the unattended vehicles.

As it was only about half way through the second half we were the only police patrolling the ground, all the rest were having a well-deserved break before the full-time chaos and mayhem that would inevitably follow the end of the match. With about twenty minutes still to go Andy and I were sitting up by Gate 8 on Shooters Way around the back of the stadium when our horses' ears pricked back and they started to shuffle around uneasily on their hooves. I looked at Andy, a far more experienced Mounted Officer than me, quizzically. He just shrugged in reply. Something was upsetting the nags but we had no idea what. As I leant forward to pat Dexter on his neck to calm him I heard a faint rumble, almost like distant thunder, building in force and coming from inside the stadium. It didn't sound like a goal celebration as there were no cheers and it felt much more threatening, almost sinister. It continued to get louder and stronger, our horses were starting to panic and it was taking a lot of effort to keep them controlled and steady. The rumble became a deafening crash behind us and we turned to see a pair of the stadium's large access doors fly open and dozens of Cardiff supporters spill out onto the road.

Before we had time to process what was happening a huge collective roar, almost a war-cry, went up and they were on us, attacking both us and our horses. More and more hooligans were still exiting the stadium until there were well over a hundred of them, all intent on fighting the police. Unfortunately for me and Andy, we were the only police around.

The sheer weight of numbers pushing against our horses made manoeuvring ourselves out of danger almost impossible. I was getting repeatedly punched in the leg, and someone had grabbed hold of my reins and was pulling hard on them. Dexter was now scared and was starting to dance around underneath me. I leant forward and smacked my elbow hard into the side of the head of the guy who had my reigns. He immediately let them drop and I started to work hard to get Dexter back under control, whilst all the time kicking and punching my attackers.

I felt another tug, this time coming from below me and to my left. Someone was trying to undo my girth. This was serious...if he succeeded I would be off my horse and on the ground underneath him and it was highly likely I'd be trampled by my own horse. I needed both hands to control Dexter so I pulled my left leg out of its stirrup and heel-kicked the lad as hard as I could to his shoulder. My leg stopped moving with a jolt as I felt a sudden bruising pain in my heel, letting me know my spur had successfully made contact with its target. The lad yelped, almost screamed "Faarrrk!" and quickly moved away.

At some point during all of this Andy had managed to call up over the radio for assistance and I could faintly hear the sirens of the first transit vans making their way to us. Help was coming, but we still needed to fight to stay on our horses. Andy and I looked at each other and nodded. Almost telepathically we side stepped our horses together to create a sterile area between us, and without a word we simultaneously went from standing still to cantering through the dangerously violent mob. We pulled up about fifty metres down the road and, exhilarated by the sudden release of adrenaline, turned to see a scene reminiscent of the parting of the Red Sea. The crowd was split perfectly in half, with a six-metre-wide channel of empty road between the two groups. The ground in the middle was strewn with Burberry caps and scarves, and the odd Adidas Samba trainer.

I let out a sigh of relief. *That'll do it* I said to myself, but my thoughts were premature and before we knew it we were under attack again, and this time they were angry, screaming and punching. Andy and I didn't wait for our second attempt at a dispersal and immediately cantered back through them, trying to buy us every second we could before the troops arrived. By now the sirens were loud and close and the crowd broke away from us to re-group and take on the foot police. Dozens of fully-kitted up public order officers jumped out of their vans and tried to push the hooligans back, but they were intent on a fight and weren't going anywhere quietly. I could hear the angry barks of police dogs and the clip-clop of my mounted colleagues arriving at the ground.

There was no time for us to recover, the mob was still out of control and in any minute the match would end and we'd have all the everyday fans and families heading out to go home. Worse, the Reading boys would no longer be safely contained in the stadium and the last thing we needed was for them to join the fight. We had to get this sorted, and sorted quickly.

The fighting was frantic with police using their batons and long sticks, and the Welshmen using whatever weapons they could lay their hands on...bottles, cans, road cones and anything else small enough to be thrown or wielded in anger. After a furious five or six minutes resulting in a number of casualties on both sides, we managed to corral the Cardiff lads into one large contained (but angry) group and the decision was made to walk them under escort the three-and-a-half miles to the railway station.

Six of the horses would be needed for the escort, but one of our horseboxes was at the ground and needed to be driven back to Reading, and that job was given to me and Vicky. We de-kitted, fed our horses and loaded them onto the box. We had plenty of time on our hands so made ourselves a cup of tea and then slowly headed back to town, getting there just as the convoy was arriving at the railway station. Predictably, small fights were now starting to break out around the town, mainly close to the station, and this led to a lot of unnecessary radio chatter about minor altercations. Irritatingly, officers were over-talking each other, making it almost impossible to call up if you really needed to. "FFS, someone needs to get a grip on this" I said to Vicky, shaking my head. "Too bloody right" she replied "but hopefully the worst of the trouble's over".

Our conversation was abruptly interrupted by the sound of car horns blasting. I looked up to see what was going on and saw some of the vehicles ahead of us and on the opposite side of the IDR (Reading's inner ring-road) were breaking suddenly and swerving to avoid a group of people running across the dual-carriageway towards us. As they got closer I could see it was a bunch of about twelve men, some of whom I recognised as Cardiff supporters I had been fighting earlier.

"Pull over" I needlessly said to Vicky, who was already breaking and manoeuvring our cumbersome four-berth horsebox to the side of the road. I wound my window down and as the group were running past us I called out "What's going on lads?" They stopped, almost reluctantly, and one of them replied in a strong Welsh accent "We've been ambushed by Reading. About twenty of them."

"So where are you running to?" I asked.

"We just want to get home without getting our heads kicked in."

"Did you come on the train?" They nodded in reply. "Okay, so we need to get you guys back to the station safely. I can get a transit to take you back there if you wait here for a minute while I sort it for you."

"Nah, fuck off, we don't want your help" snapped one of younger, smaller ones, his Stone Island jacket's zip pulled all the way up to his chin.

"Your choice mate, I'm just trying to help. But it seems to me you've had a good day...you won the footy, you had a good old scrap with us, it doesn't look like you're hurt at all...why get a kicking now? I can get you a lift and you get to go home in one piece. Sounds like a great result to me!"

"Nah, fuck you" he snarled, but he was quickly over-ridden by a much larger guy with a shaved head who shut the argument down by calmly saying "Yeah, that sounds good pal."

I waited for the radio to quieten enough for me to call up, but the stream of rubbish coming across the channel was incessant. Frustrated, I eventually pressed my transmit button to try and cut across the noise and I asked for a van to come to the IDR. I didn't get a reply, and was about to try again when the young lad said "Fuck this. I'm not waiting any longer. Let's just go and front up those Reading cunts." I looked at the big guy, but he just shrugged, almost apologetically, at me and despite my protests turned and started to walk back towards the station.

That's when I screwed up. Instinctively, and without thinking, I opened my door and jumped down from the cab to have one last go to convince them to wait.

The crew were just about to step down off the pavement to cross the IDR, so I cut in front to stop them, meaning I was standing in the middle of a busy road. The traffic on my side of the dual-carriageway came to a standstill and some cars further back who couldn't see me were angrily sounding their horns. I had my back to the railway station as I spoke to group.

"Come on lads, just give me another minute and I'll get you home safely."

"Bollocks" came the reply, but at least they had stopped moving and appeared to be considering my request. I was just about to speak again when suddenly, almost as one, their focus of attention changed from me to something behind me. A roar went up "Fucking come on then!" and their arms were thrown in the air, making beckoning gestures with their hands. One of them launched a bottle of drink over my head at whoever it was behind me. I looked over my shoulder to see a group of a dozen or so lads running towards us on the opposite side of the IDR. I immediately recognised most of them...it was the core Reading crew.

S*hit* I thought, *I'm in trouble now!*

I spun round to face them and pulled my baton from its holder on my belt. I flicked it out and was calmed by the reassuring whoosh and click as it extended and locked into place. I raised it to my right shoulder whilst I reached for my radio with my left hand. I didn't wait for a break to get in, I just said as forcefully but calmly as I could "X-ray Mike 83." (XM83 was my call sign identifying me as a mounted officer) "I need urgent assistance! I'm in the middle of the IDR just below the station. I've got about a dozen Reading in front of me and a dozen Cardiff behind me. I'm a mounted officer and I'm off my horse. I need help NOW!"

I had no idea if anyone had heard me or not, meaning that potentially my only back-up was the crew of Cardiff boys behind me. I picked out Reading's new top boy, Costar, and stared straight into his eyes. I wanted him to know that I was going to strike him hard if he got close enough. I hoped it would make him hesitate and buy me some much-needed time. I also knew that by focussing on him, by having a target, I wouldn't be focussed on my fear. This was no time to be scared and it was certainly no time to show it.

At the same time the Reading lads appeared to notice me. I guess they had been so focussed on the Cardiff supporters that they hadn't actually registered that I was there. They slowed and then stopped, their sights moving from me to the group behind me, and then back to me again, slowly eyeing me up and down critically. They looked down at my jodhpurs and riding boots and across the road to the horsebox. Vicky was still in the vehicle and I don't think they had seen her. They must have thought it was Christmas...a lone mounted officer off his horse, standing in the middle of the road and completely surrounded by hooligans. They weren't even looking at the Cardiff lads now, their attention was solely on me. I tried to fight off my growing alarm and used the only card I had left. I glanced over my shoulder and said "I'm with you. Let's have these fuckers!"

Without waiting for a reply my gaze returned to Costar. I was in full 'fight or flight' mode now, but as a uniformed copper 'flight' wasn't an option. I was left with one choice, to fight. But this wasn't Hollywood and I couldn't possibly fight them all. My brain chose tunnel vision and to reduce the perception of the threat. It filtered out everyone and everything except the group's leader. Time slowed. Automatically and involuntarily I picked a point on Costar's left temple where I was going to strike him. Every muscle in my body tensed and the pressure I felt behind my eyeballs was unbearable.

"Come on you cunt. Let's do this." I silently said to him, psyching myself up and blocking out the fear of the situation. The effect of my words was immediate and empowering. My body and my brain were flushed, no, flooded with adrenaline and endorphins. Time now almost came to a complete standstill as I had a strange out-of-body sensation...I guess my mind was trying to detach itself, protect itself, from the body that was only seconds away from a brutal beating.

I became aware of something going on behind me and was jolted back into reality when I heard Vicky shouting "Get back!" to the Cardiff boys. *Shit, don't piss them off Vicks, we need them!* I thought, wondering if Vicky was fully aware of the situation we were in. The appearance of a second officer caused a momentary hesitation in the Reading advance. I guess they were wondering if there were any more of us about to jump out of the horse box as I doubt the combination of two such physically small officers troubled them that much.

My eyes were still firmly fixed on the group's leader, who returned my stare with a mix of hate and contempt. Having Vicky behind me reassured me enough for a limited return to my senses...but it was the distant sound of horses' hooves on concrete that properly reunited my floating brain with its grounded and tensed body. The Reading boys heard the unmistakable sound too, and once again they hesitated. Their desire to make the most of their lucky situation must have been overwhelming though as, almost immediately, they resumed their hate-filled march towards me. The sound of the horses to my left was joined by the wail of sirens to my right. I still couldn't see any backup, but I knew it was on its way.

The group was getting worried now and finally stopped about three meters in front of me, just out of striking range. It looked like they were undecided whether to attack or not...this was no longer the golden opportunity they had hoped for. The sound of hooves was getting much louder and I glanced to my left to see a couple of horses cantering along the road towards us and the noise of the sirens to my right was almost deafening. A dog was barking wildly and incessantly somewhere behind me and almost simultaneously Costar and his mates turned and ran back towards the station.

I didn't move. My feet were rooted to the ground, my baton was stuck to my shoulder and my gaze was fixed on the spot where Costar had been standing. I don't think my brain had caught up and processed the fact that the threat had gone. My vision quickly filled with officers in black and I was gently brought back into the present by a reassuring hand on my shoulder.

"You okay Dillan?" asked Andy, a sergeant from the dog section. "Yeah" I exhaled. "You can put that away now" he said softly as he nodded towards my baton and smiled.

A wave of relief flowed over me as I collapsed my baton and returned it to its holder on my belt. "You lucky, lucky bastard" I said to myself. "You stupid but lucky bastard" I shook my head and half laughed as I almost floated back to the horsebox, dazed and slightly confused, my thoughts scrambling to process what had just happened. It quickly dawned on me that Vicky had saved me by not being an impulsive idiot like me. She had stayed in the vehicle and used our secondary radio (the car set) to call for assistance over a clear channel, securing backup that I was never going to be able to get over my personal radio.

Sometimes the hero of the story is the one quietly doing their job in the background, not the one stupidly putting themselves in harm's way. Another day in the job, and another life lesson learnt.

TVP officers at a different match, this one at Oxford

Kitted-up for a lively Millwall match at the Madjeski Stadium in Reading...

...and on a quieter more family-friendly day at the stadium (on Monty)

14

A Loss of Life

One thing that's hard to prepare for, and at times can be difficult to accept, is just how much time you will spend at work, away from friends and family and how many special occasions you will miss (sometimes at extremely short notice) because of shift changes or overtime. Christmases, birthdays, anniversaries, weddings, New Year's Eve parties, concerts, sports events, Friday nights at the pub, dinner parties, bank holiday weekends away, and if you're a sportsman: matches or races. Be prepared to miss out. In fact, you can forget about joining any club, class or team that has a regular meeting time. Luckily there's usually someone on your team who loves earning the overtime and will often step up when you really need to keep your day off...but even they may not want to work a night shift on Christmas Eve.

To be fair, if you don't want to work much outside your rostered duties then there are departments that don't get messed around too much. Unfortunately they tend to be the less exciting, fun or interesting places to be and I always chose my career path based on stimulation rather than regular hours.

Probably the worst place I worked for being messed around was the Mounted Section. We were a tiny team of eight full-time and two part-time constables and one sergeant. We had eight horses and the mainstay of our work was public order control, principally at football matches and demonstrations. Most matches and demos are on Saturdays, and most needed four, six or all eight horses. We had a major commitment most weekends of the year, and although on paper we had one weekend off a month, that precious Saturday at home was invariably cancelled. Not only was it cancelled, but it was also always a long day.

Those Saturdays would generally start at 6am with feeding, mucking out, grooming and finally loading the horses onto the box. We would then change out of our stable gear into our uniforms and set off for a long drive to wherever we were heading.

Our stables were in Milton Keynes, at the northern-most point of our huge force area (geographically over 2,200 square miles) and most of our commitments at that time were in the south of our force, in Reading, Windsor, Ascot, Henley and Oxford. This meant return trips of between 100 and 180 miles. To compound those distances was our feeble average speed. Our horseboxes were large, slow and heavy vehicles and to ensure the horses didn't get injured or distressed we had to drive especially carefully, anticipating every corner and almost doubling our breaking distances. Due to this we were lucky to get anywhere in less than two hours and it was often considerably longer.

Once there we would have to attend the briefing and hopefully still have time to get ourselves and the horses fed and watered before deploying.

Despite starting work at 6am we usually wouldn't mount-up until around midday! Depending on the event, we could be in the saddle for anywhere between three to six hours before we would feed and re-load the horses, drive back to Milton Keynes, put the horses to bed, clean out the horsebox, hose down the yard and clean our tack. More often than not we would finish between 7pm and 10pm, but midnight wasn't unusual. To make matters worse I lived over 50 miles away in the south of the force. I would need to leave home before 5am and would finally return over an hour after we finished (sometimes the early hours of Sunday morning). Needless to say, if that was your average Saturday (even on what should have been your 'weekend off') it didn't leave much time or energy for any sort of a normal social life.

I was fairly new on the team when Dom (my old mate from my days on shift at Windsor) told me he was getting married and asked me to be one of his ushers. I remember him looking surprised, and a little hurt, when I didn't say yes, but simply replied that I'd try to come but couldn't guarantee it. "But it's six months away!" he objected. "Just tell your sergeant you need the day off." "I wish it was that simple" I lamely replied. I checked my diary later and, as luck would have it, the wedding was on my rostered weekend off, but I knew that was only half the battle.

The next day I went to see my sergeant. "Pete, an old friend of mine is getting married next March and he wants me to be an usher. It's on my weekend off and I just wanted to check that you could guarantee I can actually go."

"How good a friend is he?" came the surprising reply.

"I'm not sure what that's got to do with anything" I said, involuntarily raising the corner of my lip and wrinkling up my nose. "It's my weekend off, I've been asked to be an usher at a wedding, I need to reply and I need to commit to it. Surely that's enough?"

"Is he a childhood friend? Is he your best mate?"

"It doesn't matter" I protested. "He's a good friend, and I need to give him an answer. It's six months away and I'm not supposed to be at work anyway. I just want you to guarantee my day off." I was starting to get pissed off.

He looked at his diary. "Sorry, it's Reading/ Millwall that day...I'm probably going to need you."

"Probably? I need to give him a reply!"

"I don't know how many horses we'll need yet, but with Millwall it will probably be eight. If I'm right then I'll need you."

"Great" I mumbled sarcastically.

"You could always book it as annual leave...I can't cancel that for a football match." He said, trying to be helpful.

"But I can't use an annual leave day on a rest day..." I said, slightly confused.

"No, but if you book a few leave days either side of your weekend, so let's say Thursday, Friday, Monday and Tuesday then you'd definitely get the weekend off."

So there it was. It was nuts, but if I wanted to go to my mate's wedding on my actual day off I had to take the best part of a week's leave. I was furious, but appeared to have no option.

When I first joined the police Andy, my tutor constable, said something that stuck with me my whole career. I think I had been moaning about having to get up at 4.30 for an early shift (I never really minded nights, it was the early starts I struggled with...I was happy to BE up at 4.30am, just not to GET up then!) "You'd better get used to it mate," he said, fixing his bloodshot and sunken eyes on me "there'll be days in this job when you'll be more tired than you ever imagined possible." Looking at him I didn't disbelieve it one bit.

I remembered this conversation one Sunday evening in July about seven years later. I had only slept in my own bed on three occasions in the previous fortnight, and I was so tired and miserable I could almost have cried. I was irritable and snappy.

"What's wrong with you?" Pete asked brusquely.

"What do you think's wrong with me?" I curtly replied. "I'm absolutely knackered. I've worked nearly a hundred and sixty hours in the last two weeks and I've hardly even been home. My mum's dying and I haven't been able to see her once. I'm tired and I'm pissed off."

"Yes, but think of the money!" he grinned with a strange, almost manic look in his eyes.

"Hmmm" I shrugged. It was all I could manage. What I wanted to do though was scream *The money? Is that all you fucking care about? I want to go home. I want to sleep in my own bed. I want to see my mum. I want to see my girlfriend. This is shit. I hate it. Fuck you and fuck this job*!

Oblivious to my thoughts, Pete rather matter-of-factly said "Anyway, your break's over, it's time to mount up and get back out there for one last patrol before the firework display starts."

We were at the Henley Royal Regatta, and it was the third (and last) of three long, sixteen-to-eighteen hour days we had had there. Just as we had done for most of the previous fortnight, we were stabling at the mews in Windsor Castle to minimise our travelling. That sounded good on paper, but in reality it made for very long days. Our mounted commitments were in the afternoon and late into the evening, but we still had be up early to muck out and feed before getting ourselves some breakfast and then cleaning and preparing our kit and horsebox for the day ahead. It also meant what little sleep we were getting wasn't in our own beds, but in shared rooms above the stables.

We had started that week at 2.30am on the Monday morning for a full 'dress rehearsal' for the State Visit of President Arpad Gonez of Hungary in Windsor. The previous day, Sunday, was my only rest day in that fortnight. I say 'rest day', but there wasn't much time to rest...I had got home at around 11pm on the Saturday night and had to leave again at 2am on the Monday morning! Following the middle-of-the-night rehearsal, the full event where we escorted the Queen, the Hungarian President and troops of the Royal Horse Artillery and the Household Cavalry, was on Tuesday. We once again spent the night at Windsor Castle.

We had spent the previous week at Royal Ascot, the UK's most prestigious multi-day horse racing event, which as the name suggests is attended by the monarch and other senior members of the royal family. Our role there was to help search and secure the processional route from Windsor Castle to the racecourse, to escort the Queen's carriage along the Straight Mile, and to patrol the carparks where many coach loads of visitors would have picnics and parties late into the evening. These parties would be flash-points for the inevitable fights (and sometimes serious disorder) that would follow long days of drinking in the sun. Thursday (Ladies Day) was the worst and seemed to bring out the most repulsive behaviour in otherwise perfectly nice people.

Royal Ascot was usually the highlight of our year. It was busy and the hours were long, but the work was high-profile, prestigious even, and utilised all our skills and training. Some of it was pure pomp and ceremony in full dress-uniform with shiny bulled boots and bridles, some of it was open-country searching, and a large part was public order control. It was also very social...we chatted to everybody, doing a great PR role for our force, and also got to catch up with old mates from the job who were either still on shift or had gone on to different departments (it felt like everyone was at Ascot...local bobbies, firearms teams, specialist search officers, royalty protection officers, dog handlers, public order tactical advisors, the list was endless). We also earned a huge amount of overtime. The down side was that yet again we were away from home, sleeping at the castle, and had to do split-shifts. We would start at 6am to carry out the necessary horse-husbandry duties and to clean and polish all our leatherwork. We would then have a few hours off before we would be back on duty to search the Long Walk. By the time we had finally finished fighting in the carparks it was often midnight before our heads hit our pillows.

We would normally pack up and head back to Milton Keynes on Friday evening but that year (1999) we needed to spend another 24 hours at the castle as there was a Royal Wedding to attend on the Saturday. Prince Edward and Sophie Rhys-Jones were getting married in Windsor the day after Royal Ascot finished so there was no chance of a day off, getting home, seeing my sick mum or even catching up on some sleep. It was a once-in-a-lifetime opportunity to escort a Royal Wedding Carriage on horseback, right in the middle of all the pageant and tradition that the British do so well. It was hard not to be completely overwhelmed by the sounds and smells of hundreds of horses from the Life Guards, Blues and Royals, Royal Horse Artillery and Mounted Police. To be immersed in the almost deafening sound of the hooves on sand-covered tarmac, and the rattling and crashing of the riders' armour, helmets and swords was unforgettable. The huge crowds filling Windsor's Union Jack-lined streets cheered as we rode past. It was magical, but my tiredness took a little of the sheen off the occasion.

Fast forward a week and a day, to my last day at Henley, and you could have offered me a training day riding on the white sands of a Caribbean Island beach and I would have told you where to stick it. All I wanted to do was be at home, sleep in my own bed and spend some quality time with my mum while I still could.

State Visit of President Arpad Gonez of Hungary, Windsor

Royal Wedding, Edward & Sophie, Windsor. On George.

15

A Matter of Perspective

As I no longer live in the UK I rarely get the chance to see or speak to old friends, so one of the great things about writing this book has been the excuse it has given me to reconnect with some of my former colleagues and chat about old times. One aspect of this that has been particularly interesting is how differently we recall some events – especially the more traumatic or stressful ones.

Police officers receive quite a lot of training around perceptual distortion, tunnel vision, red mist, auditory processing impairment, time slowing or accelerating, and other common sensory effects of high stress situations. I received further training in this area later in my career as an Authorised Firearms Officer where any perceptual distortion issues could severely impact both the AFO's judgement when faced with an armed offender, and their memory when recalling the event afterwards at an inquiry or in court. We used simulated weapons connected to computer generated screen scenarios, enabling us to play back and study our own reactions and judgements. It was an invaluable tool in helping us to understand how, for instance, we often focus so intently on the offender's weapon that other vital stimuli such as sound, distance, time and colour simply get filtered out.

Despite being well aware of all this it was still surprising for me to talk to others about jobs we had both been to and to find out that whilst one of us remembers little or nothing about a particular event, it was perceived as being a hugely traumatic (or even life-threatening) situation for the other.

One great example of this occurred when I was chatting about trauma to my good friend Jen a few months ago. I worked with Jen for a couple of years as a uniformed response officer at High Wycombe after I left the Mounted Section (the hours, excessive travel and my mum's deteriorating health had made remaining there untenable). Jen and I made a great team, we had clicked instantly and crewed together as often as we could. Due to this we had been to many difficult and testing jobs together, so I was surprised when she started talking about a job I had completely forgotten about.

She told me about a time she had been singled crewed and had attended a single-vehicle traffic accident. She said the incident hadn't affected her personally, but she had told another colleague of ours about it and twenty years later Caroline still couldn't get it out of her head even though she wasn't even there!

"It was a guy on a motorbike up near Handy Cross" she told me. "I think he was on his way home from work and had overtaken a lorry but hit some new bollards in the centre of the road and had gone under the wheels of the truck..."

"And his body was untouched but his helmet had come off and his head was squashed completely flat, like a pancake, with faint shadows where his eyes and mouth should have been..." I interrupted.

"Yes! How did you know that?" she asked.

"Because I was there!" I replied.

"No you weren't."

"Yes I was. In fact it was my job, and until Zippy showed up I was on my own. You weren't there!" I countered. (Zippy was our nickname for one of our sergeants, an ex-traffic cop who had transferred out from the Met).

"I *was* there, I remember it clearly" she said firmly. "But you weren't there, I was definitely single crewed. I told Caroline about it later and she still has nightmares about the squashed face!"

"No, no, no! *I* was there and *I* was single crewed. As it was a fatal I called up for a sergeant and Zippy turned up. It was just me and him."

"Are you sure?" she asked clearly not believing me, but now I could detect the faintest hint of doubt in her recollection.

"Yes, absolutely sure. In fact I've still got the letter of commendation that Zippy wrote to the Area Commander as he was so impressed with how I dealt with it." (Just to make sure I wasn't going completely mad I dug through my box of police memorabilia the other day and found the letter). "Maybe you turned up to help with traffic control?" I suggested.

"No! I remember the job coming in. It was a quiet evening so most of the shift were having their meal break and I went to the Noodle Bar to get dinner for everyone. I had just sat down and taken my first mouthful when the call came in about a fatal at the top of the hill. Nobody volunteered so I sarcastically said 'I'll go shall I?' Nobody answered so I stood up, threw my dinner in the bin and walked out saying 'For fuck's sake!'..."

I laughed. "I remember you doing that, but it can't have been that job because I must have already been there."

Anyway, we had to agree to disagree and accept that we were probably both there (we may even have been crewed together), but all either of us can remember is Jen not getting her dinner and the grotesquely cartoon-like image of a totally flat, almost two-foot wide blob of what had once been someone's head. I can't remember what type of motorbike he had been riding, what colour the lorry was, who the lorry driver was, what the traffic conditions were like or even who else was there. Nothing at all. Just the head.

This also highlights a very real difficulty with officers and witnesses giving statements and appearing in court, and explains why sometimes people will swear they saw something completely different to what is shown on CCTV footage of the same incident. I would quite happily have sworn under oath, had I needed to, that I attended that job on my own and I assume Jen would have done the same. Neither of us would have been lying or trying to mislead the court, but we both would have been wrong. I have often tried to explain this perceptual distortion to friends when they see CCTV or media footage on the news (particularly in public order situations such as high profile demonstrations) and say "Look! There! Did you just see that? Those officers are clearly lying. They should lose their jobs for that!" The perspective we have from watching a five second clip on a screen in the safety of our living rooms will bear almost no resemblance to what an officer standing on the front line of a violent protest is seeing and feeling.

I sometimes wish everyone could experience a few hours of facing down an angry mob, watching your friends and colleagues getting attacked whilst having abuse (and bricks, bottles and anything else) hurled at you, and then being expected to calmly remember exactly who did what and when. Not just what and when, but also what they were wearing, word for word what they said, who they were with, who you were standing next to, precisely where you were, what time it was, how long exactly it lasted and what you said and did in response. You'll also be expected to remember what the weather was like, how big the crowd was and many other forgettable details. You will then, no doubt, see the video footage at a later date and think "that's not what happened" or "why can't I see that guy punch me? It happened just before we moved forward" or, worse "Shit, it looks like I just pushed that guy to the ground for no reason. Why can't I see him kick out or hear his threats?"

Sometimes it's a simple case of the camera angle being in the wrong place or not wide enough to show the full picture, sometimes the footage is edited to sensationalise the situation and sometimes (in the case of CCTV) the lack of crucial audio portrays a different picture to reality. When you throw the officer's perceptual distortion into the mix it's not at all surprising that accounts and videos don't perfectly align. It's not the police being dishonest, corrupt or intentionally trying to mislead, it's simply a natural physiological response to high levels of stress. I really wish there was more public awareness around this issue as I think it would do a lot to help improve the low levels of trust we currently have in our police service.

With Jen, receiving an Area Commander's Commendation

Out of the Blue

16

The Kids are Not Alright

It was surreal. My brain slowed as it struggled to take in the scene and my senses were telling me so much was wrong that it couldn't be real, that perhaps I had stumbled onto a film set.

It was 2 o'clock in the morning and I was standing in my shirtsleeves in the middle of the Missenden Road, a fast country carriageway that ran alongside farmers' fields and through woodland. It should have been pitch black and it should have been cold. It was neither. It was an unusually mild, almost warm night and the scene was flooded with the yellowish glow of the emergency lighting, giving everything an eerily unnatural feel. The light pulsed and changed, brightening to bluey-green and dimming again with metronomic regularity as the flashing blue lights of one of the fire engines cut through the gloom.

Oddly, I can still hear the silence in my ears. The normally busy road (even at night) was still and silent. Except it wasn't. The silence was accompanied by the constant hum of the diesel generators that were powering the lights. And the silence was pierced by the screams and groans of the boy trapped in the driver's seat of the car. A car that was unrecognisable, bent in the middle just behind his seat, almost snapped in half where it had suddenly and violently met its final resting place, wrapped around a large tree at the side of the road.

My eyes scanned the whole picture, and were trying not to focus on the three lifeless figures that completed the horrific scene.

The front seat passenger had already been removed from the vehicle and had been carefully, gently laid on the road, out of harm's way, with a sheet draped over his lifeless head and upper body.

About ten metres back up the road was the disturbingly twisted body of his friend, who I guessed was about fourteen years old. I presume he hadn't been wearing a seatbelt as had been thrown from the car. His back had broken when his young and delicate body had slammed into the tarmac. The force of the impact with the road meant his legs were facing, almost impossibly, in the opposite direction to the rest of him. One of his arms was in a sickeningly contorted position. We didn't need a doctor to tell us he was dead.

My gaze shifted to the fourth boy, the remaining rear seat passenger. He was still sitting upright in his seat, seatbelt fastened and he appeared undamaged and intact from the shoulders down. But his neck had snapped. His head was limply hanging over the back of his seat at such an angle that he would have been looking, upside-down, at the night sky out of the smashed rear windscreen. Only he wasn't looking at anything. He, too, was dead.

Three of the four were beyond help, the only survivor was the driver who was trapped behind the steering wheel. He was screaming in pain and repeatedly saying he couldn't see. He kept calling for his mother. He had horrific facial injuries and I couldn't tell if he had been blinded or simply had blood in his eyes. The fire crew were struggling to cut him free whilst a paramedic did her best to treat and comfort him.

To be honest I just wanted to get in my panda and leave. There were enough officers, fire crew and paramedics to deal with everything and I had nothing to do but witness the horror. Unfortunately I was crewed with the Area Duty Sergeant that night and he needed to oversee the police response. So there I stood, trying not to look, trying not to hear the screams. I needed a role there, a job to do to help and to distract me from my thoughts, but there was nothing. My only role was to covey a few messages over the radio between the control room and my sergeant while I waited for it to be over.

After the longest fifteen minutes or so of my life the driver was freed from the wreckage and swiftly taken to A & E by ambulance.

The traffic investigation team arrived to assess the scene and to start collecting the necessary evidence to enable them to piece the events together and start preparing a prosecution if they deemed it appropriate. Finally we were able to leave.

I had been to many, many nasty accidents before and seen many, many bodies, some horribly mutilated. But this was somehow different. Maybe it was one too many, maybe it was the age of the boys, or maybe it was just that I was going through too much personally. Whatever the reason it was almost unbearable and was the first job in eight years of service that really affected me. I don't think I told anyone how I felt about it though. I don't think I would have known how to or what to say.

I later found out that the four friends (all 14 and 15) had been drinking at the driver's home. He had decided to 'borrow' his dad's car and take his mates for a spin. He had lost control at speed on a bend and the car spun before hitting a tree sideways. Tragically he had killed his best friends. He himself had suffered life-altering injuries but had survived.

I am still having trouble letting go of this incident. I am easily triggered by both drink-driving and people trying to justify or excuse speeding on our roads. Most people have absolutely no idea just what deadly weapons our vehicles are, and just how horrific traffic accidents can be.

Despite calls for the driver to be sent to prison, I feel only compassion for a boy who made a stupid choice with such catastrophic results. I often wonder how he is getting on and how he copes living every day with the guilt, grief, shame, regret and self-loathing. What would have been gained from a custodial sentence? What would it achieve? What further lesson was there for him to learn? What was his risk of re-offending? We often carelessly throw words like 'justice' and 'tragedy' around, but this truly was tragic, and justice, I think, in this instance would just compound the harm already done. So many lives destroyed, so much grief for the families, and so much trauma for everyone who was there that night. Why add more pain to the boy and his family?

They're already suffering enough.

Out of the Blue

17

Sometimes it Sucks

Timing is everything, and completely separating your personal life from work is not always possible, regardless of how hard you may try.

On a cold mid-November evening I was single crewed and reluctantly making my way through the darkness to a fairly ordinary job in a rural village in the Chiltern Hills.

"Control from Golf Hotel 122" I heard Jen's familiar voice over the radio.

"Go ahead 122" came the reply.

"Don't send PC Bourdillon to that last job!"

"Sorry 122, but he's the only available unit."

"I'll be finished here in the next ten minutes or so and then I can take that job." Jen insisted.

"Sorry 122, but that job has been outstanding for over an hour, it can't wait any longer. 132 is available and he needs to attend."

"Golf Hotel 132, it's okay, I'm already en route" I cut in...this was starting to get embarrassing now.

"No! Don't send him! Control, can someone please call me on my mobile..." As the argument carried on between Jen and the Control Room I quietly found the remote house. I slowly turned right, off the windy country lane, my headlights illuminating the open five-bar gate as I approached. My tyres crunched on the gravel driveway as I parked up outside a detached Georgian home next to an ambulance that was already there, waiting for me to arrive.

"Golf Hotel 132, on scene now" I called up and then turned the volume down on my radio so I wouldn't be unnecessarily disturbed and to minimise any distress to the occupants of the house. I closed my eyes, counted to five and took a deep breath before knocking on the door.

After a brief pause the door was opened by an ashen-faced and bewildered-looking woman in her mid-thirties. She led me into the hallway where an older man, I guessed in his late sixties, was standing apparently not knowing exactly what he should be doing with himself. He looked shocked, confused and extremely upset.

"She's in there" said the woman, indicating a door to our left with a sideways nod of her head. I went into the room and saw the body of a woman, around the same age as my mum, lying on her side just in front of the sofa. The paramedics from the ambulance were also in the room, waiting to speak to me.

"I just need to talk to these guys for a minute." I said to the woman "Why don't you go and make your dad a cup of tea in the kitchen."

"Would you like one too?" she offered. I smiled gently and shook my head in reply as I mouthed "No thanks".

Once she had left the room I checked with the ambulance crew that there was no further need of medical help and asked if there was anything they felt was suspicious. They were happy that everything seemed okay so I released them from the scene and called up, asking for undertakers and for a doctor to attend to certify the death. I then had the unenviable job of physically checking the body...firstly to confirm to myself that there were no signs of life, but secondly to make sure there was no indication of foul play such as an inexplicable wound, or a weapon concealed under the body. I was starting to struggle with my emotions as I rolled over and patted down the still warm and soft body, but was relieved to find nothing unusual or suspicious.

With nothing more to do in the living room, I again closed my eyes and took another slow, deep breath before I returned to the kitchen. I immediately noticed a smell of burnt food and looked at the cooker. The untouched remains of a very over-cooked Sunday dinner sat on and around the stove and I could clearly see where the potatoes had boiled over, staining the hob. The daughter hadn't got very far with making the tea, so I made a brew for the three of us (as they say...everything in life is better with a nice cup of tea) and sat everyone down at the kitchen table where I started to fill out the necessary paperwork for a sudden death.

The man told me that his wife hadn't been feeling well that afternoon, but they hadn't thought it serious. Their daughter had come round for dinner and the three of them had been sitting together having a drink in the living room when the mother got up to turn off the potatoes. As soon as she stood, she dropped to the floor, dead. I looked back at the stove and imagined the potato pan boiling itself dry as shock and confusion hit father and daughter in the living room, oblivious to the burning dinner.

I was starting to feel overwhelmed with emotion, and I had to work hard to remain detached and professional. I caught the daughter's eye and she raised an eyebrow in a momentary look of concern for me. I fought back tears and tried to reassuringly smile at her. I was there to help *her*...she didn't need to be worrying about me. Her look helped me to find the strength to pull myself together and focus on the moment and the task in hand. As I finished my paperwork there was a knock at the door. I got up to let the doctor in and I showed him to the body. He did his necessary checks and reports, and filled out and signed the appropriate sections on my form. He was just about to leave when there was another knock at the door.

I answered it to find myself face to face with a man I had met many times during my career...

most recently exactly seven days before, almost to the hour. He looked taken aback, startled even. "What are you doing here?" he asked. His face fell in sympathy as he said "I'm so, so sorry. You shouldn't be here. Couldn't they have sent someone else?" I shrugged, and for the second time that evening I tried to fight back the tears, but I was so overwhelmed I failed. I could see he wanted to console me but, terrified that I would completely break down if he did, I turned away. I wiped my eyes, took yet another deep breath, turned back to him and said "She's in the living room. First door on the left." I watched as the pair of undertakers entered the room and as soon as they were out of sight my shoulders started to shake uncontrollably as I struggled to contain my grief.

I was snapped back into the present by the sound of car tyres on gravel. I looked through the still open front door to see another panda car pull up next to mine. Jen got out, walked straight over to me and without a word enveloped me in a hug. I wept out of anguish and relief as she simply said "Go."

I looked up to see the daughter standing in the hallway behind be, with a look of confusion and compassion on her face. Of course she was confused. How could she know that only one short week before, on an identical crisp and cold Sunday evening, my own mum had died at home whilst I quietly held her hand? How could she know that the same undertakers had come to take my mum away? My dad, much like hers, had stood back and watched, unsure what to do. He, too, had appeared confused as the enormity of what had happened hit home.

Jen (so often my guardian angel) had tried her best to shield me from this emotionally triggering situation, but at the end of the day it was my job to be there. That's what we do. We serve "without fear or favour" and we sometimes, no, not sometimes but often, put ourselves in places we really shouldn't be so we can help others. We put ourselves in harm's way to help or protect others. That harm can be physical, mental or emotional, but either way it's still harm.

That may sound self-righteous, sanctimonious even, but it's not. It's simply the job. We're the clean-up team, the folk who do all the crappy jobs that nobody else can (or will) do. If there's something nasty or unpleasant that is no one else's responsibility then we'll either volunteer or get sent to do it. It's great that we can do this, but it can come at a great personal cost and we need to be very aware of the stresses and strains on our mental health. We also need to check ourselves to ensure that doing all the crap that no one else will do doesn't become a lifelong behavioural pattern, further compounding our traumatic stresses even long after we have left the job.

18

An Ending in the Middle

Rewind the clock a week, back to the previous devastating weekend, and I was on a set of early-turn shifts.

I got the call from my sister, Amanda, just as I was leaving work on a cold Saturday afternoon.

"Mum's deteriorating. I don't know how long she's got. Can you get away from work early?"

"I've just finished. I'll come now." I drove straight to my parents' house, not stopping at my tiny two-up two-down Victorian chair-maker's cottage to change out of my uniform or to feed my cat.

Half an hour later I pulled up outside the house I had grown-up in, got out of my car, and rang the familiar doorbell. Dad answered the door. He looked tired and haggard.

"How is she?" I asked. It was deliberately the wrong question. I knew how sick she was. I was asking if I had made it in time.

Dad smiled faintly, replying "She's not good" as I stepped inside out of the cold. We made our way up the stairs, past the newly-installed but hardly-used stair lift, and into the bedroom that had been my mum's entire world for the previous year.

She was lying in bed, with her eyes closed and she was struggling to take short, shallow breaths through the transparent tube that was feeding her nostrils with a constant flow of oxygen. The room was dark, and it was quiet except for sound of Mum's breathing and the faint hiss of the regulator coming from the oxygen bottle beside the bed. Amanda was sitting on a chair on the far side of the room. On seeing me she took hold of Mum's right hand and gently squeezed it as she leant in towards her ear.

"Gerard's here" she softly whispered.

Mum stirred, her eyes slowly opened and she appeared to struggle to focus. She first looked at Amanda, confused, and then saw me standing behind her. Her lifeless face lit up and she beamed the most beautiful smile of joy. It vanished almost immediately and, without saying a word, she closed her eyes and drifted back into a hazy, morphine-induced sleep. I don't think she ever opened her eyes again.

Mum had been diagnosed with fibrosing alveolitis about two and a half years earlier, shortly before I joined the Mounted section. When she broke the news to me she typically down-played it, saying it would probably shorten her life a little but there was nothing to especially worry about. She had, in fact, been given a year or two to live. I guess she didn't want me to know as she probably (and correctly) assumed that I would have turned down my dream job to spend more time with her.

However, she wasn't worried, so I wasn't worried. It was still the early days of the internet and I didn't have a home PC, so a quick check on 'Dr Google' wasn't an option. I had never heard of fibrosing alveolitis, had no idea what it actually was, and I had no easy way of finding out that in reality it was a rare and fatal disease that progressively (and irreversibly) scarred the lungs until breathing became impossible.

As it turned out, I only had to wait a few months before the seriousness of Mum's illness became apparent. I had popped over for a cup of tea early one afternoon and was surprised to find Dad on his own. I knew Mum was playing golf that morning, but she should have been back before I got there. About an hour after she had been due home there was a ring at the door. Dad opened it to find Mum's golfing buddy on the doorstep looking flustered and slightly alarmed.

"I need some help getting Joy out of the car" she said.

Together, we helped Mum into the house where she collapsed onto the sofa. Her face was flushed and puffy, she was in considerable distress and she was struggling to breathe. Once she had recovered enough to move her we took her upstairs to bed. She remained in bed for almost the rest of her life. That round of golf was the last time she left the house unaided and without oxygen.

I visited my mum one evening about a fortnight before she died. She was exhausted, tired of fighting for breath, tired of the pain and worried about the strain her illness was putting us all under. It seemed that she had finally reached the point where death had become a relief to welcome rather than a fate to fear.

As I was about to leave she asked me to pass her some writing paper. She quickly wrote a note, popped it in an envelope and addressed it to our long-standing family doctor.

I looked at it quizzically as she handed it to me.

"You know where he lives, don't you?"

I nodded in reply.

"You drive past his house on your way home. Could you deliver it for me? Tonight?"

"Of course" I said, my heart sinking. I wanted to ask what it was about, but I already knew. I decided it was better not to ask, not to make this any more difficult for her.

So, late at night, in the pitch black, I delivered the letter. Within a day Mum was hooked up to a morphine dispenser that automatically increased the dose, slowly and steadily, until she slipped into a deep sleep and quietly drifted away from the pain.

Two weeks later and there Dad, Amanda and I were, on that cold Saturday evening, by her bedside, knowing there wasn't much time left. I decided to stay the night, with my sister and I taking shifts to sit up with her in case she deteriorated further. As I was due back at work for an early-turn on the Sunday morning I elected to take the later shift from 3am until 6am, when I would need to leave for work. That way I'd already be awake, dressed and ready to go and there would be no risk of me running late.

We were short-staffed at work and, despite everything, I felt I needed to go in. I suppose I also thought it may be a good distraction for me. With hindsight I don't know what I was thinking, or why I even contemplated going in. I certainly wasn't going to be much use to anyone, and was probably going to be more of a liability than a help. It seems obvious now, but the fact that I was needed much more at home was lost on me.

I arrived at work over-tired, emotional, unshaven and wearing the crumpled shirt I had slept in. I almost bumped into my sergeant, Nigel. He took one look at me and asked "Are you okay?"

"No, not really. I've been up most of the night with my mum. I don't think she's going to last the day."

"Then why are you here? Go home and see her."

"No. We're below minimum-manning levels, and I'd rather be here right now. But if my sister calls I'll have to go."

"Yes, of course. Just say the word and you can go at any time."

I spent the morning in a state of physical and emotional exhaustion, but thankfully Sunday mornings are often notoriously quiet shifts and this one was no exception. I drank a lot of tea and tried to clear some paperwork whilst I waited for the call that finally came just after lunch. I was chatting to Jen in the main corridor on the first floor of the nick when my phone rang.

"You need to come now" Amanda told me.

"I've got to go" I said to Jen as I walked off down towards the sergeants' office. I knocked and went in, but to my surprise Nigel wasn't there. Sitting at his desk was a sergeant from Amersham who I hardly knew.

"Where's Nigel?" I asked.

"He's had an emergency at home and had to go. I'm covering for him. How can I help?"

In a daze, with my head spinning, I simply said "I need to go now."

"Go where? You know we're below our minimum staffing level, don't you? You're not going anywhere."

"Didn't Nigel tell you? He's already agreed it. I need to go."

"Sorry. Not today, no chance."

I was too tired, too worn down, too broken to argue or explain. I walked out past Jen and headed down the stairs, in the opposite direction to the locker rooms.

"Where are you going?" Jen demanded.

"Back out on patrol." I shrugged.

"What? No you're not, you're going home!" she exploded.

"Apparently not. We're too short staffed." I mumbled in reply.

"Right!" Jen snapped. She turned and in a fury stormed off down the corridor towards the sergeants' office. Without pausing or knocking she entered the room and I could hear her shouting. The door slammed shut behind her, but I could still hear the muffled cries of an argument coming from the office. Less than a minute later a triumphant-looking Jen emerged through the door and marched back down the corridor towards me. I caught her eye and then saw that she was followed by an ashen-faced and rather harassed-looking sergeant.

"I'm sorry. I had no idea," he said "you'd better go."

I didn't need telling twice. I mouthed "Thanks" to Jen, who gave me a quick hug before I rushed upstairs to de-kit and get out of there.

Thankfully I made it home in time for the four of us to have a few final, precious hours as a family. We sat around Mum's bedside, quietly chatting and saying our goodbyes. She slipped away peacefully, surrounded by those she loved and who loved her the most. And I was there to hold her hand as she left us.

19

Losing It

I've already talked about how separating your personal life from your professional one can be difficult, and sometimes keeping your emotions out of things is nigh-on impossible. There is a public perception that we as police officers are somehow trained to deal with appalling situations, and trained to control our emotions. There is no such training... how could there be? Our 'training' is going from one awful job to another, and then to another, and yet another until we become desensitised to the abuse, the violence, the misery and the horror.

This approach, although crude, tends to work for most of us...for a while. Some officers will leave either during their two-year probationary period or shortly after, but most will stay. Many who make a career out of the job will seek promotion or find departments away from the frontline to reduce the stresses of response work. Some, however, get hooked on the adrenaline and seek out ever more demanding roles, endlessly searching for the excitement of the ultimate 'big job'.

For me, the 'numbing' approach worked for the first seven or eight years (in fact I clearly remember not understanding why so many colleagues complained about being stressed) but then I started to notice the invisible load I was carrying and the cracks started to show. In 2001 I was going through a rough time at home. My dad had been diagnosed with Parkinson's disease whilst my mum was sick and he died unexpectedly within a year of her death. I was abroad on holiday when he collapsed and despite frantically trying to get an emergency flight home I didn't make it back in time. I never got to say goodbye or tell him how much I loved him. My sister and I were dealing legally with my parent's estate and would soon be starting the painful and exhausting job of clearing out our family home and putting it up for sale. In the meantime I discovered my partner had been having an affair and I had to sell my house to buy her out of it. It was still only a year since I had had to leave my dream job as a mounted police officer and go back on shift, dealing with all the crap that only response officers have to deal with. To top it off my cat had died. It felt like I had lost everything I cared about and I was back to the start of my career again.

Unsurprisingly my tolerance to any extra stress was limited...I was struggling to keep my head above water and at times my professionalism was tested to the limit.

The night I finally lost it was a couple of weeks after Dad had died. It had started much like any other Saturday night, the only thing of note was that it was our new inspector's first shift with us. I didn't get to meet her though as I was deployed to a job before I even got to our briefing. As it was an unusually warm September weekend it was a busy night and I didn't make it back to the nick until about 3am. I had just sat down to catch up on some paperwork with a much-needed cup of tea when a call came in from the hospital...the A & E department were having problems with a patient who was damaging property and assaulting staff.

"I'll go!" I said as I grabbed my keys and ran downstairs to the rear yard. Wycombe Hospital was only a two minute drive from the police station and I had my suspicions as to who the offender was going to be before I even got there. Neil Masters was a local petty-criminal who we had taken to hospital earlier that night following an incident at an illegal rave. He had had a bad reaction to something he had taken and needed medical assistance. He was a major pain-in-the-arse, and the little brother of a serious villain...a convicted armed robber with Yardie connections. He loved playing the "Do you know who my brother is?" card, trying to benefit from his brother's reputation.

More snippets of information came in during my short drive to the hospital: the offender was rampaging through A & E, had wrecked two patient cubicles and had assaulted at least two nurses and a doctor.

I pulled up close to the main entrance, got out of my panda and was about to head to the front doors when I noticed movement to my left. A small access door (marked 'Staff Only') next to the main ambulance doors opened and Masters walked out into the cool September night air. He looked surprised, almost startled to see me, then quickly regained his composure. He raised his fists in front of him and snarled as he shouted "Do you fucking want some too?"

"Here we go again" I sighed to myself at the prospect of another fist fight. I could see how violently angry he was and I knew this was no time for negotiation.

"Okay Neil" I said as I stepped towards him, almost simultaneously punching him as I swept his feet out from under him. He fell heavily to the ground and I dropped to one knee to restrain him. He was struggling violently. I knew it was going to be almost impossible to control him safely on my own so I radioed for assistance.

Masters looked at me with wild, drunken and drugged up eyes and, unfortunately for both of us, hurled out possibly the worst four words he could have said.

"Fuck your dead mother!" He almost spat the words at me.

I froze. My blood ran cold. I had an almost out-of-body experience as my brain swirled and I was overcome by a feeling of ice-cold hatred that I had never felt before.

My brain scrambled for reason as it tried to control my emotions. The best I could do was to lean down and say, very slowly, as my knee pinned his shoulder to the ground "You're talking to the wrong guy Neil. I suggest you calm down and shut the fuck up."

Unfortunately for me that gave him all the ammunition he needed – he knew he'd got to me. He gave me a long, hard look and almost sniggered as he very slowly and deliberately said "FUCK. YOUR. DEAD. MOTHER."

The ice in my veins instantly melted, quickly boiling over into a sudden uncontrollable rage. My hand trembled as I tried so, so hard to remain calm. With my left hand I took hold of the top of his head and turned it so he was looking straight into my eyes.

"You need to shut up, Neil. Do you understand?" He snarled by way of reply. Of course he understood, he couldn't believe his luck that he'd hooked me so easily. I released my hold on his head and as I adjusted my position to get better control of him my left foot slipped forward, making contact with his mouth. "Fuck!" he called out, sounding more surprised than hurt. I looked down at where my boot was and saw blood oozing out of a split in his upper lip.

"Why don't you do that again, you cunt?" he taunted. By now the rage in me was overwhelming and I was consumed by the red mist of anger that was clouding my thoughts and confusing my decisions. I was vaguely aware of police sirens wailing and of someone standing in the shadows, silently watching everything. I think it was a man in a suit, but I was so engulfed in the haze of my anger I filtered him out and focussed completely on Masters...and he had just asked me to kick him in the face. Who was I to refuse? I released my grip, stood up and took a couple of steps back. My chimp brain had totally taken over, all rational thought was gone. Common sense, procedure and training had all been replaced by a primeval desire to hurt him, to really hurt him. As I drew my right foot back to take a swing at him I heard a very loud and clear "Dillan!" behind me. Jen's voice snapped me back into the real world. I looked at her as I returned my foot to the ground. "You need to calm down" she said, looking clearly confused by my uncharacteristic behaviour. Masters was now back on his feet and lunged towards me. "Fuck your dead mother!" he screamed at me as he spat a mouthful of blood in my face. Jen's face changed instantly from confusion to realisation as she understood the situation that was playing out in front of her. "We need another unit here now!" she radioed "And tell them to bring the van." She then turned to me "Go back to your car, Dillan. Now." She immediately turned back to Masters in an attempt to verbally de-escalate everything. He was having none of it, and I wasn't going to leave Jen on her own whilst he was being so violently unpredictable. "It's okay, I'm calm now" I half-lied "and we need to get him down again."

He continued to scream "Fuck you and fuck your dead mother!" at me as Jen and I grabbed an arm each. I instantly swept his legs away and we took him back to the ground. I took hold of his wrists in an attempt to restrain him, but he was kicking out wildly and managed to kick Jen away. She recovered quickly and threw herself onto his legs, preventing him from lashing out further. Even with two of us on top of him we were having trouble controlling him – there was no way we could safely handcuff him like this. We needed more officers.

Masters continued to struggle, but knowing he wasn't going to break free decided to return to the verbal abuse. "Fuck your dead mother" became a continuous stream, and I was struggling not to be triggered by his repetitive monologue.

"Breathe, breathe..." I repeated to myself, desperately trying to regain some clarity. I could hear more sirens approaching and to my relief saw the transit van pull up right behind us. Tony and Dean got out and as soon as they had hands on Masters I got to my feet and walked away. I desperately needed to calm down and get away from the whole situation, but I knew that even the three of them were going to struggle to safely control such a violent prisoner.

I paced backwards and forwards in front of my panda, clenching and unclenching my fists as I talked to myself. "Come on Dillan, get a grip. Calm down. Calm, calm, calm down." My anger slowly started to subside as I tapped my thigh rhythmically with my right hand, helping my thoughts to become clearer.

I looked back towards the ambulance bay and saw that Dean was unlocking the rear doors of the van and opening the cage. I looked over to Masters and saw he was finally under control and in handcuffs. He was still face down on the concrete, and Jen and Tony were going to have to get him up onto his feet and walk him over to the van. I realised it would be a much easier task if I helped so I walked back over. Jen looked at me inquisitively. I nodded. "I'm okay." I mouthed as I knelt down to take hold of Masters' left arm. Tony had his right arm and Jen still had his legs.

"On the count of three we're going to get you up on your feet Neil." said Tony. "One, two, three, up!" We got him up and walked him slowly to the rear of the van.

"Okay Neil, are you calm now?" I asked. "We're just going to step you up into the van, so mind your head." The response was instant and violent. With his face just inches from mine I was splattered with blood as he screamed one final "Fuck you dead mother!" Tony's reaction was swift – with his free right hand he struck Masters in the head. My reaction was mirror-identical with my left fist also finding its mark. He sank to his knees as a fury I have never felt before (or since) engulfed me. I had a strange sense of part of me leaving my body, perhaps all of me left, all except for my rage. It was like I had lost myself and all I was had been replaced by fury. And Masters. There was nothing else. Nothing else mattered. Just my rage and him. I took hold of him and with all my might threw him up into the cage in the back of the van. There was a sickening thud as he crashed into the back of the cage, but that didn't stop me. I leapt up and into the van with no idea of, and no control over, what I was going to do. I vaguely remember saying "I'm going to fucking kill you" as I jumped into the back, intent on taking out all my pain on him. I wanted to kill him.

Someone was looking out for me that night as before I could act I was brought back to reality by a loud, shrill "What's going on here?" I turned to see an officer I didn't recognise staring at me from outside the van. Although I only momentarily glanced at her, it was long enough to register the two shiny pips on her shoulder epaulettes. It was our new inspector. Without saying a word I jumped down from the van, walked furiously over to my panda, got in and screeched the wheels as I sped away from the hospital.

By the time I got back to the nick I was a complete mess. The toxic mix of my own grief, Masters' taunting words, my violent rage, and now the relief to be away from the hospital was overwhelming. The realisation that my indefensible behaviour may cost me my job was slowly dawning on me. I was physically and mentally exhausted and needed to vent. I abandoned my car in the rear yard and walked over to the wall by the entry gate and started to punch it. My knuckles split, the pain gave me some relief so I punched harder and as the blood began to flow so, finally, did my tears. It was the first time I had cried since Dad had died, and once I had opened those floodgates there was no going back. "Fuck, fuck, fuck!" I repeated with each punch to wall, the tears streaming down my cheeks.

And then, a clam hand on my shoulder. But I wasn't ready yet. "Fuck off and leave me alone!" I half snarled, half sobbed as I shrugged the hand away.

"Okay" said a female voice softly. I looked up to see my inspector for the second time that night, concern and empathy on her face. "It's okay" she said "Jen has told me everything. Take as much time as you need here and then come and see me when you're ready."

She quietly left me alone with my emotions in the semi-darkness of the rear yard. I wiped away my tears and looked at my red and bloody knuckles. I was, both physically and mentally, a complete mess. My muddled thoughts became clearer, revealing the reality of my situation. I had assaulted a prisoner, my behaviour by any measure had been totally unprofessional and I had just told my inspector to fuck off. Most frighteningly of all though, I had unlocked a side of myself I had never seen or felt before...someone willing and able to beat another man to death.

My anger was gone and I was just numb as I contemplated the possible consequences. It seemed likely that I would lose my job. I may face criminal charges. In my slightly panicked mind I even considered the possibility of getting sent to prison. But worse than any of that was the realisation that mentally I was in trouble, big trouble. Either I was losing myself or I didn't actually know who I was anymore. With a cold, sick feeling in my gut I opened the back door to the nick and walked up the stairs to the inspector's office to face my fate.

Contrary to my expectations I was met with kindness and concern. She offered me a seat and asked "Why are you at work Dillan?"

I was confused by the question. "Because we're on nights."

"No, I mean why are you here at all?" Her response just confused me more. I was rostered to be at work, so I was at work...I had no choice in the matter.

"I'm not sure what you mean. I've used up all my annual leave for the year, so where else would I be?"

"You should be on compassionate leave" she gently suggested.

"But I've had my two days" I protested.

"*Two days?*" she looked at me incredulously. "You've lost both your parents. You're clearly struggling. Why haven't you taken longer?"

"Because I've used my two days compassionate leave and I've run out of annual leave. How could I have taken any longer?"

"No, no...two days is the *minimum* allocation, after that it's up to your supervisors' discretion. Hasn't anyone been through this with you?"

"No. I was just told you got two days. I took two last year for my mum and two last week for my dad."

"I imagine you've got a lot going on right now. Have you had the funeral yet? What about the will? And your parents' house? When are you going to clear it and sell it?"

"We buried Dad last week, but we're trying to organise his memorial service at the moment and are going through the will and probate with the lawyers. I haven't even thought about the house yet."

"How long do you need?" she asked. "I can sign you off work right now."

"But I don't want a mental health issue on my personal file. I want to get on to the Tactical Firearms Group, and that won't look good on my application."

"Don't worry, I'm not a psychologist! I can't diagnose you...I'm just going to sign you off for bereavement. It's standard policy and won't affect your career at all."

Relief flushed over me and my shoulders sank as I finally relaxed into the chair. I closed my eyes and took a long, slow breath.

"I'll give you a month" she said "and I'll come and see you at home in a couple of weeks to see how you're doing and if that time needs extending. Okay?"

"Thank you" I mumbled as my eyes welled up again. Finally someone in authority was looking after me and putting my needs above those of the organisation. My sergeants were capable and experienced officers but hadn't really done anything to help. I don't know if welfare just wasn't an issue for them or if they weren't fully aware of the regulations, but whatever the reason no one had taken charge until now.

I would later discover that my inspector's fiancée had been killed on duty, mown down by fleeing motorist, several years before. The physical and mental welfare of her officers was unsurprisingly a high priority for her, and it made her an excellent boss to work for.

"I'd like to finish my shift though...I need to sort out all my paperwork to hand over, and I'd like to go back to the hospital to take some statements and find out what actually happened there tonight."

"Okay. But I'm not letting you back out on the streets again!" she half-joked.

I left her office feeling like an enormous weight had been lifted from me. I made myself a cup of tea and sat quietly for a while contemplating and processing the night's events before writing a summary for each of my ongoing jobs.

I returned to the hospital at around 5am and was shown through to the staff area in A & E by a nurse. She introduced me to one of the doctors assaulted by Masters, who to my shame I recognised as the well-dressed man in the shadows who had witnessed my fury. My head dropped in embarrassment and self-loathing. I could barely look at him as I expected my behaviour to be judged. The doctor however just beamed at me as he shook my hand and said "How are you doing? I'm glad you're here, I wanted to thank you. I think you dealt with that little wanker extremely efficiently! I wanted to step in and help, but what with him being my patient and the Hippocratic Oath and all that..."

Again, a flush of relief. Maybe my response hadn't been as bad as I thought? Anyway, there was no time to dwell on that as I needed to take the statement.

It turns out that not long after arriving at the hospital Masters had got fed up of waiting and started to be verbally abusive to the nurses. When one of them told him to calm down he started to kick and damage some monitoring equipment and then ripped the cubicle's curtain off its rails. The nurse tried to stop him and he punched her. He then marched down the corridor to the staff area and walked in, despite the 'No Entry' signs. A nurse there told him to get out and he pushed her out of his way before punching the doctor behind her who tried to stop him. It was around then that the hospital had called the police.

Masters then made his way back down the adjacent corridor towards the ambulance doors but had stopped to enter the emergency resuscitation room where he found another doctor working on a cardiac patient. The doctor screamed at him to get out, which he did but only after he had punched that doctor too. From there he walked out of the hospital into the warm night air and straight into me, with his "Do you fucking want some too?" greeting.

That explained a lot, and went some way to help me (retrospectively at least) justify my response. Unfortunately the one thing it couldn't help with was my feeling of self-loathing, or the shock of the realisation that I could so completely lose control of myself. Lose myself to the point where I have little doubt I could have beaten another person to death.

Now don't get me wrong, I have never been shy of a fight, and at times may have been a little too eager to get stuck in. Physically hurting someone (or being hurt myself) during an arrest was not something I lost sleep over, but this was different. It had opened a door to another me. A different me who I didn't like, and a different me who scared me. It didn't take long for the sleepless nights to start, and for the nightmares to develop into flashbacks that could hit me like a train at any moment. I started to get a nagging feeling that I needed to leave the job, and I guess that it was the start of a very long end to my career.

GH01, the High Wycombe transit van, parked in the station's rear yard

20

Oil on the Boil

It was my first week back on full operational duties. It was late July and I'd been either off work or on 'light duties' (stuck in the nick doing everybody else's paperwork) since January when I had had reconstructive knee surgery following a serious assault at work. So far my knee was holding up well. The operation, months of physio and a couple of stays at the wonderful Flint House Police Rehabilitation Centre seemed to be working and I was slowly gaining confidence in its strength.

I was one of the first members of my team to arrive at work for a Sunday night-turn. I was kitting-up, putting on my belt and radio in the locker room when a call came over the air "Any unit for an immediate?" The late-turn were tired, in their last half-hour of a seven-day rotation. It was not the time that anybody wants to be off duty late, so I volunteered to go. I nudged Dan, a young probationary constable who had also got to work early "Come on mate, we've got a job!" I said as I grabbed a set of car keys off one of the late turn guys and ran down the stairs to the rear yard.

As I drove along the A40, our blue lights sporadically illuminating every building we passed, more details of the job were coming in. A man, presumably drunk, had walked into three different takeaway restaurants on a small parade of shops demanding free food. When he had been refused he had assaulted staff and smashed the shop windows. The manager from the fish and chip shop was now following him at a distance. Within a couple of minutes we had found the witness who gave us the address of the house that the man had let himself into. As it was just around the corner I killed the blue lights and pulled into the residential cul-de-sac where he was last seen.

I knocked on the door, expecting to be ignored, but to my surprise my door opened almost immediately. Before I could say anything I found myself stumbling back into the street as I was punched square in the face. Dan, who had only been in the job for a few months, was clearly shocked and didn't appear to know what to do. The occupant was standing in the doorway shouting "Fuck off and leave me alone!" I recovered myself quickly and lunged forward, grabbing hold of his left arm. Dan, following my lead grabbed his right and we pulled him towards us and tried to take him to the floor. He broke free from Dan's grip and pushed him heavily to the ground as I struggled to control him on my own. He started to lash out, punching me with his now free right hand. I had no option but to let go and push him away to create a safe space between us, out of his reach. As I did so he kicked me hard, and as luck would have it his foot connected with my still-recovering knee. My leg buckled underneath me and I fell to the ground just in time to see the offender go back into his house and slam the door behind him.

Unfortunately for him the lock must have been on the latch as the door bounced back open, allowing me to see a tiny hallway leading straight to a set of stairs that he was now climbing, presumably to his first-floor flat. At the top of the stairs he turned to his right and disappeared from my sight.

Dan and I picked ourselves up off the floor. I winced as I put weight through my right knee, the pain was almost as bad as when it had first been injured. "Shit" I said, more to myself than Dan. I knew I may be going back to more weeks of tedious light duties, and possibly further surgery. Despite the pain in my knee and the guy's violent behaviour, I still believed we could resolve the job safely. I also knew we were on an estate that was in a hopeless blackspot for our radios, and we were right in the middle of the hand-over period between the late and night shifts. The chances of us getting any immediate help were slim-to-none.

I stood on the doorstep and called up the stairs "Come on mate, we just need to talk to you. Don't make this any worse for yourself." There was no reply but I could hear the crashing and clunking of what sounded like pots and pans being banged on a hard surface. "Come and talk to us mate." I called out to him. Still no reply, just more crashing and banging from above. And then suddenly, there he was, standing at the top of the stairs holding a large kitchen knife.

"Fuck off 290!" he shouted (290 was part of my shoulder number, displayed on my epaulettes).

"Now calm down mate and put the knife down. I just want to talk to you."

"Fuck off and go away or I'll fuck you up. I'll stab you up 290, I'll fucking stab you up!" he screamed at me. I looked at Dan "We need shields. Are you trained?"

"No" he replied.

"Okay, we need help" He went to press the transmit button on his radio, but I shook my head. "No point mate, we're in a blackspot. Go back to the panda and use the car set...we need shields and full MOE kit and anybody who's trained. I am, but I don't think my knee's up to it."

As Dan went back to our car I tried to negotiate with the offender from the bottom of the stairs. He seemed to have taken a particular dislike to me and continued to threaten to stab me if I approached him. Oddly he also used an unusual threat "I'll burn you up 290 if you come in here. I'll stab you up and I'll burn you up. Fuck off and leave me alone!"

"Okay mate, but I'm not going anywhere until we get this sorted, okay?"

Dan returned and a few minutes later I heard the distant sound of a siren and we didn't have to wait much longer before the flashing blue light of the station's transit van cut through the darkness of the dead-end road. The lights and sirens were extinguished as the van parked next to our panda. Four of my shift-mates got out and started to unload shields, helmets and bags of protective equipment on to the tarmac. I limped over to them. "You okay?" asked Stuey. "Not really" I shrugged "and this guy is nuts and has got a big knife. We need to get an MOE team kitted up ASAP." Stuey grabbed a bag and started to remove bits of body armour from it, but nobody else moved. "Isn't anybody else trained?" I asked, but as I looked at them I realised they were all probationers and hadn't done any public order shield work or been through the Method of Entry course yet. "Oh FFS" I muttered to myself. "I'll have to do it then." I winced and sucked air in through my clenched teeth as I bent down to open a kit bag. I could feel my knee was already swelling up and I was losing movement in the joint, but I had no choice other than to kit up. Once Stuey and I were ready we grabbed a shield each and slowly made our way back to the open door.

"Wait a minute" I said to Stuey as I knocked on the neighbour's door. A man in his sixties answered. "Sorry to disturb you" I said "but do you know your neighbour at all?"

"Noel? Yes, but not very well. He hasn't been here long, I think he got moved because he's had some problems. I don't think he's quite right in his head."

I now had a name for him, which was a start at least. I was also now aware that he may have mental health issues of some sort. The checks we had done on the address hadn't given us any information, but that made sense now that I knew he hadn't lived there long.

"The guy's called Noel" I said quietly to Stuey. "He's got some issues and clearly doesn't like me...it'd be better if you do the talking. Okay?"

"Noel, how are you doing pal?" Stuey called up the stairs.

"Fuck off! I've got a knife and if you try to come up I'll burn you up. Now leave me alone." Came the angry reply from somewhere inside the flat.

"There's no need for that Noel. We're just here to help pal." Noel must have realised it was a different voice to mine and came out to the top of the stairs where we could see him. He was still holding the knife.

"If you come up here you're fucking dead" he shouted, but he seemed less angry and the knife was now by his side, no longer threateningly raised. Either he liked Stuey or the sight of us in full gear with shields and helmets had made him reassess his situation.

"Come on Noel, you know you've got to come with us, and you know we're not going anywhere until you do. It's your choice now, but don't make things any worse for yourself." This time he didn't reply to Stuey's calm words. "Why don't you put the knife down and then we can chat?"

Noel started to walk down the stairs towards us, knife still in hand.

"Drop the knife!" we shouted in unison. He appeared to be in a daze and carried on down the stairs giving no indication he had even heard us.

"DROP THE KNIFE!" we screamed at the top of our voices. He seemed to snap back into reality, looking startled as he let the weapon fall, hitting the stairs with a clatter. He stopped on the third or fourth step up, thinking about his next move.

"Thanks pal, now stay where you are so we can talk" said Stuey. Again he gave no reply or indication as to what he was thinking, and then suddenly, explosively, he ran down the last few steps and crashed into our shields trying to barge through us. This did him a lot more harm than us and he momentarily seemed stunned. I seized the opportunity and dropped my shield so I could grab hold of him. Stuey did the same and together we took him to the ground just outside his front door. He struggled violently, making several attempts to kick out and to get back up on his feet, but we were joined by Dan and the three of us eventually managed to get him under control. By the time we had handcuffed him and got him back up the fight had completely gone out of him, and he started to mumble apologies and talk about problems he was having. As we walked him over to the van I said to Dan "I wonder what he was doing in his flat with all that banging around?"

"I don't know. I guess we'd better go up and have a look." He replied. As I turned to walk back to the building I became aware of how bad my knee was. The adrenaline of the job had masked the injury for a while, but now that normality had returned so had the pain. It was almost impossible to walk and I knew there was no way I was going to be able to get up the stairs to his flat.

"You go mate, take one of the others. Stuey and I will wait with the prisoner."

A few minutes later Dan reappeared looking slightly shocked. "You're not going to believe this Dillan, but he was boiling up oil on his stove! He had two pans ready to go...I guess he was going to pour them over us on the stairs!" I shook my head and sighed. Experience and good judgement meant we had made the right choice by not rushing in and by using the proper protective equipment. Our injuries could have been horrific and life-changing.

Back at the nick Dr Barker, the police surgeon, was called out to assess Noel. We were concerned about his mental state and he had some bruising to his wrists from the handcuffs. When she had finished with him I tapped her on the shoulder "Excuse me Doc, could you have a quick look at my knee?" We went to the medical room and she told me to drop my trousers. "Ooh, that doesn't look good" she said as she prodded my swollen knee. "I don't think you need to go to hospital, but you need to go home immediately and rest it. You'll need to go and see your surgeon as soon as possible to check no damage has been done to the reconstruction site."

So, another two weeks off work followed...it felt like I was hardly there that year. Luckily no serious damage had been done to my knee and once the swelling had subsided I was back to work, but once again on restricted duties – this time looking after the prisoners in the custody suite.

That should have been the end to the story but a few months later I was called to give evidence in court. Noel had already pleaded guilty to the criminal damage and assault charges relating to the restaurants, but for some reason he was contesting the assault on me.

This led to a common dilemma – the circumstances leading to his arrest were now 'previous convictions' so could not be mentioned in court. All I could talk about was the arrest itself, totally out of any context.

Dan, Stuey and I waited in the police room at the court for what seemed like hours. "What a complete waste of police time" we complained amongst ourselves. Eventually Dan was called, and about 30 minutes later it was my turn to stand in the box, introduce myself and swear the oath.

The defence solicitor, a young skinny man in a badly-fitting grey suit stood up.

"PC Bourdillon, can you tell me why you visited my client's home that night?"

"Well, as you know, I can't go into details but it was in relation to an incident that occurred earlier that evening."

"Was it? Was it indeed?" he appeared to almost ask himself.

"Yes."

"And what was this *incident* you talk about?"

"As you are well aware I can't answer that, but I needed to speak to the defendant in a professional capacity."

"*Really?*"

"Yes." I couldn't understand where he was going with this, but I didn't like his snooty, condescending manner.

"I put it to you, PC Bourdillon, that you have a dislike for my client and you went to his home that night so you could antagonise him, assault him and arrest him."

I shook my head in disbelief. I almost laughed, but managed to check myself – Magistrates and Judges do not take kindly to any form of disrespect in court and I realised the lawyer was baiting me for that sort of response.

"No I did not" I replied flatly "I have never met your client before. I was sent to the address in relation to a previous matter."

"Come now, PC Bourdillon, that's not true, is it? There is no record of you being sent to my client's home. In fact you were sent to a fast food outlet on the Wycombe Road, weren't you?"

"Yes, I was sent to a fast food restaurant, but acting on the information I received there I attended the defendant's address."

"Did you now?" he replied in a talking-down-your-nose, I-don't-believe-you, sort of a way.

"Yes" I sighed.

His insinuations were starting to piss me off. I had just been doing my job, nothing more or less. As a result I had been assaulted and had to take time off work, and now my integrity was being attacked in court.

"So you say you didn't know my client?"

"No, I did not know him."

"But PC Bourdillon, you did know he was black didn't you?"

"No, I didn't."

"Of course you did, and that's why you went there, isn't it? You went there that night to harass and attack my client because of his colour. Isn't that right PC Bourdillon?"

I looked across the courtroom to Noel, a light-skinned mixed-race man. I had only noticed this fact when he had appeared with a knife at the top of the stairs.

"No. I had no idea of the defendant's ethnicity until after he had assaulted me."

"So you didn't know he was black when you went there?"

"No, why would I?"

"The witness would have told you."

"No, he didn't. He just gave me his address and described him as tall and wearing a dark hoodie."

"Come now. You know that's not true, don't you constable?"

"It is true" I insisted. The witness hadn't mentioned his colour, but perhaps in the dark he hadn't noticed either.

"So" continued the solicitor "I suggest you went to my client's home to harass and assault him because you didn't like the colour of his skin."

"No that's not true. I went to his home because I needed to speak to him about a previous matter.

I had no idea who he was, or what colour he was. I was there lawfully as part of a police enquiry."

"Then why did you illegally enter his home and drag him out onto the street before assaulting him? We have photographs of injuries to his wrists to support this."

I was getting exasperated by the questions. "I did not enter his home illegally. I knocked on the door, the defendant answered and immediately punched me, knocking me to the ground outside. I believe the injuries to his wrists occurred later when we handcuffed him."

"So you do admit to assaulting my client?"

"No." This was crazy. When were we going to talk about what *actually* happened? The punch to my face, the kick to my knee? Two weeks off work recovering and now on restricted duties? The knife? The boiling oil? I looked at the Crown Prosecuting lawyer and raised my eyebrows in an aren't-you-going-to-intervene way. His face remained blank. I looked at the magistrate. She just looked bored and disinterested. Oh well, let him play his game. We'll get to the facts soon enough.

It didn't stop though. For over an hour I was accused of the same nonsense, over and over again, back and forth like an endless game of ping-pong. Nobody stepped in to stop it. No "the officer has answered your questions, now move on." or even a simple "can you get to your point?" Nothing. It was a ridiculous waste of everybody's time (not to mention taxpayer's money) having to listen to this solicitor's fanciful and fictitious version of events.

As I stood in the box, repeating myself over and over, the incessant questioning was starting to get to me. I focussed on my breathing in an attempt to keep myself calm, but irritation and anger were festering inside me. I'd had enough of this. Not just this court case. Of all of it. The fights; the abuse; the bodies; the crap hours; the injuries; the lack of support from the public, the media, the government and the courts; the drunks; the wife-beaters; the stupid stuck-up solicitors. *It's just a game, don't get angry* I kept telling myself. *If you get angry he'll win.*

As the questions continued to repeat themselves I almost involuntarily reached into my back trouser pocket and touched my warrant card holder. Was this it? Was this the moment I had subconsciously been waiting for? The feel of my warrant card gave me both a feeling of immense strength and of total calm. As I stood there I mentally detached myself from the situation I was in, allowing a totally different one to play out in my head. I had a hugely empowering vision of producing my warrant card and holding it by my side as I looked straight at the magistrate. In a firm, steady voice I said *I am an experienced, honest and hard-working police officer. I swore to serve my community and uphold the law without fear or favour, and that is exactly what I do. I am not racist. I do not attack people for fun. I am not a bully. I refuse to stand here and listen to these insulting accusations a minute longer. I don't care if you convict the defendant or not...I did my job by arresting him. This part is up to you, not me. He's clearly got mental health issues, he needs help not punishment. Whatever, I don't care anymore, I've had enough.* At this point I pictured throwing my warrant card down on the plinth in front of me. *Here's my warrant card. Take it. I refuse to do this job a minute longer. If I'm in contempt of court then so be it. I just don't care. I resign with immediate effect.*

Of course, I didn't say any of that. What I actually said, for what felt like the hundredth time, was "No, as I have already stated, that is not what happened." And then, as if the magistrate had read my mind, she finally intervened. "I believe the officer has more than adequately answered your questions. Can we move along now?"

I finally got to recount what actually happened that night and Noel was convicted and sentenced to 30 days to run concurrently with the sentence he had received (and was already serving) for the attacks on the fast food places. He went straight back to prison from court and was released a week or two later, having served no extra time inside for the assault on me. I was, however, awarded a tiny amount of compensation which I never received as Noel never paid it.

A complete and utter waste of time? Maybe, but it is what it is, and after a while in the police you get used to results like these. It's important to focus on the fact that as an officer it's your job to put offenders in front of the court, along with the necessary evidence. After that it's up to the lawyers and the criminal justice system, not you. You have to accept the results and move on, even if it means you end up arresting the same person the following day for exactly the same offence. Is it worth at times risking your life for? I can't answer that, but the job is a vocation, a calling. You have to want to do it, to believe in it. If you just want to 'lock villains up' or get 'results' then the chances are you'll become disillusioned pretty quickly and the job won't be for you.

One of the Wycombe Vauxhall Astra panda cars

High Wycombe Magistrates Court

Being presented with Queen's Jubilee Medal! Nov 2002 - C.I. WEBB + C. Supt DONLON

Receiving my Queens Jubilee Medal at High Wycombe

Out of the Blue

21

Hen Nights and Handcuffs

"Really?"

"Yes!"

"Oh come on, do I have to?"

"Yes, it's for your own good. We clearly can't trust you out on the streets, you just can't keep yourself out of trouble" said the sergeant. "It's custody for you tonight, and I wouldn't be surprised if they keep you there for a couple of weeks or so."

So that's how I found myself in the cells at Wycombe Police Station – kept out of the way so I wouldn't get hurt again. Not quite the restricted duties I had feared, but it was somewhere my inspector thought my knee would have a better chance of healing itself.

I hated being gaoler, stuck inside checking custody records, searching prisoners, phoning solicitors, making endless cups of tea (always with four or five sugars...is there a connection between high sugar consumption and crime?) and taking our 'customers' out to the yard for a smoke. It was even worse on busy nights when all my colleagues were out blue-lighting it to break up fights and chase stolen cars.

Although I didn't need to, I kept my radio on so I would know what was going on and if we were likely to get a sudden influx of prisoners. As tonight was a typically busy Friday night I was expecting to have my hands full. I chuckled when I heard the call come in.

"Any unit for a fight in Downley?" No one replied.

"Any units available for an assault and fight in Downley?" Still no reply.

"I've got an outstanding assault that has now turned into a fight at an Anne Summers Party. It's starting to get out of hand." As if by magic the dispatcher was flooded with volunteers.

"Golf Hotel 112 making!"

"Golf Hotel Sierra 12 en route!"

"Golf Hotel Zero One making!"

So, everyone was busy until they realised they could go to a hen night where the participants would be trying on lingerie and sexy dressing-up costumes! In case you're wondering, an Anne Summers party is basically the same as a Tupperware party, but they're not buying plastic food containers. Adult toys, fancy dress and underwear are the items on the shopping list at these events.

My initial reaction was one of FOMO. These were the sort of jobs we, as young male officers, dreamed of going to! I knew deep down though that the reality was going to be far from the expectation. This wasn't going to be a house full of beautiful, slightly tipsy young professional women in classy lingerie. Oh no. It was much more likely to be a grotty flat with half-a-dozen very drunk, angry and abusive middle-aged women with smudged make-up wearing cheap and tacky French maid and school girl outfits. They'd all be swearing and snarling at each other whilst trying to flirt with the police officers who were trying their best to calm them all down. No thank you. I'm actually better off being here with my customers.

It wasn't long before I heard "Golf Hotel 112, we're Zero Nine with one. En route to Golf Hotel." Dan and James had a prisoner and were on their way to custody, so I let them know we had room for them and warned the custody sergeant that we had an imminent arrival. About ten minutes later the custody suite buzzer rang and I unlocked the heavy steel door to let them in. In walked a couple of very dishevelled looking officers and a very angry woman in a short white dress with mascara smeared down her cheeks.

"What happened to you?" I asked.

"She hit me with a dildo" said James. I laughed out loud. James seemed less amused "so I've arrested her for Assault on Police" he continued.

"Of course you did! I can't wait for this one to go to court!" I exclaimed. Dan sniggered. This was gold.

The woman, however, didn't think it was funny at all.

"What are you fucking laughing at?" she snarled at me.

"You've got to admit it's quite funny!" I replied, still chuckling.

"No, it's not fucking funny! I'm the fucking victim here! That bitch" (I guess she meant one of her friends) "assaulted me, but I got fucking nicked. And now you're fucking laughing at me!" She was screaming at me, her eyes were bulging and her face was bright red. She stank of drink and seemed to want a fight.

I tried to diffuse the situation "I'm not laughing at you. I'm laughing at him!" I said, pointing at James who raised his eyebrows and shook his head.

"You fucking pigs are all fucking wankers!" she screamed at me. I really didn't know why I was the villain in this – I was just here to look after her and had nothing to do with her arrest.

"Look, once you calm down I can get you booked in and then I'll make you a nice cup of tea whilst these fine officers can sort out what's happened and go and arrest your friend if necessary. Okay?"

Despite my best efforts to calm her down she wasn't having any of it. In fact she appeared to be getting more and more angry. She stared at me with complete contempt, her lip curled up towards her nose as she appeared to be contemplating what abuse to hurl at me next. And then suddenly she threw herself at me, yelling "Fucking pig!" I immediately stepped back out of her way, but space was limited and my back was to the wall. Her hands were at my throat. Her beautifully manicured nails were like daggers and I felt them piercing my skin as she tried to grab hold of me. I pushed her away and as she stepped back her claws ripped down my front, tearing my shirt and severing the cable to my radio's microphone. I felt a searing, burning pain down my chest as the three of us restrained and handcuffed her whilst she lashed out and swore obscenities. Now it was James who was laughing.

"You okay mate?" he asked.

"Not really. That fucking hurt." I replied, shaking my head.

"I'm not surprised" he said as he gestured to my chest. I looked down to see my torn and blood-soaked shirt, buttons ripped off, my radio mic dangling by my side and four angry red gashes running vertically down from my neck to my stomach. Blood trickled down towards my stomach. "I hope you've had your tetanus mate" he chuckled.

"FFS" I replied "I'm supposed to be down here to keep me out of trouble. I've only been back at work a couple of hours and I've been attacked already!"

The custody sergeant had got the first aid kit out. He threw it across the desk to me. "You'll want to dress that. Go get yourself cleaned up" he said with a slightly amused expression on his face. I clearly wasn't going to get any sympathy from anyone. As I buzzed the door to get out of the custody block he shouted to me "Oh, and put a clean shirt on! I can't have you in here looking like that!" I could hear him giggling to himself as I left "Priceless. Absolutely priceless!"

22

Never Judge a Book by its Cover

Six months later and my dream of joining Support Group (our Tactical Firearms Team) was finally becoming reality. 'The Group', as it was known, was seen as being the pinnacle of uniformed policing and had something of an elitist image and attitude. Their ranks were filled with officers I highly respected, and their recruit selection process was rigorous and probably the most competitive of any police department.

I had narrowly missed out the previous year, having made it through to the interview board stage but being pipped at the post by Gordy, an old colleague from my days at Windsor & Maidenhead. Having the experience of a prior Group board was invaluable and I sailed through at my second attempt. I also sailed through the Occupational Health medical and the fitness test. What I didn't sail through though was the firearms course.

The course had a reputation of being brutal, with a high attrition rate...some courses lost as many as fifty percent of its officers during the five weeks of training. Firearms courses were both physically and mentally demanding and were designed to wear you down and put you under huge amounts of stress, constantly testing your ability to cope under pressure. There were endless pass or fail assessments...a fail meant immediate dismissal from the course, which in turn meant little or no chance of ever getting on another course or becoming a firearms officer in the future. On top of the constant assessments, the firearms instructors could dismiss you at any time if you did something they considered was unsafe, if they felt your attitude was wrong, if your fitness wasn't good enough, or they just thought you weren't up to the job. With hindsight I wasn't in a good enough headspace to take on such a challenge. I wasn't anywhere near being out of the blue fog of depression and anxiety and I should have waited another year or two before applying. Looking back it was a godsend that I failed my first board...there was no way on earth I would have been able to cope the year before.

Bright and early on a dark and frosty Monday morning I arrived with some trepidation at Milton Keynes Police Station where I was given keys to a tiny bedroom that was to be my home for the next month or so. I dumped my kitbags by my bed and made my way down to the shooting range to meet my fellow recruits. The nerves, tension and excitement in the office area was palpable. I don't think any one of the dozen of us was looking forward to what lay ahead, but we all had a certain amount of pride for having got this far. The four instructors walked in and 'welcomed' us, but some of them weren't especially welcoming. It became apparent pretty quickly that there was a divided approach amongst the training staff...there were those who wanted us all to do our best and for as many as possible to pass, and then there were those who judged us on our first meeting and decided pretty much there and then who was and who wasn't going to get through. Back then there was a fairly stereotypical 'firearms officer' type and, at 5"8' and 12 stone, I wasn't it. My gut was telling me that the odds weren't in my favour and I reminded myself of a conversation I had had with my sergeant many years before during one of my first performance reviews.

"Is there any particular department you'd be keen to join Dillan?"

"There are a few I'm interested in and there are two in particular that I'm really keen to join, but I can't decide which one I should work towards." If you wanted to specialise then you had to commit to it. Your chosen department needed to be regularly mentioned in your performance appraisals, you needed to network to get yourself known to team members, and you needed to do as many courses as you could that would be of interest and of use to the department. You would also need to have attachments to your chosen team (if possible) and tailor your style of policing to fit the team you hoped to join...take on complex interviews and investigations if you wanted to join CID, or get search trained and volunteer for lots of unpleasant searches if you wanted to get onto the Underwater Search Unit for instance.

"Okay, which two?"

"The Mounted Section or Support Group." I said. My sergeant rolled his eyes.

"You don't make things easy for yourself, do you? You do know those are two of the hardest departments to get onto, don't you?"

"Yes, I've been told that, but they're what I want to do. If I don't try I won't get on, will I?" He shrugged and nodded. "Okay, so which one are you going to go for?"

"I was hoping to get your advice on that" I replied.

My sergeant looked at me thoughtfully for a couple of seconds before saying "I need you to go out of my office, turn left, go down the corridor and take the second door on your right. Go through the door, take a couple of steps to your left and then turn left so you're facing towards the wall. Then think about your choice and come back and tell me what you've decided." I was totally confused and had no idea where he was going with any of this. I thought he may be playing some sort of prank, but hey, he was my sergeant, this was my annual appraisal, so off I went. Thirty seconds later I was staring at myself in the mirror above the sinks in the men's toilets. I half laughed, half sighed as his point became clear. Back I went to his office.

"So Dillan, what's your decision? Do you think you're a jockey or a gorilla?" In their early days Support Group had the nickname of 'Gregory's Gorillas'...Inspector Gregory had formed the team, and they were all of a certain imposing size and build. Although those days were long gone, the image still endured. And I was no gorilla. For the following three years everything I did was about getting myself onto the Mounted Section. But now, with my time on the horses having been and gone, I was finally going to be an Authorised Firearms Officer (AFO) on Support Group. All I had to do was pass this course, but it appeared that some of the instructors were rather old school and still wanted a team full of only gorillas.

Luckily for me I wasn't actually the smallest of the Support Group recruits...there was a guy called Chris who was tiny (about 5'5" and slim) and at least one of the instructors couldn't restrain a raised eyebrow when they first saw him.

After a brief round of introductions and a range rules/safety brief (over the obligatory cup of tea), our first job of the day was to get issued with the necessary kit for the course. As there was a good chance many of us wouldn't make it through the course the job wasn't going to waste money on giving us nice new stuff, so we just got to rummage around in boxes of old used belts, holsters, magazine pouches, coveralls and helmets. Everything was sized L or X-L...there was nothing for the smaller officer. I managed okay by rolling up my coverall sleeves a bit and by putting a few extra holes in my belt with a leather puncher that they kept in the office for such eventualities. Chris, though, was absolutely swamped in his overalls and had to roll up both the sleeves and the legs of his firearms suit. It looked both ridiculous and comical...and made him look like a schoolboy in dress-up. This didn't help him at all and he looked like a marked man. In fact even I wondered how long he'd last. It seemed like a forgone conclusion that he wasn't going to pass the course.

After a long first day of shooting, learning how to deal with stoppages, and stripping and cleaning weapons we headed to the station bar in the evening to relax and get to know each other. I got chatting to Chris, who was softly spoken, quite shy and reserved. He didn't really want to talk about his background, but over the course of a couple of beers I found out that he was an ex-Paratrooper who had seen action at the Battle of Goose Green during the Falklands War. He had seen colleagues die and believed he had killed at least one Argentinian soldier. On leaving the Parachute Regiment he had drifted for a while before he found a faith in God. He tried to leave his military life behind him, he didn't swear, hardly drank and had gone so far as to have his regimental tattoos removed. He had joined the police and had realised that his skills could be best used on a firearms team, so here he was. It was not the story I was expecting from him...nothing about him gave away any hint of his past life. In my eyes he suddenly went from a certain course failure to probably the top student, and one I might be able to learn from.

The first week was spent entirely on the range, familiarising ourselves with the various weapons our force used...primarily the Glock 17 pistol and the Heckler & Koch MP5 carbine, both 9mm weapons. For those of us who had never really shot before it was an accelerated learning experience, and I always felt like we were playing catch-up with the ex-military students. Our one advantage was that we had no prior bad habits, as the military ways of doing things were not always the same as the police ways. The instruction style was loud, vocal and often abusive...if you did something wrong you certainly knew it! A few of us seemed to be shouted at a lot more than the others, and despite his military experience, Chris found himself on the wrong end of an outburst more than most. He never argued back, but I could see his head go down and as the week went on he withdrew further into himself.

Week two was our first taste of tactical work, and the part of the course that I had actually been looking forward to as I thought my high level of fitness would be a real advantage. The tactics we learnt were fairly basic...camouflage and concealment, building containments, moving under cover from fire and cover from sight, removing armed offenders from vehicles, building entries, and the feared 'open country search'.

Open country searches involved firearms teams moving in formation across open ground, following a tactical firearms dog who was tracking an armed offender. It was feared by students as, on the course, the search could go on for miles and was conducted at a fairly high pace...the 'suspect' was obviously running away from us, and we had to keep up. Running, in formation, wearing full ballistic kit (including body armour, helmets etc.) whilst carrying weapons and ammo wasn't easy.

It was usually conducted across farm fields and through woodland. The terrain was seldom flat, and the ground surface was never compatible to running in heavy boots. There was no good time of year to do it either...in winter the ground was slippery and muddy and the cold air burnt your lungs as you desperately sucked it in; and in summer the mud had dried into rock-hard ridges and potholes, and you sweated and boiled under all the kit. At any moment you would come under fire and would have to dive into any available cover and then deal with the threat as you deemed necessary.

The whole scenario would inevitably end up with a building containment (a siege type situation) and we would have to safely arrest, or maybe shoot, the offender. As with all parts of the course it was a pass-or-fail module, but this particular module presented so many opportunities to fail...be it for your fitness, your communication skills within the team, your grasp of the tactics, your weapon-handling, your teamwork, your concealment skills at the building containment, your ability to keep calm and make sound judgements under extreme pressure, or for how you conduct the final arrest.

And all of this whilst being screamed at that you're useless, you're not good enough, you're not fit enough, you don't deserve to be on the course, and lots and lots of " What the fuck do you think you're doing?!" "What the fuck was that?!" and "Get a fucking move on!" Of course, if you did get a *fucking move on* then you'd get a "Slow the fuck down! What sort of fucking team player are you? Don't you ever fucking leave your Tail End Charlie behind, you fucking idiot!" The first basic rule of open country search was that you only go as fast as your slowest team member, but the second rule was that you keep up with the dog at all times...a real juggling act. And nobody wanted to be the slowest member of the team!

Our first attempt at an open country search was a wake-up call for many of us as to just how hard the course was going to get, and how we needed to be at the top of our game to get through.

We were nearing the end of the scenario – we had tracked the 'offender' for several miles across difficult ground and were all physically and mentally exhausted. It appeared that the subject had taken refuge in a derelict farmhouse a few hundred meters ahead of us, just across a field to our right.

Breathing heavily from the exertion, we were keeping as low as we could, following a hedgerow to give us some cover, when a couple of shots were fired from the building. Just as we had been trained to do, we dropped to the ground, crawling and scrambling to get behind any hard cover we could find. Some threw themselves into a ditch that ran along the edge of a field...not bad cover but unfortunately for them it had about a foot of filthy, freezing water at the bottom.

We were just a few metres short of a gate-sized gap in the hedgerow and we knew that we had no option but to get safely past this danger if we wanted to contain the farmhouse. Chris and I were closest to the gap, having both taken cover behind a large oak tree about five metres from the hedge. We decided to crawl over to the edge of the opening to get a proper look at the problem and the building.

We got there unseen by the 'offender' and had just started to discuss our options for getting the team to the other side when one of our instructors appeared beside us. Any credit I may have hoped we'd get for taking the initiative, not being stuck in a muddy ditch, and being first to the gap evaporated immediately as he screamed "What are you going to fucking do now?" Before I had time to answer, his question was followed by "It's not a fucking coffee morning at the WI! Stop fucking gossiping and get a fucking move on!"

I looked from Chris to the gap and back to Chris again. He nodded. "We need to cover the gap so the team can get across" I suggested.

"So why haven't you fucking done that yet?" barked the instructor. The rest of the team were now assembling behind us, crouched behind the hedge so I briefed them. "We've got to get past this gap so we can maintain cover all the way to the back of the farmhouse. We'll have to cover and move...Chris will cover me as I move across, and then I can cover from the other side until we're all across safely. Okay?" No one objected to the plan, and the instructor remained quiet so it was time to go.

Chris knelt down at the end of the hedge and dropped his camouflage netting over his helmet so that he was out of sight from the building but still able to see it. He raised his MP5 to his shoulder, looked over the sights and flicked off the weapon's safety catch.

"Ready!" I shouted as I tapped him on the shoulder.

"Move!" he shouted in reply as he nodded his head. I sprang into action, running across the gap as quickly as I could before diving behind the cover of the hedge. The silence was shattered by the deafening crack of three shots fired in close succession from right behind me.

"Stop!" boomed the instructor. "What the fuck was that?" he screamed. I looked up to see who he was shouting at. It was Chris. "What the fuck are you doing?" Chris looked shocked and tried to answer "I was covering Dill..." but was cut off "That's not fucking covering, that's suppression fire! You don't EVER pull the fucking trigger when you're covering!" Chris tried to explain "That's how we cover in the army..." but that just made the instructor even angrier "You're not in the fucking army now! We didn't teach you to fucking do that, you fucking clown!" Chris had gone white, and his head dropped. I could see he wanted to explain himself, but knew there was no point. "Hand over your weapon" said the instructor. Chris made his weapon safe before lifting the sling over his head and handing it over.

My heart sank, I assumed he was getting kicked off the course and it was clear Chris thought the same. We all waited in silence whilst the instructor walked away to chat with one of the other instructors. We watched them, trying to lip read what was being said, but apart from a few head shakes and shoulder shrugs we were none the wiser. A minute or two later he came back over, handed Chris his weapon back and told us to start the manoeuvre again. I looked at Chris and raised my eyebrows, in return he shook his head indicating he had no idea what was going on.

We completed the exercise and successfully arrested the suspect at gunpoint without any further dramas (other than being told what a "shower of shit" we were, and how we "couldn't organise a fucking piss-up in a brewery" at the de-brief). Sitting in the back of the van, our trip back to Milton Keynes was subdued. We were physically and emotionally drained and none of us had any idea if Chris (or anyone else) was going to get kicked off the course that night. And that had just been a practice run! The actual open country search assessment was still a couple of weeks away.

I spoke to Chris in the bar that night. They hadn't got rid of him, but it had been made quite clear to him that it was unlikely he'd get through the course. He wanted to quit, but I tried to talk him out of making any rash decisions.

"I'm over this mate" he said. "I'm not a sixteen year old recruit anymore, I'm nearly forty. I don't need to go through this again. Guys with over-inflated egos screaming and shouting and swearing at me. They don't know anything about me or what I can do. They just want to make me feel small so they can feel like big men. I've had a lifetime of this rubbish. I just don't need it."

"Don't give up" I pleaded. "Prove them wrong. Show them what you've got. You've got so many skills and so much experience that we can all learn from." He agreed to think about it, but I could tell by the look in his eyes that he had made his mind up.

The following morning he wasn't at breakfast and we were informed by the lead instructor that Chris had removed himself from the course. I was gutted for him, but was also concerned about how much longer I would survive. I tried to supress the nagging thought in my head that said "You're next" but it wouldn't go away.

Later that day I was talking to some other members of the course about Chris and his background. Everyone knew he was ex-army, but no one knew his full story. While I was chatting away I noticed one of the firearms instructors was craning his neck to listen in to the conversation. After a couple of minutes he came over to join us. "Who are you talking about?" he asked.

"Chris" I replied.

"Chris was a Para?" he asked in disbelief. I nodded.

"And he was at Goose Green?"

"Yep"

"Fuck!" he exclaimed as the penny dropped. He jumped up from his seat and went straight to tell the other instructors. I guess Chris hadn't mentioned any of this on his application form. I presume he had glossed over his military career as he didn't like talking about it and was trying to distance himself from his past.

As I understand it, once the Firearms Training Department found this out they tried to get him to change his mind and re-join the course, but he refused. It really was a classic case of never judging a book by its cover.

As for me, I did make it through the course (if I remember correctly only six out of twelve of us did), but my head was still such a mess after the trauma of the previous couple of years that it was (probably correctly) recommended I didn't go straight onto the Group, but had an attachment to Protection Group first. I was fairly indignant about the posting as protecting members of the Royal Family and high-profile politicians was not something I was interested in, and the firearms course had made me seriously consider whether I even wanted to be an AFO. Ultimately though

I had no choice if I wanted to realise my dream and join Support Group, so a new and unexpected chapter in my career began.

The six survivors...Last day of the Basic Firearms Course

Upper Heyford, Oxfordshire. Firearms Training site

Firearms officers training at Upper Heyford

Out of the Blue

23

Who Needs Protecting?

Despite being posted to Sunninghill in Berkshire where my 'principals' (the VIPs we were assigned to protect) were the Duke and Duchess of York, one of my first jobs as a Protection Group officer was to protect a very different type of famous person from the one I would had expected. Actually, not famous so much as infamous.

Ian Huntley was probably the most hated man in Britain in 2003. He was on remand at HMP Woodhill in Milton Keynes, charged with the murders of two ten-year-old girls, Holly Wells and Jessica Chapman. The girls' disappearance in August 2002 and the subsequent search and police investigation had gripped and shocked the nation. The case was headline news for much of the summer and became known simply as the Soham Murders. After the horrific discovery of the girls' bodies in a ditch nearly two weeks after they first went missing, the investigation started to focus on Huntley and his girlfriend Maxine Carr, who had been the girls' teaching assistant at the local primary school. Both Huntley and Carr had been in the media extensively prior to the bodies being discovered, portraying themselves as spokespeople for the concerns of the community, but their behaviour drew suspicion from both the press and the police. Searches of the couple's home and car uncovered a wealth of forensic evidence that directly tied Huntley to the deaths and he was charged with their murders on the 20th August. Carr was charged with attempting to pervert the course of justice and assisting an offender. Although she had not been present when the girls disappeared (she had been on a night out with friends in Grimsby) she had provided an alibi for Huntley, claiming she was at home with him at the time.

So why were we, police firearms officers, protecting a double child murderer nearly a year after his arrest?

Huntley was called to appear in court for his initial hearing in June 2003, but due to the seriousness of the offence the plea was to be heard at the Central Criminal Court (the Old Bailey) in London, and at that time he was in prison in Milton Keynes...sixty miles away. The case still regularly dominated the news, and as Huntley had been so visible in the media with his lies and crocodile tears, he was universally despised. He was hated in such a way that is reserved for only the most sickening of criminals - paedophiles and child killers - and many death threats were made against him. We took these threats seriously, and whilst he was relatively safe in an isolation cell in prison, on a sixty mile trip down the M1 motorway and through central London he was not.

Cat. A Runs (transporting Category A prisoners) were a high-adrenaline ride. These operations would usually comprise of three or more Armed Support Vehicles (ASVs) driven by armed Class 1 advanced drivers specially trained in evasion and extraction driving techniques, with at least one armed crew-mate. The tactic was designed to prevent or minimise the risk of ambush and was used for vulnerable prisoners (like Huntley) and for those prisoners with terrorist or organised-crime links where an assisted escape attempt was likely.

The ASVs would escort the prison van (containing the high-risk prisoner) from either one prison to another, or from prison to court. The route would be pre-determined, and one ASV would be the pilot car, leading the way at extremely high speed, lights and sirens going, clearing the route for the van and its escorting ASVs. The escorts would also be travelling at high speed, just inches from the front and rear of the van so trust, concentration and clear, instant communication between all the vehicles was vital. There was little or no time for reactive braking...all changes in traffic conditions and speed had to be immediately communicated to each driver. If you were in the rear escort position (behind the van) all you could see was the back of the van and you had to have one hundred percent trust in the skills of the other drivers. Any additional vehicles assigned to the run would leapfrog ahead to close off junctions to keep us rolling forward smoothly.

The role of the passenger was hardly a passive one either. Fully armed, with your MP5 on your lap and Glock 17 on your hip, you were constantly on your radio, communicating with the other vehicles, whilst monitoring the satnav and scanning the road ahead and behind for potential hostile vehicles and any other dangers. Your window would be wide open, with your yellow gauntleted left arm continuously waving around manically, directing other motorists to slow down, speed up, move out of the way or change lane. The first fifty miles of our escort that morning were straight down the M1 and at the break-neck speeds we were travelling we got to the outskirts of the capital in less than half-an-hour.

Once we were off the motorway we headed into central London down the A1 and then via more minor roads. Our drop in speed was dramatic as we navigated our way through heavy morning traffic, and as we entered ever-more built up areas the risks, and the stress, increased accordingly.

After what felt like the quickest sixty mile London rush-hour commute in history we deposited Huntley at the Old Bailey. Other than a few angry protesters outside the front of the court, the trip had passed without incident. Now we just had to wait until he had made his first court appearance so we could repeat the whole process to get him back to the safety of his prison cell.

Once back in Milton Keynes I mentioned to my crewmate Smithy that it felt odd spending a day at work being so unproductive...I hadn't visited any victims of crime, I hadn't taken any statements, I hadn't arrested anybody, I hadn't dealt with any domestic disputes, or missing people, or sudden deaths, I hadn't pulled anyone over or issued any tickets. In fact (other than signing out my weapons) I hadn't done any paperwork at all. Smithy looked at me and smiled.

"Welcome to life on Protection Group mate! Let me ask you something..."

"Go on..."

"Did both you and your principal make it to the end of your shift alive and well?"

"Yes..."

"Then you've successfully protected your principal. Job done. There are plenty of other cops to deal with all the other crap out there, that's not your problem now...keeping the people you're protecting alive is."

During my time on Protection Group I reminded myself of his words on many occasions, when either I had the nagging guilt of not *doing* enough or if I was simply cold and bored patrolling the back lawn at Chequers in the middle of a freezing winter's night. And, to be fair, I don't think I ever missed doing the endless mounds of paperwork that response officers are faced with every single day. I may not have chosen this job, but I was starting to see its advantages.

A TVP Vauxhall Omega similar to the ASVs used in Huntley's Cat A run

24

The Three Ps

When I first joined the police we were taught about the perils of the Three Ps. Historically there were three things that were most likely to get you in trouble or cause you to lose your job, and coincidentally they all began with the letter P... Property, Prisoners and Prostitutes.

By the time I was at training school the list had officially been updated to Property, Prisoners and Paperwork, but to our instructors and tutor constables paperwork was replaced by the far greater danger of our *penises.* So, the Three Ps of Property, Prisoners and Penis were what we (as young male officers) needed to fear the most. If you could manage and control these three things well then you'd be fine. But if you couldn't (or didn't) then buckle-up sunshine because the fan's going full blast and someone's about to throw something brown and nasty at it.

Property

Probably the easiest of the three to get right, although an alarming number of officers fail to be pedantic enough with it. I guess this lack of care is out of complacency, although it's possible they somehow missed the numerous Three Ps lessons at Training School.

'Property' is basically any physical thing that a police officer comes into possession of: stolen property, drugs, prisoners' belongings, forensic evidence, cash, clothing, weapons, lost property, CCTV footage, interview recordings, etc. Whatever it is, it needs to be properly and precisely documented, given a unique reference number (usually your initials followed by a sequential number), bagged, labelled and booked into the register for the appropriate storage area (Crime Property, Found Property, Firearms etc.) where it gets locked away securely. You then need to note all this in either your pocket notebook or a statement, detailing when, where, how and why it came into your possession and where it is now.

Time consuming? Yes.

A bit of a pain in the arse? Yes.

Absolutely essential to cover your arse should said item of property get lost or stolen? YES!

So, property...follow the procedures, document everything fastidiously and never, *ever* just stick it in your pocket to deal with later, or simply throw it in the bin because "it's just a bit of weed", or "he's never going to ask for it back". Do it right and you'll be fine. Fail to do it right, particularly when it comes to money or drugs, and you're looking at a whole world of pain.

Prisoners

Now this P is much harder to manage. Property is inanimate, so if things go wrong it's through no fault of the item itself. But prisoners? Well, they've got a mind of their own and as I've previously mentioned will sometimes go to extraordinary lengths to engineer a complaint against you, particularly if they think it will help them get off whatever it is they're being charged with.

Malicious accusations and lies against you? No problem.

Self-harm and then claim assault? Why not?

Claim you've planted evidence on them? Of course!

In an ideal world all arrests would be made calmly, using little (or no) force, and with either a second officer or an independent witness present to corroborate events. Everything would be perfectly and contemporaneously documented in your pocket notebook with either CCTV or bodycam footage to support your notes. Actually, in an ideal world officers would always be 'double crewed' and would never carry out an arrest alone.

In reality, however, arrests are often violent, messy affairs with just you and the prisoner present.

Both of you are totally committed to an opposing outcome...you to making the arrest, the offender to escaping. Often both of you will get hurt. There will be no CCTV. There will be no witnesses, or worse, the only witnesses will be mates or accomplices of the offender. You'll have no time to make notes... you'll be a little too busy wrestling to worry about that! Despite all this, you will usually 'win', getting the offender under control, into handcuffs and into the back of your panda. Once back at custody you can catch up on making your notes and hope that, despite the red mist and perceptual distortion, you can recall everything clearly. This is where the complaints usually start and, particularly if the prisoner has any injuries, and mates willing to back him up, it can be very hard to negate what they claim. Just about every officer goes through this a number of times in his or her career, and it can be extremely stressful.

But, much like property, if your documentation is fastidious and written as soon as possible after the event, and the force you used during the arrest was reasonable and justified, then you'll be okay in the end. Unfortunately, a mix of complacency and the time pressures of the job means that sometimes these notes don't get made, and that can leave you very exposed to a malicious complaint.

So, Property and Prisoners done. Now onto the final P, the one that could have lost me my job and landed me slap bang on the front page of a Sunday tabloid...

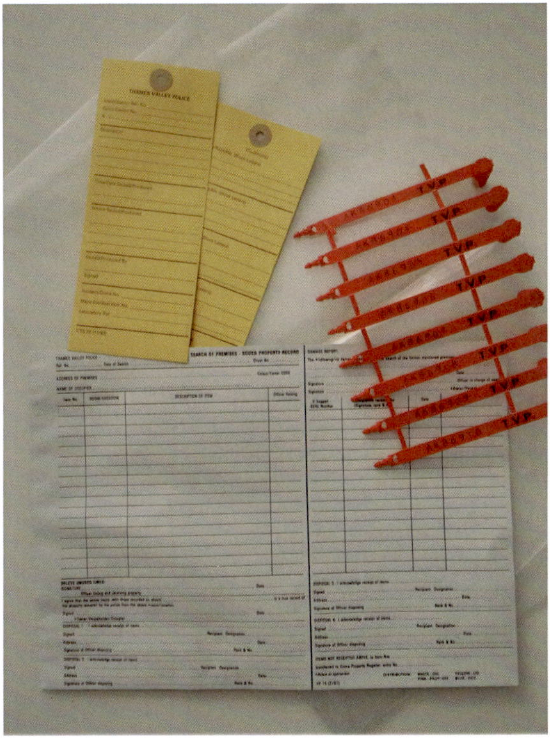

Just some of the many bags, tags, seals and forms needed to safely deal with property

25

The Third P

It started with a random phone call from a friend of a friend, Jonny, on a Sunday evening. Jonny was a successful and charismatic property developer, but he also had smaller subsidiary businesses in IT and high-end party management.

"Dillan, I need a favour mate."

"Go on..." I replied, wondering what he could possibly need from me.

"I'm organising a big secret ball near Regents Park next weekend. It's an invitation-only do for the rich and famous, a bit of a who's who of London's celebrities, and I need to keep the tabloids out. I want all the guests to be able to relax and enjoy themselves without having to worry about press taking photos."

"Okay, it sounds like a great party, but what's this got to do with me?"

"My usual security firm have just cancelled on me and I'm struggling to find a replacement..."

"Okay..."

"...and I was wondering if you and Suzie could do the door for me?"

I shut him down immediately. "Sorry mate, no. There are just too many issues here. As a copper I'm not allowed to moonlight, or do any work outside the job. And I guess you'd want us to search the guests? What happens if I find drugs? I can't just ignore that, I'd have to seize them and call the police. I'm sure you're not going to want that. It's just too much of a minefield. Sorry."

"I understand all that. Look, if I don't pay you then surely you're not technically *working*, are you? I'd only need you guys for a couple of hours, and after that you could come in and join us, and food and drinks would be on the house. It would definitely be worth your while."

"That might cover the moonlighting issue, but there's still the issue with drugs. It's just too big a deal. I'm not happy with it all. Sorry mate, but it's going to have to be a no."

"Okay. Look, all I need you to do is to keep the press out and to stop anyone bringing in cameras or any sort of recording devices. If I get you some metal detectors then you wouldn't have to actually search anyone and so you wouldn't find any drugs anyway." He really wasn't taking no for an answer and I was starting to get a bit annoyed. Suzie, my partner, had come into the living room and was listening intently to my half of the conversation... she was clearly interested.

"So, which day is it?" I asked him as I opened my work diary.

"Next Saturday. In six days' time."

I turned the page and let out a sigh of relief. "Sorry Jonny, even if I wanted to help I couldn't. I'm on an early on Sunday morning, I'll have to be at work at 6.30. Oh, and Suzie's on nights all weekend so it's just not possible."

As soon as I had hung up Suzie started to bombard me with questions. She loved a good party and couldn't believe I had turned down the opportunity to go to the event of the year for London's 'it' crowd. "I could see if I could get leave for Saturday night" she suggested, ignoring all my other concerns.

"You'd be lucky to find cover at such short notice" I said "and even if you can, I can't take Sunday off. The Queen's at chapel and I'm rostered for the briefing at the castle first thing."

"One late night won't kill you" she persisted.

"Forget it. Jonny wants us to work the doors until he closes them at about 10.30. If you want to actually go to the ball after that then it'll be a very late night...we wouldn't get home until at least 2am, and I need to be up at 5.30. It's just not going to happen. Sorry."

That was that. Or I thought it was until my phone rang on Wednesday afternoon.

"Dillan, Jonny here. Sorry to ask again but I'm desperate. I just can't find any door staff that I can trust. I've been told that the press have had a tip-off and are wanting passes so they can get photos for the gossip pages."

"So don't give them tickets. Easy." I suggested.

"I'm obviously not going to give them tickets, but now they know about it they'll either try to get in or will pay guests to smuggle in cameras and take photos for them. This is going to be a huge ball and we've got some real A-Listers coming... footballers, politicians, TV stars...I just can't risk having the press ruining the evening." He wasn't giving up "All you'd need to do is to make sure everybody has got a ticket and nobody brings in a camera, phone or recording device. The guests all know they have to be in by 10.30 and after that the doors are closed...no exceptions. Once I've locked the doors you're free to enjoy the evening. Trust me, you won't want to miss this, it's going to be *the* party of the year!"

I sighed "Okay, leave it with me. I'll speak to Suzie and get back to you tomorrow. No promises though."

Suzie could hardly contain her excitement "I'll phone the duties department to see if I can get Saturday off" she chirped.

"There's no point in me even trying. Sunday will be a struggle but at least I've got Monday off to recover." Despite my reservations, Jonny had sold it well and I was actually quite excited about the possibility of going to a secret celebrity ball.

Against all the odds Suzie got the evening off, so on Thursday afternoon I called Jonny. "We're on. We won't stay long though as I've got an early start the next day."

"Great! I guarantee you'll be free from 10.30, so hopefully you can hang around long enough to enjoy the evening. It's going to be legendary!" There was a pause, and then he threw in the hand grenade. "By the way, I haven't managed to get the metal detectors...have you got some you can bring?"

"No. Why would I have metal detectors?"

"For all your search stuff at work."

"Obviously we've got that sort of stuff at work, but I don't have my own."

"Can't you just borrow some from work then?" he asked in a way that only someone who works in private industry (and has no idea how the public services work) would ask.

"No chance, I could lose my job for that."

"Oh well, I guess you'll just have to physically search everyone then" he replied very matter-of-factly.

"No way mate. I'm not touching anyone. I've been through this with you...it just puts us in too much risk with drugs and complaints. You'll have to contact everyone who's coming and tell them not to bring their phones or cameras. If they bring them they'll have to hand them in as a condition of entry, and you're going to have to provide a safe or secure box to keep them in."

"Okay, I can do that, but it would still be much easier if you could just bring a metal detector with you..."

Now I was pissed off. Why had I agreed to this? Nothing is ever as straightforward as it seems. I was in a 'damned if you do, damned if you don't' situation. If I borrowed the metal detectors I would be in breach of Police Regulations, but if I didn't I was putting myself at real risk of finding myself in a compromising situation. Either way could have potentially serious consequences.

After a fairly sleepless night I decided to check our office storeroom the following day. We never actually used the small handheld, wand-type of detector and I wasn't even sure we still had any. After a few minutes of hunting around I managed to find three – one hanging up behind the storeroom door, and two in a box at the bottom of a shelving unit at the back of the room. I turned them on and none of them worked. I took them out of the gloomy room and into the light of the office to have a better look at them. One of them was corroded inside the battery compartment – someone had put it away without removing the old battery – so I scraped away the corrosion and popped a new battery in. To my surprise it worked. I replaced the batteries in the other two devices and they sprang into life. I started to feel a bit better about what I was doing...I was only borrowing them overnight (when no members of the search team would even be on duty) and at least I had serviced and fixed the damn things. And they clearly hadn't been used in years.

I hung one of the now-working wands back behind the door and put the other two back in their box, intending to take those two home with me after work on Saturday afternoon before returning them at 6.30 on Sunday morning. In the highly unlikely event that someone may need one on Saturday night then there was now a fully working detector hanging up where it should be.

Saturday evening finally arrived and as we pulled up outside the venue I was already impressed. It was a beautifully white-washed four-storied Georgian town house in Park Crescent with a columned entrance. It had previously been used as an embassy building and was immaculately looked after. I wondered if Jonny's company owned the building. My knock at the large glossy black wooden doors was answered by Jonny who, wearing a very expensive looking suit, welcomed us in.

"I've just got to sort out an issue at one of the bars...why don't you have a quick look around the place first and I'll meet you back here by the doors in a few minutes and I'll show you what you need to do." He scurried off and we followed him out of the small entrance hall into a cavernous double-story lobby with an amazing mahogany staircase winding its way up to the first floor. The stairs were lit by an enormous crystal chandelier hanging high above us, illuminating a full-sized gilded harp at the bottom and hundreds of red rose petals scattered over the steps. As I stopped to take in the scene a very tall and attractive woman in her late twenties, wearing only deep red, expensive-looking lace lingerie and killer heels walked up to the instrument, sat down on the chair positioned next to it and started to play it.

"Okay, Jonny was right, this isn't like any party I've ever been to. This place is amazing!" I could see a large room off to my right which appeared to be the ballroom, complete with bar and dancefloor, and behind that another room with a bar, but much smaller and more intimate. A number of bar staff were rushing around, making sure everything was perfectly prepared before the doors opened, and waiters in immaculately pressed white shirts and black trousers were starting to bring out trays of delicately delicious-looking canapes.

"Do you guys want a drink before you start?" I looked behind me to see Jonny grinning and holding a glass of champagne.

"No thanks mate, we're fine" I replied.

"Okay, the doors are opening in five minutes so let's get you in place and ready to go."

The set-up by the door was easy. The entrance hall was cosy, but big enough to house the two of us and a small table which had a box and a clipboard on it.

"Everybody has a ticket. No ticket, no entry" Jonny explained. "All the guests have been told not to bring electronic devices of any kind, but if they do then we'll hang on to them until they leave. All you need to do is check the tickets, cross the names off the list on the clipboard, ask them to hand over any phones or cameras they have and pop them in the box. Give them a quick check with the metal detector and if they're clear let them in."

"Okay, that sounds simple enough" I said "but aren't we giving them some sort of receipt or token for their phones?"

"No. They've been told not to bring them. They know what's going to happen if they bring them anyway. Don't worry about it."

I wasn't happy. What if a phone got lost, or someone took home someone else's by mistake? I didn't want any accusations coming my way...this was a property nightmare and my Three Ps alarm bell was ringing loudly. Jonny could see I wasn't impressed. "Don't worry mate, it's my job to look after the box and to hand back everything to the guests when they leave. It sounds like you'll be long gone by then. It's my responsibility, not yours, so don't stress about it." His words helped but I still had major reservations and looking at Suzie I could tell she felt the same. Before I could argue further there was a knock at the door and the first guests entered the building.

I was keen to see who the famous people coming were, so I quickly scanned the names on the clipboard. To my surprise it was a list of first names only, and all in couples... 'Mike and Sophie' or 'Christian and Helena'. I re-read the names in the hope of seeing 'Posh and Becks', 'Hugh and Liz', or any of the other current 'it' couples, but there was nothing to give me any clue as to who was coming. I would just have to wait and see who came through the doors.

A steady stream of beautiful and elegantly dressed couples arrived over the course of the following two hours. I vaguely recognised some of them, but to my disappointment none were the A-Listers I had been expecting. The system we had going worked well. In stark contrast to the behaviour of my usual professional clients, all the guests here were friendly, relaxed and happy to cooperate with us. Almost all of them had left their phones at home and no one had brought a camera. The metal detectors worked a treat...Suzie checked the women and I checked the men but, much to my relief, neither of us had to actually touch anyone.

Before I knew it Jonny came in and locked the doors. "It's 10.30. That's you all done – come in and join the party!"

"But there are still about a dozen couples that haven't arrived yet" I said as I passed him the clipboard. He didn't seem surprised and looked like he was about to say something but thought better of it. He simply said "Oh well, the doors are closed now. Go and enjoy yourselves...all the food and drink is on the house!"

We entered the main ballroom and went straight to the bar. As the designated driver with an early start I just got a soft drink while Suzie got herself a glass of bubbles. As we looked around we were surprised to see the place was much emptier than expected. A couple of hundred people had come through the doors but less than a quarter of that number were in the ballroom. Some were dancing, some were in small groups chatting and it was hard not to notice that some of the guys' shirts were either untucked or hanging open, and many of the girls were stripped down to their underwear.

Suzie caught my eye "Glad we came?" she asked with a grin. I smiled back "Let's go and wander around and see where everyone else is" I suggested. "Lots of people are going upstairs, there must be more bars up there." As we reached the first floor we saw a couple of guys in suits standing in front of a closed door across the landing. The smaller one of the two smiled broadly and held out his hand "I just wanted to thank you for doing a great job on the door, that really makes our life a lot easier" he said in a strong Manchester accent.

I was confused "Sorry, who are you?" I asked, wondering how this guy knew who I was.

"We're the security team for this event. It's great having professionals like yourselves helping out."

I ignored his reference to my job, and told him that I thought Jonny couldn't get any security and that's why we were there.

"Oh, we were brought in at the last minute" he answered rather unconvincingly before turning his attention to Suzie. The other guy, a softly spoken man with closely cropped hair approached me. "Do you do this often?" he asked me, grinning. I assumed he was asking about door-work so replied "No, this is a one-off. It's just a favour to Johnny."

"Jonny?" He didn't seem to know who I was talking about. "Oh, the property guy?" He quickly returned the conversation to me. "Well, you're really good at this, very professional. You should do more of it, we could use someone like you."

"No thanks. As I said, this is just a one-off as a favour."

"So" he pressed "Where do you work? Are you in the Met?" I was feeling very uncomfortable with these guys, they seemed to know a lot about us but I didn't know anything about them.

"No, not the Met." I replied flatly.

"So where do you work?" he persisted in his soft manner.

"Not round here" I replied as vaguely as I could.

"Where's that then?" he smiled.

"Not here" I said, trying to shut the conversation down. I looked over to Suzie, who was on her third glass of champagne and appeared to be chatting freely to the first guy. I hoped she wasn't talking too openly and giving away any personal details.

"So what exactly do you do in the Police? I can see you're very good at dealing with people" he asked me, clearly hoping a bit of flattery would get me talking.

"Firearms stuff" I replied, hoping my answer was both vague enough to give nothing away, but specific enough to shut him up.

"Ah, that explains your professionalism. So where do you do that?"

"Not round here." I had had enough of the conversation so I took Suzie by the arm and said "Let's have a look around up here" and I pushed the door open. "Enjoy yourselves" the first guy said with an oddly huge grin on his face.

The room was dark and it took a few seconds for my eyes to adjust to the low light, but even the darkness couldn't disguise what was going on. There must have been close to fifty naked or semi-dressed people either standing around in small groups chatting or lying on what appeared to be an enormous bed in the centre of the room.

"Wow" I said to Suzie "Well, this is obviously where everybody is! No wonder Jonny didn't want any cameras!"

We were just about to leave the room when a very attractive couple, dressed only in their underwear, approached us. "We hoped you'd be joining the party once you'd finished at the door" the guy said. His partner looked me straight in the eye, tilted her head to one side and smiled.

"We're just having a quick look around before we leave. We're not staying long" I countered. I hadn't been expecting the evening to turn out like this and I was far from being in my comfort zone. All my anxieties about agreeing to help Jonny and around borrowing the metal detectors were flooding back. The direct questions from the guys outside the room had made me uncomfortable and now we were being approached by this beautiful couple in a room full of naked people. My brain was struggling to process it all and I was starting to freak out. "So, are you two lovely people interested in playing?" the girl asked. "Sorry, no. We need to go soon." I blurted out as I took hold of Suzie's hand and left the room.

It was only about 11pm and I was hoping to leave there and then. If I was lucky I might actually get five hours sleep...a couple of hours more than I was expecting, and I was getting desperate to get away from the party. Suzie was less keen to go though "Let's just get one last drink" she suggested. "We might as well make the most of being here!" I reluctantly agreed and we went back downstairs to the ballroom and she got herself another glass of Möet and then asked me to dance with her. I started to relax a little. Quite a few couples were on the dancefloor and the atmosphere was buzzing, almost electric, in a way that I had never experienced at a party before. After a few minutes she said "Why don't we go back upstairs? It could be fun!" My spider-sense was tingling, telling me to go home, but temptation got the better of me and I silently followed as she took my hand and lead me back up the rose petal covered staircase to the bedroom. We quietly found an empty corner of the giant bed and, without even looking at anybody else, quickly undressed each other, had sex, dressed ourselves and went back downstairs. Jonny caught us as we were about to walk out the front door. "Thank you guys so much, I really appreciate all your help! I hope you guys got to enjoy yourselves!" he said with a devilish glint in his eye.

"Well, it's been a night I won't be able to forget for a while!" I replied, totally unaware of how true my words would become.

The following morning, a little tired and grumpy, I got to work early, returned the wands to the storeroom and checked my weapons out from the armoury, all ready for my day at work. That should have been the end of the story, but unfortunately it wasn't. A brief phone call six days later turned my world upside down and told me just how far from over that story actually was.

I had just got home from an uneventful Saturday early-turn when my phone rang. "Hello" I answered. I was met with a vaguely familiar softly spoken voice that I couldn't quite place. "Hello, this is Dan." He told me he was calling from a national Sunday tabloid newspaper. "This is a courtesy call to give you the opportunity to comment on the fact that you were moonlighting at a sex party last weekend." I felt the blood drain from my upper body as the shock of what he had said sunk in. I went cold and scrambled to process my thoughts before I answered him.

"Sorry, I wasn't moonlighting, I was just doing a favour for a friend and I had no idea what sort of a party it was."

"Well, you're a police officer, you were working the door at a sex party and you engaged in sexual activity at the party. This is your opportunity to have your say."

I realised why I recognised the voice, I was talking to the security guy with the cropped hair. "You're the bouncer from upstairs, aren't you?" I asked. He didn't reply, but just said "Do you want to comment before we publish?"

Publish? He's not just digging for a story, he's about to print one! My head started spinning and I was struggling to control my panic.

"I don't know what to say. I wasn't working...I wasn't paid. I didn't know it was that sort of a party, and the only sexual activity I had was with my long-term partner. Are you really going to publish? You're going to destroy my career, my whole life... just because I had sex with my girlfriend?"

"We haven't decided yet. This is your chance to comment."

"I've told you what happened. Are you going to publish this? When's it going to be in the paper? Why do you want to destroy me like this?"

"I'll get back to you later" he lied as he hung up on me.

I called Suzie immediately. It was her weekend off and she was out shopping. "You need to get home as soon as you can...we've got a major problem!" I said as calmly as I could manage, trying to mask the total panic that was engulfing me.

After an agonising half-hour or so pacing the house I finally heard Suzie's little MG pull up onto the driveway, quickly followed by the rushed slamming of the driver's door. I was already waiting by the front door to let her in, by now engulfed by nausea and an enormous stress-induced migraine. It was a miracle I hadn't actually been sick. At least the delay in her arrival home had given me some time to fully process what was happening, and what we needed to do next.

As I told her about the phone call I could see the shock, panic and fear appear in her eyes. She struggled to hold back tears as she said "Maybe they won't publish it. Maybe they're just digging. Why don't we just wait and see what happens?" I think she was trying to calm herself, reassure herself that everything was okay. But it wasn't. I shook my head. "We can't wait. This is too serious. What happens if they print tomorrow? I've got to phone work and warn them." Suzie looked like she was going to collapse on the floor and I thought I was going to throw up as I picked up my work phone and called the Superintendent in charge of our department.

"Hello Sir, its Dillan here" I said as cheerily as I could muster. "Are you sitting down? I'm afraid I'm about to ruin your Saturday evening." I proceeded to tell him everything that had happened and that there was a distinct possibility that we were going to be in the Sunday tabloids the next morning.

He listened quietly, punctuating his silence with the odd "Okay", "Right" or "uh-huh" as he waited for me to finish.

"Right, is that it? Is there anything you haven't told me?" he asked. I could hear the exasperation in his voice.

"I borrowed a couple of metal detectors from our store cupboard."

I heard him sigh. "Where are they now?"

"I put them straight back the next morning. I only took them overnight."

"Okay. Anything else?"

I took a deep breath. "We had sex."

He replied with an even louder sigh, almost a groan. "Just you and Suzie?"

"Yes."

"Not with anybody else?"

"No, just us."

"Well, I'm going to have to call the Chief Constable to let him know. Apart from the metal detectors which could be a problem, this seems to be a private matter, not a police one. You two have gone to a party whilst off-duty and had sex. My view is that what my officers do in their spare time is none of my business...as long as it's not illegal. I can't guarantee the Chief will agree, but I suspect so." There was a pause whilst I exhaled with some limited relief. At least we were being supported by our boss. “Have you got somewhere to go?”

“No, why?”

“Because the press will turn up at your house tomorrow morning if it’s printed.” My brief relief vanished as panic quickly returned. “If you’re going to stay at home then draw your curtains, bring your rubbish inside, lock the doors, and don’t answer your door to anyone. Oh, and don’t use your mobile phones and disable your voicemail. Be very careful who you speak to and what you say. It’s safe to assume that you’re already being watched and listened to.”

I came off the phone completely freaked out. The press were following me, watching my house, listening to my phone calls and going through my rubbish? As a police officer I had no power to do any of this to a known criminal, but it was okay for the gutter press to do this to me? Seriously? I was angry and I was panicked.

My next call was on the landline to Jonny.

“What the fuck’s going on?” I asked him. I was stressed, angry and scared, and he was getting the brunt of it. What had he known? Why did he so desperately want us there? How had the press got in? Why had so many of the guests failed to turn up? Where had the press got our names and phone numbers from? What other personal information did they have about us? Had we been set-up?

"Shit, sorry mate. I had hoped you guys would have been left out of all of this."

"All what?" I barked.

"Well it turns out the whole thing was a set-up from the start. I was co-hosting the event with Emily, a girl I've worked with a couple of times before. She's a party organiser, but she also runs swingers parties on the side. It turns out she's got some massive money problems and set this whole thing up so she could sell a juicy story to the tabloids. She used her society contacts to invite a whole load of celebs and people in the public eye, and then sold exclusive access to the party to one of the Sunday papers. It was supposed to be a huge scoop...politicians, footballers, government advisors all involved in one big sex scandal."

He paused for breath. "The word got out a couple of weeks ago that the press were sniffing around. That's why I called you...I needed someone on the outside who I knew I could trust to keep them out. I had absolutely no idea that they already had a way in and had rigged the place with cameras and recording equipment. Anyway, once the word got out the more famous and influential guests stayed away. I don't know why the press are after you, but I guess stitching up a couple of cops is just a consolation prize after they lost the big scoop."

"You should have told me, we would never have agreed."

"I know. I'm sorry. It just never occurred to me that the press would be interested in you, and I really thought you'd be able to keep them out."

"You know we could lose our jobs. This is serious."

"I'm sorry mate, I really am. We've been filing injunctions all week...there were some very prominent government and parliamentary figures there who have been scrambling to keep their names out of the papers. I feel like I've spent all week in court...it's been crazy! Unfortunately for you, I guess you guys were just an easy target at the bottom of the pile."

"So what are you doing about Emily?"

"She's vanished" he said. "I had been letting her stay in my flat for the last month or so as I knew she was going through a difficult time financially. On Monday my flat was burgled and all my computers, hard drives, phones, diaries and address books were stolen. She disappeared the same day and isn't replying to any of my messages. My guess is she faked the break-in so she could give all my devices and contact lists to the press. I assume that's where they got your name and phone number from. I feel awful mate. I'm so sorry I got you involved in all of this."

I came off the phone feeling slightly less angry. Jonny should have warned us, but to be fair he had no way of knowing what was actually going on, much less what was going to happen. He was suffering too. He'd been betrayed by someone he trusted, he'd been burgled and lost much of his digital data (at a potential cost to his business) and it looked like he was going to be publicly shamed in the media too. But he *should* have warned us and I was in no mood to forgive him just yet.

I had only just hung up and was still processing everything Jonny had just told me when the phone rang. It was my superintendent.

"Right Dillan, I've spoken to the Chief. Our official stance on this is: 'What our officers do in their own time, as long as it's legal, is their own business.' If the press ask us to comment we won't. I'm afraid that you're going to have to take some time off though, and if this gets published tomorrow then I will have to refer it to C and D for investigation."

My heart sank. C & D was our internal complaints and discipline department, now known as 'Professional Standards'. If they were to become involved then serious disciplinary action, including losing our jobs, became a very real possibility. And a suspension from duty was humiliating. I prided myself on my professionalism and the thought of such a stain on my personal file was painful. To fight the nauseous anxiety in my gut I tried to focus on the positive. At least the Chief Constable wasn't particularly interested and so far the job appeared to be supporting us.

"I'll call you in the morning once we know what the damage is" he continued. "Try to get some sleep."

I didn't, of course, get any sleep. Even for someone used to working through the early hours it was an excruciatingly long and tortuous night. I tossed and turned, the knot in my stomach growing as the minutes ticked agonisingly slowly by. Finally, just as I became aware of the first glow of dawn seeping around the edges my firmly-drawn curtains the phone rang. I sat up with a jolt, my heart racing as I answered it.

"Have you seen the papers yet?"

"No sir, you told us not to go out of the house."

"Some of it's online, so you can read it there, but the worst of it is in print. I'm sorry, but it's not good. You two aren't just *in* the story, you *are* the story. Make sure you look after Suzie, she's going to need your support...it focusses mainly on her and some of the quotes that it claims from her are quite worrying. There are also photos of you both that appear to have been taken outside your house, so that confirms my fears that you're being watched and possibly followed." I was starting to freak out again. The press were blatantly invading our privacy and actively trying to destroy our lives.

Why? Because we had gone to a party and had stupidly had sex with each other whilst we were there? This was insane.

"I'm afraid we're going to have to ask you both to hand in your firearms tickets and take two weeks leave until this blows over. Our position hasn't changed, but the Met are now involved and the head of Royalty Protection there wants you gone. He can't tell us what to do, but he does have a lot of influence and is already putting us under pressure to get rid of you. Try not to worry too much, but I thought I'd better warn you."

"Thank sir, I really appreciate all your support."

Shit. We're front page news in a sex scandal, we've had our firearms authorisation revoked, we've been suspended from duty, we're under internal investigation, we're being watched and listened to by the press, and now the Met want us sacked. The shame, the embarrassment, the regret, the self-loathing, the anger and the fear were overwhelming and I wanted to be sick. My head was spinning as the phone rang again.

"Is that Dillan?"

"Yes" I replied nervously. I didn't recognise the number so assumed it could be the press.

"It's Chris here, the Duke's PPO." Relief as I recognised the voice belonged to one of the Duke of York's Personal Protection Officers.

"Hi Sarge" I said, wondering where this conversation was going to go…Chris was a Met, not a Thames Valley, officer.

"Look mate, I'm just phoning you on behalf of the Duke. He's worried about you and Suzie and knows you're only being attacked because of your relationship to him. He thinks the press are just using you to have another pop at him, and knows that much of what gets printed isn't actually true. Anyway, the bottom line is he's pretty angry right now and he wants you to know that you have his full support and he'll do whatever he can to make sure you don't lose your jobs."

Well, I wasn't expecting that. The one positive thing I could try to hang on to was the fact that those who were attacking us didn't personally know us, and those who did were offering us support. That was, at least, some source of comfort.

So, the press published their story. The basis of it was true: there was a high society swinger's party; we were there; some pretty influential people were there; we worked on the door for a few hours; and we had sex. The rest of the four-page spread was a salacious and sensationalised mix of misquotes, false assumptions, half-truths, incorrect personal information, photographs and lies. It was designed to be as scandalous as possible, and in that respect it didn't disappoint.

I felt violated. My privacy had been invaded. We had been followed, filmed, recorded and photographed without our knowledge or consent. Our home no longer felt safe and secure. Personally we had been very publicly humiliated and professionally our reputations were in tatters.

Ultimately though the press moved on and we became the clichéd fish and chips wrappers, yesterday's news. The sickening anxiety of waking up every Sunday morning faded over the following weeks as no follow-up stories were published.

The internal police investigation was mercifully quick. The investigating team went to Fleet Street to speak to the journalists and to view their material. Suzie and I separately attended Langley Police Station to be interviewed on tape by experienced detectives. To be sitting on the wrong side of the table and having to answer, not ask, the questions was a shameful and humiliating experience, and one I never expected to find myself in. The investigation concluded that the whole thing was largely akin to the proverbial storm in a teacup, but issues around the metal detectors and moonlighting needed to be addressed. After a few weeks our suspension was lifted and we returned to work, re-instated as firearms officers and back on our teams. I understandably, and rightly, received a formal written warning for misuse of police equipment and for not declaring a secondary employment.

In typical police style, the day I returned to work I was met by a swing hanging where my desk should have been. As I remember it was suitably decorated with our names and several hearts and bows. I've never quite been allowed to forget about it, but over the years the comments from my close colleagues have been the perfect balance of brutality and hilarity...police humour at its best.

It was the only time I faced disciplinary action during my career and, being an officer used to receiving praise and commendations, I took it quite hard. It added another straw to the already sizable but invisible load my camel was carrying on its back, and further removed a little more of what was left of the love and optimism I felt for the job. I had taken another step forward along the long road to leaving the police.

The worst part was the shame and the feeling that I had let both myself and my family down. For the only time since their passing I was relieved that Mum and Dad were dead...at least they wouldn't have to deal with the humiliation and, although it's cowardly, I wouldn't have to face them. It's taken me many years to come to terms with this.

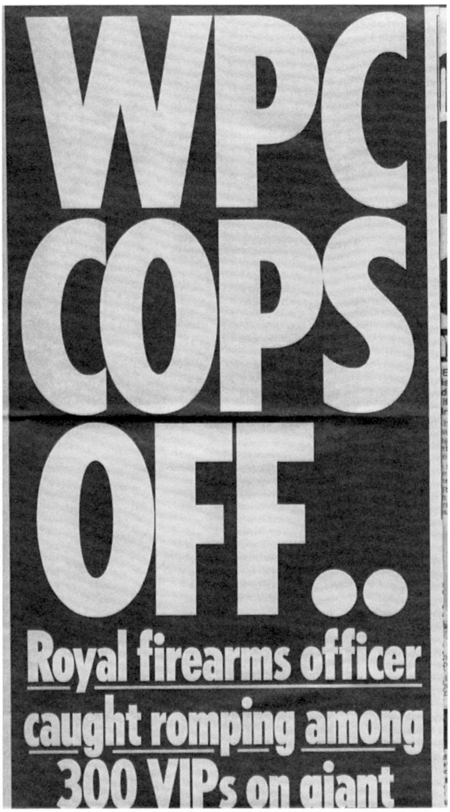
WPC COPS OFF..

Royal firearms officer caught romping among 300 VIPs on giant

One of several headlines in the Sunday paper that focussed (in typical misogynistic fashion) on the female officer, not the male one

Out of the Blue

26

Princes and Prime Ministers

I hadn't intended to write about my time protecting members of the Royal Family (or other dignitaries), but the recent death of Her Majesty the Queen brought back a flood of memories to me.

Right from the start of my career I found myself regularly performing Royal duties of some sort...being based in Windsor it was just a regular part of everyday policing. Most early shifts required attending the Changing of the Guard, either to stop the traffic or to escort the soldiers through town from Victoria Barracks to the castle and back again.

We also had duties at Royal Ascot, the Royal Windsor Horse Show, and official state visits of foreign heads of state to meet with the Queen. As such, seeing senior Royals was a fairly regular occurrence.

Later, during my time as a mounted officer, my interactions were closer still. During Royal Ascot week we would billet and stable our horses in the Queen's Yard at the Castle Mews, opposite the Queen's personal stables. Back then she still rode most days so we would occasionally see her riding through the yard on her way to the Great Park. On those days we would call out a cheery "Good morning, Your Majesty!" or, if it seemed more appropriate, we would greet her with a more subdued and less formal "Morning, Ma'am" accompanied by a respectful nod of the head. Our greetings would be met with either a smile or a simple "Good morning" by way of reply.

One of the highlights of my Royal duties whilst on the mounted section was, as I've talked about earlier, escorting the wedding procession of Prince Edward and Sophie through the crowded streets of Windsor. Riding alongside the castle with the Household Cavalry and the Royal Horse Artillery in full dress uniform whilst following a gilded carriage was something quite special and an experience I'll never forget.

However, for me the greatest privilege was at the Royal Windsor Horse Show when the 'Musical Ride' Troop of the Royal Canadian Mounted Police came to put on a display ride. Like us, they stabled at the castle and so we spent quite a bit of time getting to know them, chatting and trading bits of kit (I managed to score a pair of their brown lace-up riding boots for a traditional bobby's helmet).

It was my job to escort them from the Queen's Yard, through the grounds of Windsor Castle, past the East Terrace Lawn and around and down to the showgrounds at Home Park. It was dusk on a gorgeous summer evening, the sun was low in the sky behind us getting ready to set beyond the castle walls, and I was riding with a troop of Canadian Mounties, complete in their iconic red tunics and Stetsons. As we slowed to make a sharp right-hand turn under a turret I noticed a small figure half-a-dozen meters away standing watching us. She smiled and waved and as I nodded in reply I was slightly surprised to see that the Queen looked not just happy but truly overjoyed to see the troop.

Many years later I found out that Her Majesty's favourite horse was a mare called Burmese. Burmese was an RCMP horse who had been trained by the Musical Ride in Ottawa and was gifted to the Queen by them when they came to perform at the Royal Windsor Horse Show in 1969. She went on to ride Burmese at the Trooping of the Colour every year from 1969 to 1986, and when asked if she had ever had a favourite horse, the Queen answered "Burmese" without hesitation. I guess seeing the RCMP's Musical Ride was always a special experience for her.

Less than a month later I was lucky enough to have a second equally brief but equally magical moment. Again it was in Windsor, but this time I was about a mile away on the Long Walk, and I was riding George, not Dexter.

George was my favourite horse on the yard. He was a stocky chestnut Welsh Cobb with a cropped mane and white flash on his nose. He had a lovely temperament, would always do what you asked and had a very endearing habit of resting his head on your shoulder.

It was Ladies Day at Royal Ascot and I had just completed a search and secure patrol along part of the route the Queen would take from Windsor to the races. I had ridden the length of the Long Walk, from the castle gates to the Copper Horse at the top, and had taken up my point by Warden's Gate, about mid-way between the two. It was a stunning summer's day, and unusually hot for June in England. There was barely a cloud in the sky and I was desperate to get out of the sun, but I didn't have time to worry about that as I only had a few minutes to get into full dress uniform before the Queen came through, ready to throw up a salute as she passed.

I looked down to check my riding boots and I was pleased and relieved to see my reflection looking back at me from the glassy-black mirrors of the bulled toe-caps. Despite the morning's ride the polish hadn't cracked or scuffed. I picked a few horse hairs off the thighs of my jodhpurs and then slowly undid the leather straps that were securing my carefully rolled-up tunic to the front of my saddle. There was no way I could have worn such a heavy navy woollen jacket all morning in that heat so I had chosen to carry it the best way I could. I had carefully pressed it the night before, making sure it had perfect razor-sharp creases running the length of each sleeve, and had meticulously removed every last speck of dirt and hair from it. As I unrolled it I quickly checked it for any hairs or spit that George may have deposited on it. It was amazingly clean...I just had to shake it out and pick off a couple of hairs before sliding it over each arm and fastening the shiny silver and crested buttons

I looked down to check George hadn't drooled all over his bridle (he had to look his best for Her Majesty too!) and I gave him a quick pat before putting on my white gloves just as I saw the Queen's convoy leaving the castle. As I sat waiting, I noticed that a herd of around forty Red Deer had approached us and were standing on the opposite side of the Long Walk, several of them staring intently at us. A few of them appeared to be startled by a familiar roar from above us and I looked up to see Concord, flying low but slowly ascending into the clear, still, summer air. It left a perfectly straight and white vapour trail in its wake, splitting the otherwise clear blue sky into two. I watched it disappear out of sight just as the Queen approached the Warden's Gate. I saluted and the deer scattered as the vehicles sped by. Hours of preparation for a few fleeting seconds.

But what a few seconds. I was sitting on my favourite horse on a beautiful sunny day, in full dress police uniform, looking down the Long Walk past a herd of deer towards Windsor Castle as the Queen approached and Concord was flying overhead. Could you get a more quintessentially British experience than that? It occurred to me that if you could 'bottle' such an experience it would be almost priceless. And I was getting paid to be there! It certainly beat the usual abuse of attending a drunken Friday night domestic dispute.

A few years later I found myself back on Royal duties again, but this time on a more full time basis as a firearms officer on Protection Group. Along with protecting several Prime Ministers at Chequers and at their home addresses, I primarily guarded members of the Royal Family. Initially it was the Duke and Duchess of York at Sunninghill Park, then briefly Prince Harry at Eton College before returning to the Duke of York at the Royal Lodge in Windsor.

Many of my stories from these times are not for print, but one amusing event stands out, and I don't think anyone involved will mind me sharing it.

On a very dark, cold, wet, windy and generally miserable winter's evening I was at the gatehouse at the Royal Lodge. I was settling in for a quiet, uneventful Friday evening as the principals

(Prince Andrew and the princesses) were away until Sunday afternoon.

"Do you want a brew Steve?" I asked my crew-mate as I went into the kitchenette to put the kettle on.

"Please matey" he replied, briefly looking up from a report he was writing on the computer.

"After that we could do an armoury check" I suggested. As one of the site armourers it was my job to regularly check the armoury's inventory, to physically check the weapons and ammunition, and to strip and clean the guns.

"Sure" he mumbled, just as a familiar alarm sounded. "There's someone at the gate" he said, slightly surprised.

"I'll go." I grabbed my coat and pulled it on as I opened the door, and braced myself as I walked out into the freezing rain. I could see there was a silver Mercedes SLK waiting on the other side of the gates, its engine was running and headlights were glaring. The lights cut through the darkness highlighting every single raindrop that was falling heavily and almost horizontally in front of them. I pulled my hood up and yanked my zip up to my chin as I approached the car, a futile attempt to keep myself dry and warm. As I bent down by the side of the vehicle the driver's window partially opened, allowing me to see there was only one occupant, an attractive female in her late thirties.

"I'm here to see the Duke" she said impatiently, before rudely adding "and I'm already late", implying this was somehow my problem. She had already failed the attitude test, but I smiled regardless and as politely as I could I said "You must have made a mistake, the Duke isn't here."

"I'm here to see the Duke. Let me in, I'm late" she replied, apparently having failed to either hear or believe what I had just said.

"I can't let you in. Nobody has told me you're coming and the Duke isn't here." I inwardly sighed as she shot daggers at me from her perfectly made-up eyes. "If you wait here I'll go and call down to the house and see if you're expected" although I already knew she wasn't.

"Well, can you hurry up, I'm late" she said to my back as I turned to go back into the gatehouse.

"Steve," I said as I shook my arms to disperse some of the water that had pooled in the creases of my sleeves "can you call the house mate? This woman thinks she's seeing the Duke tonight."

"But..." he started. I cut him off.

"I know, I know. But just check for me, would you?"

Steve called the house. The staff knew nothing about her and weren't about to take in an unexpected guest. Like us, they were looking forward to a quiet evening without the boss.

The weather was rapidly deteriorating and reluctantly I went back outside into the now driving rain which stung my almost numb face and hands. I again bent down beside the car, but she didn't open the firmly closed window, and made no attempt to acknowledge my presence. She was talking rather excitedly to someone on her mobile phone and continued to ignore me. I could feel the rain trickling down the front of my neck and my trousers were soaked. I had had enough of her rudeness. I straightened myself up and had just started to walk back to the warmth of the gatehouse when she opened the window a fraction. I turned around.

"We've spoken to the house..." I started to explain, but she interrupted me with an abrupt "Here" as she slid her phone out of the tiny gap. I held it up to the side of my face, under my sodden hood, and said "PC Bourdillon here" not knowing who I was speaking to.

"PC Bourdillon, what are you bloody playing at?" The crisp, curt and angry voice of the Duke barked in my ear.

"Stop fucking about and open the bloody gates."

"But..." I started to lamely protest, but I was cut down.

"Just bloody do it" he snapped and then hung up. I handed the phone back to the woman, and without a further word I went back inside and pressed the gate release button. Steve looked at me, raising his eyebrows in a "what are you doing" sort of a way. "Don't ask mate" I said as I shook my head and hung my soaking wet coat on the back of the door. My attention was briefly taken by three pools of water that were rapidly forming on the floor, one under each arm and one larger one under the main body of the waterproof jacket. The repetitive drip and splash as the droplets landed in the puddles was strangely calming.

I glanced up at the camera monitors and saw that the Mercedes which had sped through the open gates was rapidly slowing down. A faint glow illuminated the inside of the car, suggesting she was using her mobile phone. The vehicle came to a standstill about fifty meters down the driveway and didn't move for about a minute or so.

The penny dropped. I looked at Steve, grinning. "She's gone to the wrong place. She's supposed to be at the Palace, isn't she?" We watched as she very, very slowly did a three-point turn and crawled back towards us. I could have opened the gate in time for her to just roll through, but I was really pissed off with how I'd been treated so I waited until she had actually stopped before I pressed the button. As I stood in the doorway she sat there, staring dead ahead not wanting to look at me – and definitely not wanting to apologise or explain.

The gates finally opened, she disappeared off into the miserable winter's darkness, and I returned to the warmth to find a cup of tea waiting for me.

"Have a cuppa mate, that'll cheer you up" Steve said cheerily.

"Cheers. What a stupid cow." I was wet, cold and irritated. After fifteen years in the job I was very used to people like her talking down to me, but getting a bollocking from the Duke was another matter, particularly when I hadn't done anything wrong.

The phone rang.

"Gatehouse, PC Bourdillon" I wearily answered.

"Ahhh, PC Bourdillon, just the man. It appears I need to offer you an apology. I've behaved somewhat like a complete cock." The Duke sounded jovial and sincere. "The stupid cow thought the Lodge was the Palace. God knows why she went to the wrong bloody place, but there we go."

"No problem, Sir" I replied "and thank you for taking the time to call me."

"Well, I couldn't leave it like that now, could I? Goodnight." He hung up.

Now, I know that the Duke isn't a particularly popular member of the Royal Family, and that most people have a fairly strong opinion about him. I have no idea whether he is guilty or not of the accusations against him. I can only comment on how I found him, and I found him to be a personable but hot-headed man. He would occasionally stop for a chat and could be very good company, but he could also at times be extremely rude, particularly if he felt something wasn't being done to his expectations.

For him to phone to apologise, though, showed me another side to him. That act, together with the support he offered when I was on the front page of a Sunday tabloid, is something I deeply respect him for. He didn't need to make either of those phone calls, and many others in his situation wouldn't have done so, but he did. That to me says a lot about the man.

As I mentioned before, I also had to perform armed protection duties for three former Prime Ministers, Tony Blair, Gordon Brown and David Cameron. I had very little to do with Brown, but had many interactions with Blair and Cameron. Our involvement with them at Chequers was limited, but at their homes our close proximity meant we got to know the pair of them much better.

I'm not going to make any character assassinations or political comments, but the difference between the two couldn't have been greater.

Blair was always friendly and personable. He would always smile and greet you, and occasionally would make time to chat, find out a little bit about you, and enquire after your family.

At Christmas and Easter he would send gifts (such as chocolate or wine) down to the officers who were working that day, and the kitchen staff (presumably at his request) would also send down servings of the Christmas dinner and slices of cake. The Duke and Duchess of York would do the same, in fact they would send out personal Christmas cards and small gifts to all the officers who protected them.

Cameron, on the other hand, appeared to despise us and made no attempt to hide his feelings. He never looked us in the eye, never smiled, turned his back on us at every opportunity and never thanked us for anything.

I spent one unusually cold Christmas Eve at his home in Oxfordshire. It had snowed heavily in the days leading up to his arrival, and when we got there to open up and prepare for the Prime Minister we found the driveway was under about a foot of snow and ice. There was nothing for it other than to spend an hour breaking our backs shovelling away the snow and salting the drive. Dressed for a long cold night in thermals, fleeces and our firearms suits, we were in a horrible sweaty, boil-in-the-bag mess by the time we finished. The snow had made our gloves sodden and useless and we could hardly feel our fingers. Once we stopped shovelling we quickly cooled and the waterproof coveralls trapped the moisture from our sweaty underclothes, making us feel the cold even more acutely. It was miserable.

When Cameron arrived he appeared not to notice the work done and, true to form, totally ignored us as he alighted his car and went into the house. His wife Samantha, however, looked at the piles of snow to the side of the driveway and nodded and smiled sweetly to us. She appeared to be slightly embarrassed by her husband's rudeness.

Later that night two of us were standing in the freezing cold just outside the back door. The lights came on as the Prime Minister and his father-in-law, Sir Reginald Sheffield, entered the kitchen. They chatted away for a couple of minutes before Sir Reginald suggested "Why don't you go out and wish the lads a Merry Christmas before we head up?"

"Well, if you want to, you can bloody do it" came the terse reply, apparently annoyed that his father-in-law had even suggested such a thing.

Cameron left the room and then the door opened and Sir Reginald stepped out into the cold dark night. "Mr Cameron just wanted to wish you all a Merry Christmas and to thank you for all your hard work."

"Thank you sir, and Merry Christmas to you all too."

He went back inside, shut the door and turned out the lights. We shook our heads in disbelief.

"What a wanker." We certainly weren't expecting presents, slices of Christmas cake, or even a simple mince pie, but some basic good manners would have been nice. Even that seemed to be beyond him. To quote William Horman, ironically a former headmaster from Cameron's old school Eton, "Manners maketh man". Unfortunately I'm guessing our former PM must have missed that particular lesson...

On duty at the Royal Lodge

Changing of the Guard in Windsor as a young PC

Waiting for the Queen on the Long Walk, Ladies Day, Royal Ascot week

Escorting the RCMP Musical Ride through Windsor Castle (on Dexter)

27

Family Matters

Despite all the glamour, excitement, violence and trauma, sometimes it's the most every-day or innocuous moments that are the most memorable.

Later in my career as a Protection Group officer I qualified as a Police Search Advisor (or PolSA). Following selection for the role, prospective PolSAs attended a three-week residential course at the Bramshill Police Staff College in Hampshire. This was an intensive pass-or-fail course, and was unique in that it was run jointly by the Army and the Police. As such it was a very old-school style of course, and much like the Firearms and the Advanced Driving Courses I had been on, you could fail at any stage. The work-load was high and it required working late into the night to research and prepare for the following day's exercises and assessments. It was both mentally and physically demanding.

Once qualified, the role involved the planning and preparation of counter-terrorist, major crime and missing person searches, and advising senior officers on search strategy and execution. For our force a major part of the PolSA's role was to plan and execute the pre-searching and securing of major events like Royal Ascot and State Visits to Windsor. It also required being on call to give advice when necessary.

Suzie and I had finally split up a couple of years after the party scandal. I discovered she had had another affair, this time with a sergeant from work, and we had gone through a very acrimonious year-long legal battle where I tried (partially successfully) to keep my parent's inheritance and my police pension, both of which she wanted half of.

I had subsequently met Gretchen, a lovely Kiwi physiotherapist, at a triathlon in New Zealand and we had married a year later. We had three beautiful baby boys, but tragically we lost the second, Sammy, as a full-term still birth.

The distress of the break-up, the hurt of the betrayal, and the fear of losing my home and my inheritance was awful. For this to be followed several years later by the unbearable pain of losing a baby (and burying him beside my Mum and Dad) added considerably to my underlying PTSD, anxiety and depression. I knew I needed to take drastic steps to reduce stress in my life and that, despite the amazing support I had received from my workmates, maybe my time in the police was coming to an end.

One damp and cool early summer afternoon I was enjoying a rare day-off at home with my two boys. The eldest, Archie, was three, Oscar was just five months old.

Gretchen was at work and I was on call. It was time to feed the little one, so I heated up a bottle, checked its temperature and had just stuck it in his hungry mouth when Archie (who we were in the process of potty training) declared "Need a poo Daddy."

I put the bottle down, causing an immediate piercing scream of protest, and quickly took my older boy upstairs to the bathroom and put him on his bright blue plastic potty. I ran back down to the kitchen and put the still-warm bottle back in the baby's mouth. The howling was immediately replaced by desperate (and satisfied) sucking noises.

My work phone rang. I shook my head and sighed in disbelief at the timing. I briefly considered ignoring it before putting down the bottle for a second, and clearly inexcusable, time. I was met with furious screams of disgust and shaking of tiny arms. I reached for the mobile that was on the kitchen bench.

"Hello, PC Bourdillon speaking" I said, fumbling to place my thumb over the microphone in an attempt to dampen down the wails in the background.

A confused-sounding senior officer replied "Have I got the right number for the duty PolSA? Aren't you at work?"

"It's my day off but I'm the on call PolSA today."

"Oh" then a pause. "You sound busy. Is there someone else I can talk to?"

"No sir, just me. How can I help?"

He then proceeded to brief me about an extremely vulnerable and elderly man who had been reported missing from his care home. He was trying to locate him and wanted me to set priorities and parameters for the search. With a now-quiet baby under one arm, the bottle in my opposite hand and the phone wedged between my shoulder and ear I tried to advise him as best I could.

"Have officers checked the care home?"

"I think so, yes."

"You need to confirm that first. Before we do anything else I would strongly advise you to get a team of officers to do a proper search of his room, all communal areas of the home including the gardens, and someone to go door-to-door to every bedroom and see if he's just visiting a friend or in his confusion he's gone into someone else's room by mistake. The care staff will tell you they've already done that, but it probably hasn't been done properly. Most MisPers are found at, or very close to, home...you don't want to start an extensive search until you've bottomed that out."

Without maps there wasn't a great deal more I could do so, reluctantly, I put Oscar back in his high chair and put the still-unfinished bottle down in front of him so I could get my laptop out and bring up our mapping systems. I thought he was angry the last time, but this was off the charts. His face flushed deep red, his mouth flew open, he pounded his tiny fists on the table, his little legs kicked and he screamed. And screamed. And continued to scream.

"It sounds like someone wants your attention, do you need to go?"

"No sir, I'm fine. I'm just loading the maps now. I'll have them up in a minute" I replied, desperately trying not to sound as stressed as I was feeling. "

At that moment I heard little steps coming down the stairs and realised I had totally forgotten about my eldest in the bathroom who was now on his way back down.

There I was, with my cortisol levels already through the roof, standing in the kitchen, laptop open on the workbench, a hungry baby violently screaming, a phone stuck to my ear, trying to stay calm and give professional advice to an Area Commander as my three-year-old very proudly (and loudly) announced "DADDY, I DONE A POO!"

The phone went quiet for a second, and then "PC Bourdillon, are you sure you don't need to go?"

"No sir, everything's fine" I lied. "Now, looking at the map I can see there's an area of low, open ground about 100 metres south east of the home. It appears to have direct access to the river..." I was interrupted again as my toddler entered the kitchen "DADDY, LOOK! I DONE A POO!"

I looked. And he was right. There sitting in the cupped hands that Archie was proudly holding out in front of him was a warm, brown and very smelly lump which he desperately wanted to show me.

"Shit. Sorry sir, I've got to go! I'll call you back as soon as I can" I garbled into the mouthpiece. I heard chuckling on the other end of the line as I almost dropped the phone and rushed across the kitchen to deal with the imminent domestic emergency.

Ten minutes, two plastic bags, half-a-dozen anti-bacterial wipes and a lot of soap and water later I called him back.

"Ah, PC Bourdillon, I was just about to call you back. We found him. Just like you said he was still at the home. He was sitting quietly, in his pyjamas, on a secluded bench at the back of the garden. He was soaked to the skin and almost hypothermic and had no idea where he was. Well done, your advice was spot on." A brief pause and then another chuckle "I hope your crisis at home has been successfully resolved too?"

I laughed. "Nearly sir...I've got one full and one empty boy here, once I've emptied the full one and filled the empty one I think I'll have averted any major disorder!"

Despite the undeniable humour of the situation, as I hung up I was acutely aware of how stressed and overwhelmed I actually was. My heart was pounding, my breathing was fast and shallow and my head was spinning and unable to form any coherent thoughts. I felt physically sick and I was exhausted. My physical responses to the previous twenty minutes were at least as acute as any I had experienced at any point during my entire career, and I had been in many, many situations far more stressful that this. I knew I had finally reached my tolerance limit and I couldn't see a way out other than to leave the job.

My time as a police officer was nearly up and I started to dream of a new, reduced-stress life in New Zealand with my young family.

A quick stop at home to see my little man

28

Olympic Escapades

In 2012 the Summer Olympics came to the UK, and although most events were held in London (and therefore the Met's responsibility, not ours) the rowing and kayaking races took place at Dorney Lake, an impressive rowing facility on the outskirts of Windsor that is privately owned by Eton College.

Our team, Protection Group Specialist Search (PGSS), with the help of the Underwater Search Team, was assigned the enormous job of searching and securing the 400 acre site, all its buildings, structures and the lake itself. To complicate things further, we would also have to search, secure and sign-off all the construction work of the temporary stands, restaurants, bars, toilet blocks and other port-a-cabins that would need to be built for the athletes and spectators. We were used to planning and carrying out the searches of major events at large venues, but this was physically the biggest job that any of us had been involved in as PolSAs.

We started the planning process in July 2011, as soon as Royal Ascot had finished. This gave us just over a year to tackle the monster, fitting our work on the project around our usual firearms and search commitments. It also allowed us to get into the site before any of the temporary construction work began, meaning we could literally work from the ground up (all the underground and confined spaces bits were down to the Underwater Search Team who seemed to enjoy crawling through drains and sewers).

We split the site into different zones and allocated each zone to a PolSA. Once all the main buildings and construction sites were dished up I, as the most newly-qualified PolSA, was given the crappy job of everything that was left. That meant *all* the open ground (including the lake itself), approximately 350 of the 400 acre site. The plus side was that the Underwater Search lads were allocated almost exclusively to me, and they were an excellent and highly professional team.

Remember Tony from Chapter 10? With his fondness of effing and blinding and using the 'C' word when addressing senior officers? Well, despite that he was given the co-ordinator's role of head PolSA (or Mr Olympics, as we liked to call him). He moved to the Olympics operational planning HQ at the Taplow Traffic base where he was given a desk in a room full of high-ranking officers. Each one was responsible for one of the many logistical aspects of policing such a large public event (traffic management, major incident response, public order response, firearms response, site security, staffing levels and shift patterns, feeding officers on site...the list is almost endless). Tony's job was to oversee the whole search operation, attend all the briefings and liaise between us and senior management, keeping everybody informed and updated as necessary.

It was amusing to see Tony readily adjust into a management position and morph (albeit in a tongue-in-cheek, self-depreciating way) into a caricature of a senior officer.

His favourite thing was to meet with us after a briefing and use all the latest management buzz words and phrases that he'd just picked up. If we asked him something that he couldn't answer, rather than simply say "I don't know" he would always reply "We don't know what that's going to look like yet." This would be followed by a brief pause accompanied by a deadly-serious, "shut the fuck up" sort of stare. He would then invariably shrug his shoulders, roll his eyes, laugh and say something like "I asked that too, but those fucking useless bastards hadn't even considered it. They're going to get back to me apparently. Don't hold your fucking breath though."

We arranged for our Air Support Unit to fly over the area and take a comprehensive set of aerial photographs from their helicopter. Once we had the images my first job was to pour over them and try to identify exactly where every single structure, drain, lamp-post, inspection cover, culvert and any other vulnerable point was.

My next job was to go and actually find all these points, see exactly what they were, and assess if they required any further investigation or if they could simply be ignored. Once on site it became obvious just how big an area it was and how long it would take me to cover every inch of open ground on foot. I went back to the office feeling dejected and slightly overwhelmed by the sheer scale of it.

I phoned Tony.

"Get the Underwater Search cocks to do it. There's eight of them and they love that sort of shit."

I called them up. "Yes mate, we knew you were going to ask so we've already been to the lake and have done a recce. It'll take us about a week, and we need to fit it around other jobs, but all going well we'll get it done by the end of the month."

"Great. Thanks mate. If you can do a detailed map and a comprehensive list of all the points then I can take it from there."

"Yeah, yeah. Don't stress, we know the drill."

I came off the phone relieved that at least I didn't have to worry about the mapping side of things, but I was a new and relatively inexperienced PolSA and was daunted by the amount of planning I still had to do for a job this big. There was plenty for me to get on with for now, but I couldn't really get stuck into it until I received the maps. I would just have to wait.

Over the next month all the other PolSAs were busy working on their areas, regularly visiting the lake and were making real progress. I was feeling totally left behind and starting to panic a bit. The other PolSAs picked up on my stress and, with typical police humour, very kindly added to it whenever possible. Almost daily Tom or DWC would say “I got so much done yesterday, I can’t believe how well this is going. We’re running out of time but I’m still on schedule. How’s your area going Dillan?” Frankie and Tony were considerably more blunt “Isn’t it about time you did some fucking work? The Olympics aren’t going to wait for you, you know.”

My response was to immediately call the Underwater Search Team, but I invariably got the answerphone, and they never returned my calls or emails.

The month they had promised came and went, and I found myself running a MisPer search along the banks of the Thames. I was looking for a suicidal teenager whose car had been found abandoned by the river. There had been no recent usage of either his phone or his bank account and we were assuming the worst. I called out the Underwater Search guys as it was likely we were looking for a body in the river.

As soon as they arrived, before I had even briefed them, I asked them when my maps would be done.

"Don't stress Dillan" Rodders said with a slow grin. "We'll get it done in plenty of time."

We'll get it done?!!" I said to myself. *What the fuck does that mean? Haven't they even started yet?* I felt myself starting to panic.

"You have started, haven't you?" I asked him.

"Just chill out mate. It'll be done in time." He wasn't giving anything away, and no matter how much I pushed for clear answers he wasn't going to tell me anything. I had to drop it and focus on the job in hand.

We searched several miles of the river over the following couple of days with no result. All my other enquiries came back negative too. I stood the team down whilst I considered my other options, and hoped they would finally go to Dorney Lake and map the vulnerable points for me.

I got a phone call at home that night from Control Room. "Sussex Police have found your young lad. Apparently he got on a train to Brighton and has been sleeping on the beach. His parents are on their way down there to get him now." He had no known connections to Brighton, so I have no idea why he ended up there, but he was safe and well so that was all that mattered.

A couple of days later I got a call at work from Rodders. "Dillan, it's all done mate. I'm going to email everything over to you now." Relief flushed over me. Luckily I was in the office so I immediately opened up the file.

I looked at it in horror. The 400 acre site had been roughly sketched out on a tatty piece of A4 paper with a couple of dozen or so crosses, stars and circles dotted around what I assumed was the lake. At the top left hand corner was a scribbled key indicating the crosses were inspection covers, the stars were lampposts and the circles were other structures. A few arrows on the page pointed to the culverts. The whole thing was barely legible, not to scale and was of little or no use to me.

My tolerance for this sort of stress was zero. I exploded. "What the fuck are they playing at?" as I threw my pen across the room. Tom and DWC looked at each other and grinned. "What's up matey?" Tom asked me.

I showed him the map.

"Oh" he said, trying to supress a smile. He shrugged his shoulders "I think you need to call them, you're already well behind. Maybe you should have just done it yourself."

I didn't need to hear that, I was stressed enough already. I picked up the phone.

"Underwater Search. Rodders here" came the cheerful answer.

"What the fuck is that?" I asked. "Have you even been to the lake? I thought you guys were professional. I thought I could rely on you to do a proper job. You do know you're the ones who are going to be actually searching all these drains and culverts, don't you. This is the Olympics...don't you fucking care?"

I thought I heard a slight snigger, but I couldn't be sure. "Calm down mate. It's fine" he said. It wasn't fine and I wasn't going to calm down...I was angry and wanted an apology. Most importantly I wanted my maps done.

"You need to go back and do it again. I need those maps ASAP. If you can't do it I'll get the Mounted Section to do it. I know I can rely on them."

"Yeah, okay mate" he said, sounding like he didn't have a care in the world. Then he added "Oh, I've just sent you another email."

I kept him on the line whilst I opened it. It had about a dozen attachments. I opened the first one. A perfectly executed map appeared on my screen. And another as I clicked on the next. And another and another. And then spreadsheets with list after list of every vulnerable point, each with an appropriate identifying marker corresponding to the maps.

Rodders was giggling on the other end of the phone. I looked up to see Tom and DWC laughing their heads off.

"You wankers" I laughed. "You fucking wankers. Do you know how stressed I've been?"

"Yes" said DWC. "That's what made it so funny"

"We actually got it finished before we did the MisPer job with you last week. Martin felt sorry for you and wanted to give it to you then, but I thought we needed to wait a few more days!" Rodders laughed in my ear.

"Wanker" I replied, already wondering how I could get him back.

So, fast forward four months and all the work was done. The whole site had been mapped, sectioned, searched, sealed and secured. The racing had started and we were allocated shifts to be on site to deal with any security issues as they arose. I, as the junior PolSA on the team, got the short straw and was given the night shifts. I would spend two weeks at the Olympics but wouldn't see a single race.

The government had, slightly controversially, awarded G4S (Group 4 Security) the contract for providing over 10,000 guards to back up the police and to carry out gate security and bag searches. Many thought the police or the army should be performing those roles, not casual security staff, but the government were pushing an austerity agenda and G4S were cheaper than the professionals. As it turned out, despite being the largest private security firm in the world (and the British Government being their biggest client), G4S had bitten off more than they could chew. With only a week or so to go they finally admitted that they were only able to provide just under 6,000 of the 10,000 staff required.

It was an absolute shambles and as a result 1,200 military personnel (mainly Royal Marines and Paratroopers) had their leave cancelled and were promptly posted to the Olympics. At Dorney Lake they were responsible for patrolling and securing the perimeter of the site and we liaised closely with them to ensure everything ran smoothly. It didn't take long however for inter-agency rivalries to surface and this led to a challenge being thrown down that I couldn't resist.

The London 2012 organisers had lent us and the army a number of BMW mountain bikes to get around the venue on, and on one of the first nights a bored squaddie from the Parachute Regiment decided to see how fast he could ride the 5 kilometre road loop around the lake. After a few attempts he recorded a pretty respectable time and asked if any of us wanted to try and beat his time. A couple of the lads on the team tried, but couldn't match his time.

Excessive exercise (to the point of it being obsessive) had been a cornerstone of my stress-management practices for the best part of a decade. On top of that I had also been a keen and competitive triathlete for almost twenty years and had actually raced at Dorney Lake a dozen-

or-so times at the Eton Super Sprints triathlons. I knew how quickly I could do a lap so I fancied my chances. I decided to go for a quick spin to try the bike out before I committed to the challenge... riding a mountain bike in the pitch black of night in full police uniform was clearly going to affect my times. It was a horrible, heavy, clunky bike that I guess was sponsored (and not actually made) by BMW and I couldn't believe how slow it was compared to my tri bike. I nearly changed my mind, but figured the army lad had exactly the same handicap as me, so why not?

As I mounted the bike at the starting line the motivating comments from my team didn't actually help. All the "You'll kick his arse" and "Does he know how fast you are?" just put the pressure on. Thames Valley Police's reputation was on the line here and I was determined not to be beaten by a squaddie twenty years younger than me.

It was a warm, humid and still summer's night and it wasn't long before I was sweating heavily into my coveralls. The lack of moonlight made visibility poor and I nearly rode right off the road on a couple of the bends. My ankles couldn't flex properly in my work boots and I could feel the sweat trickling down my legs into my socks. The effort required to get the bike moving quickly was enormous, the risk of crashing was high (I didn't even want to think about how would try to explain my injuries and a broken bike to my supervisors) and I hated every minute of the ride.

As I rounded the last bend I changed back into the biggest gear and pushed as hard as I could for the final couple of hundred metres. I was struggling to catch my breath as I was met on the line by cheers and a few pats on the back. I was told I'd beaten the Para's time by about twenty seconds. Olympic gold to the Police, silver to the Army. Excellent. Time for a cup of tea to celebrate.

When I got to the lake to start work the following night Frankie was there to hand over to me. After he'd briefed me on what needed doing during the shift he congratulated me on my race.

"Mick's well pleased mate. You've done us proud." Mick was our sergeant and took great pride in our team. "He's liaised with the Army and he's got a favour to ask you."

It turns out the squaddie wasn't happy to let it rest there. Apparently he was about to go through SAS selection and being beaten by an old copper had seriously put his nose out of joint. He now wanted to move the goalposts and turn this into a triathlon...two more events to go before I could claim my victory.

"So Mick's told them you're an Ironman, you've run across the Sahara Desert and you've done lots of other stupid shit like that. He said you're going to destroy their lad. They laughed and said you haven't got a chance against their man." I shook my head and rolled my eyes...why did he have to tell them that? Now I felt more pressured to win. Secretly though I was revelling in the challenge.

"Mick's asking if you can bring your wetsuit in tomorrow night to do the swim. Two widths of the lake...that's about 200 metres or so."

I shook my head again. "No."

Frankie looked surprised.

"I'm not saying no to the race, I'm saying no to the distance. I'm not going to all that trouble for 200 metres. If he wants to swim against me then we're doing the length of the lake...two point two kilometres."

Frankie grinned. Now it was us throwing down the gauntlet, not them.

"Okay, I'll get Mick to sort it out. Don't forget your wetsuit tomorrow though, that lake's bloody freezing."

Twenty four hours later and I'm back at the lake, my wetsuit, cap and goggles packed carefully in my kitbag. This time it's Mick, not Frankie, who's handing over to me. He looked serious.

"We've got a bit of a problem" he said. "Someone's been talking and the Public Order Commander's not happy about your race."

"What's it got to do with him?" I asked. We were there purely for the search and secure operation and to deal with any suspicious items that could pose a threat. The Public Order Department had an entirely different remit and quite frankly I didn't really care if their commander was happy or not.

"As Chief Inspector he's the most senior officer here right now, in fact he's the Silver Commander tonight and I'm afraid as such it's got everything to do with him. It may be best if you postpone the swim for a few days."

"Oh. Bugger. We may not get another chance...this is my last night here this week as I'm in the ASV over the weekend. I've got no idea if the squaddie will even be here next week when I'm back on site." The ASV was our Armed Support Vehicle, and there was no way I could park that up one night to go for a quick swim! It was tonight or never.

"Okay. I really want this race to happen. I haven't been given a direct order to tell you not to do it, all I know is that Silver's heard about it and doesn't like it. If you think you can get away with it then do it, but keep it quiet and do it in the early hours, maybe around two or three am?"

"Perfect!"

"Just don't get bloody caught. I don't want to be up in front of the Chief for a bollocking, okay?"

"Right-oh, Sarge" I grinned "I'll be careful. The last thing I want is another PSD interview..."

Mick left after he'd fully briefed me about a number of minor issues I needed to deal with during the night. After he'd gone I headed over to the temporary staff canteen to get myself a cup of tea and a biscuit.

Actually, not a biscuit but a Nature Valley muesli bar. Nature Valley must have either been an Olympic sponsor or had done a deal with the organisers to supply their bars to venue staff and volunteers as there were hundreds and hundreds of boxes of them. I particularly liked the dark chocolate bars, with the maple syrup ones a close second, but to my dismay there were only the honey ones on display.

"Surely you haven't run out of the other flavours?" I pleaded to the guy behind the counter. He laughed. "No chance mate, there's bloody thousands of them out the back. What ones do you want? I'll go and grab a few boxes for you...you can take one back to your van for your team if you want."

"Thanks mate, you're a star."

He disappeared out of sight and I wandered over to the hot water urns to make myself a brew. I was struggling to squeeze out my tea bag with a pathetically bendy white plastic spoon when I felt a tap on my shoulder. I turned my head expecting to see the canteen guy holding a box of Nature Valley bars, but was surprised to see the Silver Commander and his bag-carrier, one of the Public Order Instructors.

"Pc Bourdillon?" he enquired.

"Yes, boss" I cheerily replied.

"I've heard a rumour you've got some sort of competition going with the army."

I sighed. "Yes sir. It's just a bit of fun."

"Are you winning?" he asked, smiling.

"Yes sir, I am so far."

"Jolly good!" He looked genuinely pleased. Maybe he wasn't going to put a stop to it after all.

"Please tell me you're not planning on getting in that lake tonight..."

"Ummm, well...."

"Because I can't allow that. Too much of a Health and Safety risk. I can't have anyone drowning on my watch, it wouldn't look good in the papers, now would it?"

I sighed again. "No sir, it wouldn't." One last chance "But I'm not going to drown, and neither's he. He's up for Selection and I swim twice that far several times a week. In fact I've even swum in this lake multiple times before."

"That's as maybe, but sorry, you're not swimming tonight." My heart sank. "Look on the bright side. At least you've already beaten him."

It wasn't much of a consolation. I loved my swimming, particularly in the open water. To properly race at an Olympic venue, in the moonlight, was like a dream.

I returned to the van feeling totally dejected...I felt like I was carrying a wooden spoon, not a box of my favourite muesli bars.

"What's up mate?" I was asked as I stepped up into the back of the transit.

"I've just been tapped up...the race is off."

"What? No way!"

I shrugged. "Yup, I'm afraid so." I slumped down into my seat as I dropped the Nature Valley box onto the small grey table between the two rows of facing bench seats. "If anyone wants to go and grab a brew I'll mind the van."

Nobody moved. "Why don't you do it anyway?" somebody suggested. "We can cover for you. It's pitch back out there, as long as you're quiet no one's going to know."

I shrugged again. "Everybody knew about the bike race. You can't keep a secret here. Even if we all keep our mouths shut the Army won't. I'll never get away with it. It's just not worth getting stuck on for. Sorry."

I knew it was the right decision, but I was gutted.

I'd spent the best part of a year planning for the Olympics. It was a once-in-a-lifetime event and should have been one of the highlights of my career, but I didn't get to see a single race. I didn't get to witness or really appreciate all the fruits of my labour. I never mingled with the crowds, experienced the atmosphere or felt the excitement of the racing. I didn't see any medal ceremonies, in fact I never even saw an athlete. The only medal

I saw was one that I was given (like all the other police and military personnel involved) as a thank you from the Prime Minister. As it turned out, thanks to governmental austerity cuts the medal was downgraded to a medallion, meaning I couldn't wear it alongside my Queen's Jubilee medals. To further add insult to injury the Prime Minister who issued it was bloody David Cameron.

10 DOWNING STREET
LONDON SW1A 2AA

THE PRIME MINISTER — December 2012

Please accept this commemorative medallion as a symbol of our gratitude for your efforts in helping deliver the safe and secure London 2012 Games. Thank you for a job well done and be proud of your contribution to this spectacular moment in our history.

Yours sincerely

My Olympic 'medal'

Exiting the swim at Ironman New Zealand (l), in the Sahara desert at the Marathon des Sables (r) and competing in the ITU Long Distance World Champs in Immenstadt, Germany (below).

Out of the Blue

29

The Big Job

One question I get asked a lot is "What was your biggest gun job?" or words to that effect.

In the firearms world, just as in all areas of police work, the definition of 'biggest' or 'best' is subjective. Is it the job that made it onto the BBC? Is it the job involving the most officers? The one with the most arrests? The job where you actually save someone's life? It is the one with the longest, most exhilarating pursuit? Is it the most exciting job, or the most satisfying one?

It really is hard to pick and choose, mainly because so many incidents you attend could fit the criteria. In this book, rather than pick the 'big' stories, I've focussed on the jobs that impacted me the most, those that defined my career, that shaped what sort of copper I became, and those that affected my mental health the most. Although what I'm about to write could definitely be considered a big job, it's much more about my state of mind on that day.

I was crewing one of our Armed Response Vehicles (ARVs) on a mid-week early shift. An indication as to just how tired, stressed and burnt out I was is that I cannot, for the life of me, remember who I was crewed with, or who any of the other officers involved were. I do remember that they were all from the Tactical Firearms Group (TFG) which was the latest re-branding of Support Group and as the only Protection Group officer, I was the outsider. I was the designated driver for one of the ARVs, and for the sake of the story I'll call my crewmate 'John'.

We were patrolling some of the villages to the south of Aylesbury when a call came in about a suspected gunman in a car parked up near Bracknell. A member of the public had seen what he believed was a handgun in the driver's door pocket of a small red hatchback. It wouldn't have been a particularly high-priority job (reports like that are relatively common and are usually cases of mistaken identification of toy guns, cameras or other items), but the same vehicle had been involved in an armed robbery several days earlier and we had been actively looking for it.

Despite being almost 30 miles away we were the closest armed unit available. I immediately flicked on our blue lights and sirens and put my foot down. We were off at break-neck speed and John was furiously typing the location into our sat-nav so he could direct me. It's hard to describe the intensity of deploying to an instant-response armed situation. The frantic activity in the vehicle combined with the sudden adrenaline rush of being deployed is both exhilarating and stressful beyond almost anything else I have experienced...and I say that as someone who, amongst many other stupid things, has dived with great white sharks.

The radio is relaying a constant stream of information in your ear. The make, model, colour and registration number of the vehicle. The number and descriptions of occupants. The type and location of the weapon seen. The exact location. The number of witnesses. The volume of members of public in the location. The known history of the vehicle. The details of whom the vehicle is registered to. The owner's police record. Their criminal record. The list is almost endless and control room never give us all the details we need. Where's the driver's home address? Does he have any accomplices or family in the area? Does he have a firearms licence? Does he have a history of violence? Has he ever been arrested at gunpoint before? Is there any CCTV at the location? How many other units are on route? Do we have an RV point, and if so where? Do we have authorisation to deploy with firearms? Is the helicopter available? What about a tactical dog handler?

The conversation is too much just for the radio, so we're using mobile phones too. We're talking to the control room, to the Silver Commander, to the other ARVs. The sat-nav needs updating. I'm driving at speeds of well over 100mph (where the conditions and safety allow). The lights are flashing and the sound from the sirens and wailers is almost deafening. My crewmate is opening the firearms safe between our seats, removing our Glock 17 handguns and loading them. He hands me mine. I reach over with my right hand and grab it, dropping it swiftly into my hip-mounted plastic holster and flicking over the locking mechanism to keep it secure. Both my hands are quickly back on the steering wheel and John now removes the MP5 carbines from the safe and loads them too. He turns on the HDS sights, checking the batteries are good. He dumps my carbine on my lap. The information is still coming in. It's relentless.

There are two occupants. They're back in the vehicle. *Shit.* We're still at least five minutes away. Are any other units there yet? No. We'll be the first. I press my right foot down a touch more, squeezing a little more speed out of the ARV. Bang. Too fast. I clip the kerb.

"What the fuck?" shouts John. It's my first mistake of the day. He's never worked with me before and is now wondering if he can trust me. My stress levels rise another notch. *You fucking idiot* I chastise myself, inadvertently increasing my stress even further. Luckily the tyre doesn't blow and we carry on. I'll have to deal with the damaged wheel later, there's no time to think about it now.

Another update. They're leaving the car park. *Shit.* We're still a couple of minutes away. Let's hope they come this way. I kill the lights and sirens so we don't scare them off. *Please come this way, please, please.* They don't.

The witness is on foot and doesn't know which way they went. Still no other units on scene and the helicopter isn't up yet. It's a total loss. *Shit. How much time did I lose by clipping the kerb?* It's only seconds. It wouldn't have made any difference, but I hate myself all the same. I've let myself down and I'm embarrassed.

I slowed down to match the speed limit and we started a laborious search of all the surrounding roads and car parks. A second ARV arrived and we agreed a search plan. At least I could use my expertise and local knowledge to positively help now, and the TFG officers were happy with my plan.

After an hour or so of fruitless searching we decided to head into Bracknell nick to grab a very late breakfast. Once parked up the first thing I did was check my front wheel. It wasn't good and it would need replacing, but we couldn't leave our commitment to take it to our workshops yet. We were still needed in Bracknell in case the vehicle was sighted again.

Once inside the nick we found a kettle, made ourselves a brew and sat down to finally eat. Predictably, we had hardly started when a call came in.

"ARV 8?"

"Go ahead"

"A local unit has just spotted the suspect vehicle heading out of town on the London Road. They're just approaching the Coppid Beech, travelling towards the A329(M)."

We were on our feet and running before the call ended. Half-drunk cups of tea and almost untouched sandwiches left on the table. Back into the ARV. Lights and sirens on, impatiently waiting for the back yard gate to open. Out onto the road and my foot's down again. More updates over the radio. Mobile calls to Silver and to the other ARV. He's heading towards the motorway. We need traffic (Roads Policing) units and we need the helicopter. Now. If he gets on the motorway we're going to need a rolling road block and the slip roads blocked. Have we got enough traffic units? If not, can local units cover the slip roads? We need to prepare for a possible hard stop on the motorway. We need it clear of all other traffic. Guns and motorways are an exceptionally dangerous combination. We need to make this as safe as possible.

We kill the blues and twos as we close in on the hatchback. We don't want him to know he's being followed. Despite our frantic efforts of the last few hours the occupants of the vehicle probably have absolutely no idea we're even looking for them. Softly, softly. We don't want him spooked. I reduce my speed to match his, and make sure there is at least one vehicle between him and us. The second ARV is another three or four vehicles back, hopefully completely out of sight.

We're on the A329(M), heading towards Reading. We're approaching the junction with the M4. Which way's he going? Wait. Wait. It looks like he's going straight on. Into Reading. No. *Shit.* He's changed his mind. First exit. Left, left, left. Onto the motorway, heading towards Slough and London. Has he seen us? No. No change in his speed. This isn't a pursuit, we're still just following at a safe distance. The plan is being furiously discussed and approved over the air. The helicopter is up and only a minute or two away. We have multiple traffic and local units on their way. The slip roads onto the motorway are being blocked off. Suddenly there are no vehicles on the opposite carriageway...a traffic unit has blocked the west-bound lanes of the M4 somewhere close to Junction 6 at Slough.

Finally the suspect realises something is going on. He's been driving at, or close to the speed limit and sitting quite innocently in lane one, the slow lane of the motorway. The traffic travelling in our direction is rapidly thinning out. Somewhere out of sight, a mile or so behind us, a couple of Roads Policing cars have set up a 'rolling road block', slowing all the vehicles travelling in our direction down to a walking pace. Pretty soon we'll have a sterile motorway. The only vehicles anywhere to be seen will be the hatchback and two ARVs.

We're on a real time frame now...we have to get the suspects stopped before we get to Slough. On top of that every second the motorway is shut costs a small fortune. We're shutting down the main transport route connecting London to Cardiff, via the large centres of Slough, Reading, Newbury and Bristol...that's a massive economic disruption for the country.

Now the driver decides to try to get away. Maybe he's gained confidence by seeing an empty motorway ahead of him, a virtual racetrack. He's away and has swerved into lane two, the middle lane. We can't stop him there, we've only got two vehicles so we need to sandwich him against the central reservation barrier, boxing him in. I flick the lights and sirens back on, instantly drowning out the whoop, whoop, whoop of the helicopter that has just arrived somewhere overhead. The second ARV comes flying past us on the inside and within seconds has caught the hatchback, sitting right alongside it in lane one. We come right up behind it, so the suspects have one police car close on their nearside and one on their rear bumper. Together we gently guide the hatchback to its right, into lane 3 and then further right still until it's up against the central barrier. The lead ARV pulls up diagonally across the front nearside of the hatchback as it slows to a complete halt. The suspect car is trapped.

"Strike, strike, strike!" comes the command from the front ARV. We're already out of our vehicle, MP5s raised, pointing directly at the threat.

"ARMED POLICE! KEEP STILL!" we scream in unison as we approach the vehicle. The other two AFOs, being at the front of the car, deal with the two known occupants in the front seats. John and I are covering the unknown...the rear bench seat and the boot.

The helicopter is hovering noisily above us, ready to track anyone who tries to escape, and filming the entire operation.

The two suspects are shocked and totally compliant. They are quickly out of the vehicle, arrested and handcuffed. Now it's our turn. We don't need to talk to each other...despite never having worked together before, our training and experience means we know exactly what to do, and what each other is going to do. John covers the boot as I approach the rear driver's side window, weapon raised, and look in. It's clear. There are no passengers sitting in the back, no one hiding in the floor well.

"Clear!" I shout. I carefully take a few steps backwards, my MP5 still raised, as I return to the rear of the vehicle. John looks at me. I nod. He slings his weapon behind him, crouches low and moves up to the nearside rear bumper. My weapon is pointed directly at the boot, my gaze fixed at where I'm aiming. In my peripheral vision I see John look at me again and nod. He's ready. Without looking at him I slowly nod three times. On the third nod he opens the boot and swiftly moves to the side, out of harm's way.

Now, there are three possible situations here, and three clear commands depending on which one you face. That way all the other officers know exactly what's going on, and how to respond. If the boot is empty you shout "Clear!" and there's no need for anyone else to get involved. If there's someone hiding in there you shout "Armed police!" and carry out a full armed challenge with the support of your crewmate. If the boot is sufficiently full of stuff so you can't tell if there's someone in there or not, then you shout "Search!" and your crewmate will search the boot while you keep it covered with your firearm.

You'd think, what with me being both an experienced firearms officer and a search specialist that 'search' would be a nice, easy command to remember. I don't know if I was slightly complacent (as we had been told there were only two occupants) and was expecting to shout "clear" as the boot would be empty, but more likely my mind just went blank with the stress. Not so much the stress of that morning, but the accumulated stress and trauma of the previous decade. Whatever the reason, when the boot opened and I saw it was full to the brim with clothes, sleeping bags, tools, food and rubbish I froze. I simply could not remember the command. John glanced at me, confused. He needed to know what to do, but couldn't see into the boot from where he was standing. My head started to spin as my brain desperately searched for the right word. I almost stuttered as I forced the wrong phrase out of my reluctant mouth. "Not clear!" I shouted, like a fucking idiot.

John now looked slightly panicked. What the fuck did that mean? Was there someone in there or not? He stepped to his side, raised his weapon and leaned his head around to look into the boot. "SEARCH!" he bellowed, looking at me with complete disdain as he shook his head. We had apparently now switched roles. I slung my MP5 behind me and searched the boot. There was nobody there. And there were no firearms. The only item of interest we found was five hundred quid hidden in the driver's sock.

We split the prisoners up, one in each ARV, and took them to Maidenhead Police Station where they would later be interviewed by CID about the armed robbery. The car was seized and also taken to Maidenhead where it could be properly searched and forensically examined. The helicopter left and the Roads Policing units let the motorway traffic flow once more.

We drove back to the nick in silence. We should have been buzzing, but I was crestfallen and embarrassed, and John was pissed off. It was an uncomfortable ride, with none of the humour or banter that would normally be present after a job like that. My head felt like it was full of cotton wool. I was drained, tired beyond belief and could hardly think, let alone make witty conversation. The only thought I seemed capable of was "You're an embarrassment and a liability. You shouldn't be doing this job...you're not up to it. *You're not good enough.*"

Yet again destructive feelings of self-doubt and self-loathing started to take hold of me, and started to eat away at any last strands of positivity I had been clinging onto. Leaving the job and moving overseas was becoming much less of a nice dream for the future. It was rapidly becoming an essential priority for my mental well-being. I knew I was done.

30

A Bloody Mess

One thing that really annoys me is the throw-away (mis)use of superlatives and 'big' words.

At one end of the scale words like 'hero' and 'legend' are regularly used to describe pop stars, sports people and celebrities, leaving few words powerful enough to describe those who do actual heroic deeds.

At the other end 'depressed', 'traumatised' and 'suicidal' are bandied around by some seeking sympathy without any real understanding of what going through a mental health crisis really entails.

If you have been truly depressed, traumatised, or suicidal, or if you have had first-hand experience of dealing with people intent on killing themselves (or those who have succeeded) then the casual use of these terms can be something of a trigger.

Part of my motivation to write this book was to document my own struggles and to hopefully give hope or help to others dealing with their own demons. Although I have often had suicidal thoughts, I would never have considered myself to be suicidal. I have never planned to kill myself, and don't believe I would ever actually enact those darkest of thoughts.

I have, though, come into very close contact with genuinely suicidal people, those of us right on the edge, and it's painfully sad to see their desperation. Throughout my career I have dealt with the impact of severe mental health issues on individuals and their families.

As a response officer I have attended countless successful hangings, gassings, overdoses and wrist-slashings. As a PolSA I have searched for and found, both dead and alive, suicidal missing people. As a response officer and as a Firearms Officer I have had to attend medical interventions on suicidal individuals and on occasion actively stop both men and women from killing themselves.

I was part of the search team that found the body of Dr David Kelly in woods near his Oxfordshire home in July 2003. Kelly was a Biological Warfare specialist and had been a UN Weapons Inspector in Iraq. He had killed himself after appearing at a Foreign Affairs Select Committee investigating the leaking of confidential information regarding Weapons of Mass Destruction in Iraq to the BBC.

In 2001 I, along with three colleagues from High Wycombe (Jen, Tony and Chris) received a commendation for pulling a suicidal woman off an M40 motorway over-bridge just as she was about to jump. We had tried in vain to talk her down, and suddenly found ourselves in the extremely dangerous position of having to wrestle her off the outer-ledge of the bridge. To compound things she was a larger woman and was bleeding heavily from her wrists, which she had already tried to slit. Grabbing her arms was like trying to grip onto a greasy pole, and pulling her to safety was a monumental task. Any one of us could have gone over the edge at any point. Somehow though we managed to haul her back to safety. The only casualty that night was Chris's back which he pulled badly. He was off work for the rest of the month recovering.

The last serious mental health case I had to deal with as a police officer was in the last year of my career.

I was crewing one of our force's ARVs with an old colleague from my days at Wycombe, Matt. We were on a night patrol just outside Aylesbury when we got a call for assistance from a local unit.

The double-crewed panda had attended a welfare call to help an ambulance crew transport a twenty-year old man to hospital. He had tried to kill himself at home but his parents had found him and had called for an ambulance. He was intent on finishing the job and wasn't going to go to hospital quietly, so the paramedics called the police.

One of the young officers went in the back of the ambulance whilst the other followed behind in the panda. About halfway to Stoke Mandeville hospital all hell broke loose as the patient decided to have another go at killing himself. The copper and the medic tried their best to restrain him, but came under a vicious and relentless attack. He was absolutely determined to end his own life, and he wasn't about to let anyone stop him.

The ambulance driver quickly became aware of what was going on in the back of his vehicle and put his blue lights on and pulled over to the side of the narrow country lane they were travelling on. The panda driver realised there was a serious problem and sensibly immediately called up for assistance. As luck would have it we were just round the corner and arrived on scene in less than a minute.

Matt was driving so I was first out of the ARV. I rushed to the now open rear doors and couldn't believe my eyes. It's clichéd to say it, but it really was like a scene from a horror film, a literal bloodbath. Almost every surface inside the ambulance was covered in blood, including the white shirt of the young cop and the green coveralls of the paramedic, both of whom were ashen faced and clearly in a state of shock. There were two bloody handprints on the windows of the rear doors, with long streaks of blood trailing below them, giving the impression someone was clawing to get out.

As I tried to step up into the back of the emergency vehicle the suicidal male pushed me away and jumped down in a bid to escape. Luckily Matt was right behind me and managed to grab hold of him. It was pitch black on a moonless night. There was no street lighting and the lane was surrounded by woodland and fields. If he got away from us now we'd have little or no chance of finding him alive.

He struggled violently and was kicking out at Matt. I jumped on his back and we fell to the ground. He was incredibly strong and quickly broke free from my hold, viscously punching and kicking me as he got back on his feet. Matt reacted quickly and swept his legs out from underneath him, taking him back to the ground. I don't remember exactly how long it took for us to get him under control, or what we had to do, but it was fairly brutal hand-to-hand fighting. This guy was desperate and incredibly unwell. He was totally fixated on killing himself, and he would do whatever it took to achieve his aim, even if that meant killing us or the paramedics in the process.

But restrain him we did, and once the handcuffs were on he fell silent and gave up struggling. I couldn't believe that it had taken such enormous effort, violence even, to stop this guy from taking his own life. I really felt awful that we had hurt someone who was already in such pain, both mentally and physically.

The paramedics reluctantly agreed to finish transporting him to Stoke Mandeville, but thistime he was handcuffed and I went along too, with both the ARV and the panda following along.

Once back in the ambulance the guy's personality changed. He slowly became aware of his surroundings, of reality I guess, and asked if he'd hurt any of us. He could clearly see we were covered in blood and I think he already knew the answer. Shame was written all over his face. He apologised over and over again, and I had to tell him not to worry about us, and to focus on himself. I asked him about his life, his family and his job. He was intelligent, articulate and well mannered. The transformation from ten minutes earlier was extreme and I started to really like the guy.

When we got to hospital the paramedics had to go to change their vehicle for an uncontaminated one, and the panda got re-deployed to another commitment. Matt and I were left with the young man, unable to leave and praying that a firearms job didn't come in.

He was seen quickly by A & E staff for his wounds, which were cleaned, stitched and dressed, but then came the long wait for a mental health crisis team.

I got the three of us a nasty coffee in a thin plastic cup (the sort that was impossible to hold without burning your fingers) from the hospital vending room, and we sat and waited. We were getting a lot of confused glances and raised eyebrows from patients and staff. I can't imagine what they thought had happened, but here were two cops and another man who they probably assumed was our prisoner, all covered in blood and mud, with ripped clothes, enjoying a coffee and laughing together.

Eventually he was whisked away to be assessed and probably sectioned (detained under the Mental Health Act). The assessment itself could take up to 36 hours so someone had to tell his parents. True to form in the "doing all the jobs that no one else can or will do", that someone was us.

So, just before six o'clock in the morning two very dishevelled looking officers were standing in the dark knocking on the door of a lovely country cottage. A yappy dog barked and a man in his late fifties answered the door in his pyjamas, dressing gown and slippers.

"Are you here about our son?" he sighed as his wife joined him by the door.

"Yes" I replied. I proceeded to tell him what had happened and where he was now.

"Hopefully they'll keep him there for a while and once he's more stable he can come home" I suggested.

"He's not coming back here" scowled the dad. "We've had enough. He'll have to find somewhere else to go. We've done everything we can. It's up to him now. We're done with him."

I wanted to fight his case, to give their son a chance to return home, but I could see how beaten they were. They really had had enough.

I felt desperately sad as we walked back to the car. There wasn't going to be any happy ending here, and my gut told me the lad would succeed in killing himself before too long. There was no one there to look out for him, and the chances of this medical intervention working weren't great.

"What a bloody mess" I muttered as we drove back to work to hand the car and weapons over to the early crew.

"Yes, what a bloody mess" agreed Matt.

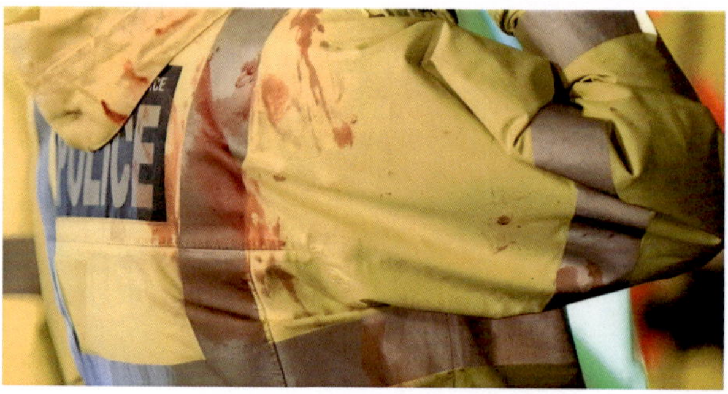

Crewing the Armed Support Vehicle

Receiving commendation for pulling suicidal woman off M40 motorway over-bridge

Out of the Blue

31

A Lonely Goodbye

So, my mind was made up. It was time to leave. Almost exactly twenty years after I had joined the job my house, my car and my collection of classic scooters would be sold and I would be getting on a plane to a new life in New Zealand.

We had taken a gamble and bought a house on-line (and un-seen) by the beach just outside Auckland. Gretchen and I were going to set up our own small boutique health and fitness business, she would be practicing as a physiotherapist and Pilates instructor and I would be doing run coaching, swim coaching, bicycle set-ups and boot camps. My work would be part time so I could take over the primary care role of the boys, pretty much a full time job in itself as we would soon be getting an autism spectrum diagnosis for my eldest.

The six months before we left were quite a juggling act, between my work (including being on call), Gretchen's work, two pre-school boys to look after, packing up and selling our home in preparation for an international move, sorting out passports and visas, and planning our future business. At times I questioned why we were doing it...I certainly wasn't feeling any less stressed yet.

A couple of weeks before we left I had my leaving do at a pub in Windsor. Old colleagues from all the different teams and departments I had worked on turned up to say goodbye over a pint or two. It was a strange evening for me.

On one hand I couldn't wait to leave the police and start a new life, but on the other I was deeply sad to know I would never work with these amazing people again. To leave such a close-knit team, one where you often trust your life to you colleagues, is daunting. I remember feeling like I had been cut adrift and was suddenly very much on my own. It was a similar feeling to how I had felt when my mum and dad died, and to be honest the evening wasn't the celebration I had been hoping for. I went home slightly drunk and very dejected.

My final day at work was much less social, and was as un-ceremonial as my very first day all those years before.

That last-ever day was a Sunday, and I was into the last eight hours of an uneventful weekend of being the Duty PolSA. I spent the day in the office, alone, waiting for the phone to ring. It didn't. I had no future jobs to plan, no patrols to do, no armoury checks to carry out, no weapons to clean. All I had to do was be ready to answer the phone and to empty out my locker and bag up all my uniform and kit. It was soul-destroying.

By four o'clock it was already starting to get dark as I punched in the code to unlock the sergeant's office. Once inside I piled up the large, clear property bags full of black clothing, body armour, pouches, holsters, baton, handcuffs, radio, helmets and other assorted bits and pieces. I took my warrant card out of my pocket and carefully placed it, along with my firearms authorisation card and my locker key, in the middle of the sergeant's desk. I took one last nostalgic look at all my stuff as I closed the door.

I wandered back into the locker room for a final check to make sure I hadn't left anything behind. As I closed my locker there staring at me, stuck to the front of its door, was an A4 print of a hipster-styled man riding a scooter with the caption 'Vespa: For the Man Who Loves the Feel of the Wind in his Vagina'. One last typical joke from Tony. I laughed out loud as I left the room.

I picked up my coat and my old and battered Batman lunchbox, took one last glance around the office in, I guess, some sort of vain attempt to imprint every detail of it onto my memory. And then I turned out the lights. I felt liberated and yet deeply sad as I pulled the main door shut behind me, got into my car and drove out of the gates into the darkness of the Great Park.

No fanfare, no farewells, no good lucks.

Several months later I received a certificate in the post recognising my years of service to the community, with a covering letter from the 'Head of People Services' confirming the date I'd left the force and to thank me for my service.

That was it. I was out of the blue. I was a civilian.

Epilogue

Washing it All Away

As I walk barefoot down to the beach, my senses are awoken by the cool grass, wet with the morning dew. I feel grounded and alive.

The joy of walking across the park, particularly when the grass is overdue for a cut and is a little longer, allowing it to hold more droplets of water on each blade, is overwhelming. If I'm really lucky the sea will be flat, the tide will be high and the sun will just be rising.

The feedback from my feet changes abruptly as I step down onto the beach. It's much less pleasant now as the sharp, harsh grittiness of the sand replaces the refreshingly cool dewiness of the grass. My feet are already wet and the sand sticks, squeezing into the spaces between my toes. But it doesn't bother me, I know it will be washed away as soon as I reach the water's edge.

As I stride across the beach I put on my goggles and swim cap in preparation for my swim. I don't slow my pace or hesitate, I don't want to think about the temperature of the water. It's not that cold, but for six months of the year it's cool enough to take your breath away. The cool water is what I crave though, and I can't wait to get in.

The water hits my feet and I breathe in deeply. I wade in and then gasp as the sea reaches my waist. I need a few seconds to adjust to the cold, but I don't take them. Instead I dive under the surface and immediately feel all my worries and stresses wash away. I become one with the sea, engulfed and supported by it. My other life - the one on land, the one weighed down by physical gravity and mental trauma, anxiety and grief - melts away.

I start to swim. I head east directly towards the rising sun, drawn to its warmth and glow. Its light blinds me, but guides me. I forget about trying to sight, to see where I'm going and instead I focus on my breathing and my form.

I relax into my stroke. My physical aches and pains vanish as my body absorbs, and is held perfectly horizontal by, the salts and minerals in the water. As I find my rhythm I stop thinking and start to count. One, two, three, breathe. One, two, three, breathe. As I settle into my stroke this breathing every three strokes becomes every five strokes. Eventually I stop counting and start thinking about my kicks, keeping them light, relaxed and even. Then I'm onto my arms, relaxed but powerful. One, two, one, two, one, two. The regularity of my hands pushing forward into the blue is metronomic and meditative. Soon I'm not thinking or counting at all.

The water is holding me and is washing away everything I don't need in my life.

I turn for home and the sun that was guiding me is now behind me and slightly higher in the pinkish-blue early morning sky. It's over my right shoulder and catches my eye every time I roll to breathe. I can feel its warmth on my back and shoulders. Bizarrely, rather than making me feel warmer it just heightens my awareness of how cold I am and so I increase my pace to generate some extra heat.

As I round the small wharf, I swim wide to avoid hitting the lines of the fisherman who's also been enjoying the sunrise. As I reach the shallows I stand. My first few steps out of the blue are wobbly as I adjust to being upright again. I remove my cap and goggles and I'm greeted by my first irritation of life on land...I can't see without my glasses.

But I feel great. Refreshed, alive, strong. My demons are, temporarily at least, banished...I've left them out at sea.

I'm ready to face the morning. I have taken control of how the day is going to be before the day has been able to take control of me. I am empowered.

I can breathe again.

Out of the Blue

A Final Thought

It has been a few months now since I completed this book and I have had time to sit back and reflect on the effect writing this memoir has had on the symptoms of my own trauma. It has been something of a revelation.

Since writing the book my flashbacks and nightmares have (so far) completely gone. It appears that by documenting each incident I have been able to release the event from my sub-conscious. Writing has allowed me to 'keep' the memory, but in a secure place outside my brain. I no longer feel the need to hang on to those destructive thoughts... if I need to revisit them I can pick up the book and read about them. This has been liberating and truly transformative.

Unfortunately, the writing appears to have had little or no effect on my anxiety, and my frustration, irritation, and anger remain. I have found other strategies for dealing with these and, as I mentioned in the epilogue, cold open water swimming is one.

I start just about every day with a swim in the sea and I never wear a wetsuit. The cold in winter is almost like shock therapy and when I get out of the water my anxiety has gone. Sadly it's only a temporary fix...it will slowly creep back in as the day goes on and I inevitably wake the following morning in a highly anxious state. But as long as I can swim I will be able to cope with most of what the day will throw at me.

I have also rediscovered my love of art and music, and the simple pleasure of riding my Lambretta. I have almost returned, full circle, to the passions of my youth. They served me well then and do so again now, bringing a little joy to each day.

To further help myself I have learnt to avoid stressful situations, and to give myself plenty of time to either get things done or to get to somewhere I need to go. I exercise regularly, I eat well, I work on my breathing and I practice gratitude daily. I try to avoid alcohol as it never helps and often makes things far worse. I have found that personally the CBD and THC contained in a cannabis brownie are far more beneficial than any drink (or prescription medication), but sadly that option still remains illegal in most countries. The irony of an ex-police officer considering breaking the law in order to cope with the trauma of upholding the law isn't lost on me. I feel this is an important conversation that needs to be had.

So, my point is what? I didn't want this book to be a 'How to Fix Trauma' guide, or a sales pitch for cold water swimming, and I'm certainly not suggesting anyone should go and start taking cannabis. But...if you're suffering from any sort of trauma then I would highly recommend writing about it. You don't need to write a book, you could start a journal or make regular entries in a diary. Alternatively you could write a letter to yourself or to the person who inflicted the trauma on you (you don't need to actually send it), or you could just scribble down random thoughts in a notebook. Whatever works for you is great. For me the effects have been revolutionary and the benefits have gone far beyond any counselling or medication ever have. It has been life changing.

Acknowledgements

This book would never have happened if it wasn't for the influence and support of some amazing women, and these women need to be at the very top of my 'thank you' list.

Firstly, my mum. When I joined the police she told me to keep a diary "One day you'll write a book about all your experiences". I did as she suggested, but sadly for only the first few weeks of my service. I recently found the battered notebook containing a dozen or so pages of my pathetic ramblings when I was searching for old police photos to include in this memoir. It was of little use, other than to remind me of her words. I wish she was still around to see me, thirty years later, finally publishing the book she always knew I'd write.

Next comes a pair of conspirators...my lovely wife Gretchen, and her dear friend (and our ex-next-door neighbour) Carolyn. Without their encouragement I almost certainly would never have written a single word. Gretchen tricked me into agreeing to a weekly "writing morning" with Carolyn, who also had aspirations to write, at our local café. We met up, and over the course of a coffee (or two) started to scribble a few tentative paragraphs. She never turned up to any more meetings. Their objective had been achieved...I had finally started my book. They have both proof-read each chapter along the way and have tirelessly encouraged me to keep going.

I need to thank my sister, Amanda, for an extremely thorough proof-read and edit of my (almost) final version. She uncovered an abundance of typos, spelling mistakes and missing words that I would probably have never noticed.

Harmony, the barista at the local Beach Café, needs a special mention not just for her excellent coffee but also for tolerating me nursing a single large flat white for several hours each morning as I lost all concept of time whilst recounting my memories.

Next up is Kirsty from the Publishing Launchpad who, despite not taking on any new clients, has kindly offered to make an exception and get me published. Her professional help, knowledge and guidance have been invaluable.

Shelley, for her marketing expertise and extensive help with my website and social media. Her enthusiasm and vision have been amazing, and she has brought some much-needed clarity to my muddled plans for actually getting the book out there.

Finally, as you will now no doubt be aware, I may not have even survived my policing career, let alone written a book about it, without Jen. It is difficult to put into words how indebted I am to her, but for a few terrible years she was crucially there for me at every turn. She was my guardian angel.

Aside from these special women there are, of course, many others who need recognition. One of my oldest fiends, Paul Richards (himself a writer) has provided a wealth of professional help and guidance. My local readers Jim Hainey, Jenny Groom, Brett Plummer and Richard Webster whose feedback, support and advice have been invaluable. Frankie and Jen have helped with prompting long-forgotten memories, reminding me of important details and providing photographs. But from within the job itself I need to acknowledge not just Jen and Frankie, but every single officer I have ever had the privilege of working alongside. My respect and admiration for every past and present member of the ever-thinner blue line is enormous. I hope this book helps to shine a tiny light onto the enormity of the challenges they face day in, day out, often without the support of the public, the press, politicians or even the criminal justice system itself.

My last (and emotional) acknowledgement is two friends who feature in this book but who tragically died far too young. Dom and James will sadly never get to read about their exploits, both having left us in the six months prior to publishing. Rest well my friends, this book is for you.